The New Regionalism in
Western Europe

The New Regionalism in Western Europe

Territorial Restructuring and Political Change

Michael Keating

Professor of Political Science
University of Western Ontario
Canada

Edward Elgar
Cheltenham, UK · Northampton, MA, USA

Published by
Edward Elgar Publishing Limited
8 Lansdown Place
Cheltenham
Glos GL50 2HU
UK

Edward Elgar Publishing, Inc.
6 Market Street
Northampton
Massachusetts 01060
USA

A catalogue record for this book
is available from the British Library

Library of Congress Cataloguing in Publication Data

Keating, Michael, 1950–
    The new regionalism in Western Europe : territorial restructuring
and political change / Michael Keating.
    Includes bibliographical references.
    1. Regionalism—Europe. 2. Regional planning—Europe. 3. Europe—
Politics and government. I. Title.
JN94.A38R4343   1998
320.54'094—dc21   97–47520
                                                                  CIP

ISBN 1 85898 527 7 (cased)

Printed and bound in Great Britain by Bookcraft (Bath) Ltd.

Contents

Figures

Preface and Acknowledgements

The end of territory as a factor in social and political life has been predicted regularly over the last hundred years, yet somehow it keeps on coming back. At the close of the twentieth century, we are once again being told that economic, technological and social change have broken the bounds of space, severed its link with time and function, and are the heralds of a borderless world. Certainly, the European state is undergoing profound changes, its authority and powers challenged by continental integration, the advance of the market and a panoply of effects subsumed under the term globalization. The central argument of this book is that these changes have affected states' roles in territorial management but, far from effacing territory, have encouraged a new regionalism, defined not merely in relation to the state but also in relation to the market and the continental regime. This process is uneven and mediated by differing state traditions, the power and resilience of some states, and by region-building projects in specific places. We are not headed for a Europe of the Regions, in which the states will give way to smaller units, but we are witnessing a new stage in the territorial politics of the European state. Regions are not the only element in this, and elsewhere I have written about cities and stateless nations, but regions are an important part of the functional and institutional apparatus of the new Europe.

Territorial politics is not a new phenomenon, but is rooted in the very construction of the European state. That is why, after a general introduction, I discuss some historical issues, arguing that territorial effects have been a constant presence in European politics, but that too often social scientists have simply not looked for them, or defined them out of existence where they conflicted with successive modernization paradigms. Then I look at the postwar model of territorial management in the Keynesian welfare state era, before examining its breakdown and the emergence of the new regionalism. The last two substantive chapters examine regions and economic development politics, and regions in the

European Union.

I have received a great deal of help and advice in this project. Sean Loughlin read and commented on the draft text. Some parts reflect earlier work and publications with Liesbet Hooghe, Sean Loughlin and Sylvia Pintarits. Others who have helped with advice, discussion and criticism are: John Agnew, Francisco Aldecoa, Harald Baldesheim, Richard Balme, Marleen Brans, Emmanuel Brunet-Jailly, Enrico Buglione, Udo Bullman, José-Luis de Castro, Stefaan De Rynck, Wilfred De Wachter, Lieven De Winter, Frank Delmartino, Carlo Desideri, Elizabeth Dupoirier, Howard Elcock, George France, Felipe A. González, Jürgen Grote, Tore Hansen, Christopher Harvie, Stefan Immerfall, Gurutz Jáuregui, Charlie Jeffery, Bart Kerremans, Beate Kohler-Koch, Hans-Peter Kriesi, Jan-Erik Lane, Neils Lange, Patrick Le Galès, Alvaro López Mira, Gary Marks, Jörg Mathias, Paul McAleavey, James Mitchell, Francesc Morata, Luis Moreno, Francesc Pallarés, Antonio-Carlos Pereira-Menaut, Simona Piattoni, Enzo Santantonio, Allen Scott, Jim Sharpe, Wieslava Suraszka, Alex Ugalde, Elke Versmessen, Ron Wintrobe, Vincent Wright.

Funding was provided by the Social Science and Humanities Research Council of Canada. Much of the work was done while I was visiting fellow at the Norwegian Nobel Institute in 1996. Institutional support and hospitality were also provided by the University of Western Ontario; Nuffield College, Oxford; Istituto di Studi sulle Regioni, Rome; the European University Institute, Florence; Mannheimmer Zentrum für Europäische Sozialforschung; University of Strathclyde; Universidad del País Vasco. The network of the ECPR Standing Group on Regionalism is a constant source of support and ideas.

Papers arising from the project were presented in 1994, at the Conference of Europeanists, Chicago, USA; the European Consortium for Political Research, Madrid, Spain; the International Political Science Association, Berlin, Germany; the German Political Science Association, Potsdam, Germany; the European Science Foundation, conference on integration and disintegration in Europe, St. Martin, Germany; a conference on European Integration, The Hague, Netherlands; in 1995 at the European Consortium for Political Research, Bordeaux, France; at a colloquium on *Les Regions en Europe*, Rennes, France; in 1996 at the European Consortium for Political Research, Oslo, Norway; at the Northwest Seminar, Ålesund, Norway; at a Conference on Regionalism in Europe, Wroclav, Poland; at the Foundation Europe of the Cultures conferences in Leuven, Belgium and Dublin Ireland; in 1997 at the International Studies Association, Toronto, Canada; at a conference on Territorial Politics in Europe. A Zero-Sum Game?, European University Institute, Florence, Italy; at a conference on Exploring Sustainability,

University of Karstad, Sweden; and at the European Community Studies Association, Seattle, USA.

I also presented the material at seminars and lectures at the University of Karlstad; the ARENA project, University of Oslo; the University of Mannheim; St. Anthony's College, Oxford; the Catholic University of Leuven; the University of Geneva; the University of the Basque Country; and the Asociación Galega de Estudio Europeos.

Michael Keating
London, Canada

1. Territory and Politics

IN SEARCH OF TERRITORY

Territory is in many respects a fundamental feature of political and social life. It provides the framework for politics and social interaction. It underpins systems of authority, in the state, whether at national, subnational or supranational level, and in a wide range of non-state structures, including the religious, the social and the economic. The sovereign state is a territorially-defined political unit, whose authority and legitimacy are limited to a given territory. Within the state, power is usually divided and government organized, on a territorial basis. Citizenship and rights are bounded by the territorial state and representation is typically organized by territory (Paddison, 1983). Territory is thus fundamental to two key aspects of the modern state. It underpins the state as a principle of domination and control; and it structures the system of representation and participation within it.

Territory is also a key element in economic exchange and the structure of markets. Spatial proximity encourages exchange, facilitates communication and generates complementary activities, while access to materials, labour and markets is structured by territorial factors. Innovation and learning are conditioned by territorial relationships. Equally, territory is a factor in the production and reproduction of culture, language and customs. It is the basis for identity, providing symbols, spaces and myths for collective representations and solidarity.

Given this centrality of territory to the understanding of politics, it is perhaps surprising that territory has so often been neglected as a factor in the social sciences (Gottmann, 1980). Perhaps the ubiquity of territory leads to its being taken for granted or merely discounted

1

as a source of variation in political life. More consciously, theorists of modernization have often seen territory as a feature of 'traditional' society, whose significance would diminish under the influence of social and economic change (Paddison, 1983). Durkheim was one of the first, but not the last, to argue that the territorial criterion would give way to a functional one in the division of labour and organization of society, adding that 'we can almost say that a people is as much advanced as territorial divisions are more superficial' (Durkheim, 1964, p.187). Political sociologists after the Second World War argued in much the same vein, predicting that territorial cleavages would give way to economic ones as peripheral territories were incorporated into national political and social systems (Deutsch, 1966). If territorial distinctiveness remained, this was the result of an incomplete process of integration, and must refer to events and processes in the distant past, rather than present conditions. Economists, too, have tended to dismiss territory, except in so far as distance is a cost of production. Their world is that of the unrooted, individualistic actor concerned with maximizing individual utility, and of the market as an anonymous system of exchange which takes essentially the same form everywhere. The revival of spatial economics in recent years has been largely the work of geographers, planners or sociologists.

In the 1990s, the modernization thesis has returned in a different form, in the argument that modern communications systems reduce the effect of space by erasing its connection with time. The penetration of territories by global influences in economics, culture and politics has destroyed their cohesion, while political movements operate across old boundaries (Badie, 1995). Economic production has been liberated from its spatial ties to sources of materials and technology has freed communication from the constraints of proximity. Political and institutional restructuring have broken the link between territory and politics, undermining the territorial state. It is always difficult to discern trends, particularly in a time of rapid social change such as the 1990s, but previous predictions about the demise of territory have proved well wide of the mark. Nineteenth century sociological accounts of the disappearance of territory in the face of modernization preceded an explosion of territorial political movements at the end of the century (Keating, 1988). The diffusionist accounts of the 1950s and 1960s with their confident assumptions about increasing homogeneity were followed by another crisis of territorial representation and the rise of urban, regional and minority nationalist forces. In the rest of this book, I shall argue that the current era is similarly witnessing not the end of territorial politics but their reconfiguration and re-emergence in new and potent forms.

Part of the problem with the recurrent modernization thesis is that the relationship between function and territory is ill-specified, so that they are presented as alternative principles of organization. In the heyday of the nation-state, scholars, especially in the Anglo-American world, often simply forgot that the state itself was a territorial framework, historically contingent and never entirely free from challenge, and so confused national integration with the spread of universal values and processes. Others, especially those brought up in the French Jacobin tradition, consider the nation-state to be the only relevant territorial framework so that the escape of social functions from the state framework is seen as the equivalent of the end of territory itself (for example, see Badie, 1995). In fact, territory and function are linked in complex ways and the territorial logic of functional processes is constantly reasserting itself, often at new and unfamiliar territorial levels. At the end of the twentieth century, economic, technological and social changes are serving not to destroy territory but to reshape its social importance and reconstruct territorial systems of action.

Another reason why territory always seems to return is that it is intimately linked to identity and politics, although this too is often ignored because it is so fundamental. Political identities are complex and increasingly multiple, but do tend to be linked to territory, a place, a homeland. Territory is the principal basis for political mobilization, because of its link to identity and for purely practical reasons. It is also the main foundation for political representation and accountability. Finally, it is the basis for political action and public policy. The link between these elements and territory is also being reshaped in the present era, but it is not disappearing.

More generally, the problem is perhaps not that spatial effects are absent in social science, as that social scientists simply have not looked for them. The aspatial approach has long been dominant, with similar effects postulated for similar variables in different places. This is no doubt due to the influence of modernization theorists and ingrained assumptions based on the conditioning effects of living and working within nation-states (MacLaughlin, 1986). It also reflects practical considerations. Surveys and other studies become extremely expensive once territory is factored in, as sample sizes have to be very large. Conceptualization and model-building are greatly complicated. Data tend to come in national sets, biassing inquiry again. The extent to which research is driven by convenience and the drive for parsimony in explanation is not widely discussed in social science but can have distorting effects. Studies which have addressed the issue of place directly are rather unusual, except perhaps in France, where the rich tradition of political geography and the *annales* school of historiography have generated a wealth of data on place-based activities over time. Unwillingness to recognize territory as a factor in human behaviour also stems from the intellectual commitment to universalist explanations in social sciences and the aspirations to scientific rigour, predictability and parsimony. It owes a lot to the normative association of universalism with liberalism and particularism with reaction. The Cold War, pitting two universalist ideological systems both derived from the scientific legacy of the nineteenth century may have reinforced this tendency. The end of the Cold War has led to a revival of interest in particularism (Agnew, 1996), and the manner of its ending certainly brought into question the claims of social science to be able to predict on the basis of universal laws.

Some scholars have dismissed the importance of territory for politics, arguing that in itself it does not add anything to explanations of social and political processes. It may be that social classes, or religious or ethnic groups, are distributed unevenly in space but the source of variation is class or group identity, not territory itself. These studies have sought to test for the presence of a territorial effect by comparing different territories and then controlling for the standard functional and social variables. If there is still a difference unexplained by these variables, it is attributed to the independent effect of territory. This mode of analysis is applied to the study of political behaviour, to see whether territory has an effect independent of class, religion and the standard non-spatial factors, often concluding that the territorial effect disappears once everything else is controlled for. It is applied in economics in the form of shift-share analysis, which seeks to measure the amount of variation to be explained by the structural composition of regional economies and the amount which remains unexplained and can therefore be attributed to the territorial factor. These analyses suffer from a common set of problems. First, in treating territory as a residual, that which remains unexplained by other factors, they fail to address the territorial effect directly. It is merely assumed that territory somehow explains what cannot be explained otherwise, without specifying just what the territorial effect is or how it operates. Yet territory is a ubiquitous factor which structures and gives meaning to social factors everywhere, so that there is no non-territorial control group with which to compare. Shift-share analysis, for example, compares the economic performance of a territory, not with a spaceless economy outside, but with an aggregation of other spatial economies, normally grouped arbitrarily into states and regions. Studies of the territorial effect in voting measure regional effects against a norm defined by the largest regions and so often end up concluding that territory does not matter for most people, only those in the smaller, marginal or peripheral regions so that, for example, the Scots vote 'territorially', but not the southern and midland English. A second problem with these studies is that they try to infer territorial effects and processes from individual-level behaviour and so risk falling into the 'individualist fallacy' in making inferences about units larger than those for which observations are made (Rose and Urwin, 1975). This produces discrepancies, for example, between survey-based analyses of voting behaviour and ecological approaches which start from territory, and between analyses of firms' investment decisions based on surveys, and analyses of regional economic performance as a whole. The problem is that in the survey, the decision is taken out of context, factors which interact in space are separated analytically and the social construction of meaning is lost.

If there is a territorial effect, it is a complex and dynamic one. Firstly, it is the very combination of other factors within a given place, and so cannot be considered to be independent of them. Secondly, it is a compound of these effects and their dynamic interaction, which produces an effect which is more than merely the sum of its parts. Thirdly, territory is an intervening factor, which moulds the other structural variables and determines their meaning. So, for example, religion is a factor in political behaviour in some places and not in others. In some places, Catholicism inclines people to vote for the right, in others for the left. Small farmers in one context are conservative, in another radical. So territory may need to be seen not as an independent variable conditioning social life alongside class, religion and other structural factors, but as a mediating factor through which these other factors are perceived and given meaning.

There are several ways in which territory can structure political, economic and social life. One is by providing a frame of perception for policy issues. These are appreciated via a system of values and cultural assumptions which in turn are rooted in territorial society. The territory, as a system of communication, reproduces these values, disseminates them and incorporates new issues into the value framework. Failure to appreciate this underlies many of the failures in state-sponsored regional development policies over the years, for example the assumption of French governments that the peasants of lower Languedoc could painlessly move into the tourist service economy, or the belief of British Conservative governments in the 1980s and 1990s that coalmining and steelmaking communities could transform themselves into nurseries of independent small business people. An inability to understand the nature of territorial communities also underlay the fiasco of the poll tax, in which the Thatcher government sought to extract an individualized, per capita payment from residents of poor working class communities with traditions of active and passive resistance to authority.

To the degree that a territorial society has a cohesive identity, issues will be assessed by their local impact, as well as their impact on socially-defined groups such as classes, ethnicities or genders. Social solidarities and collective responses may in turn be structured by territory. By constituting collective actors and structuring perceptions, territorial identities can thus define the terms of rational action itself. For example, a transnational corporation engaged in global restructuring may have a rational interest in closing a plant in order to maximize profit. The local community have an equally-rational interest in keeping it open to retain economic activity locally and, in so far as they think as a territorial community, this is a common interest. Economists and others who dismiss place-based solidarity on the ground that most local people do not have a direct stake in the threatened sector and, as consumers and taxpayers, should be in favour of the global efficiency-maximizing strategy, miss this very point.

Territory can also define the limits of the public and private domains. Much of politics concerns control over physical space and the resources, power and opportunities that come with this. Territorial politics can thus take the form of the private appropriation of space, the monopolization of space or the exclusion of others from space. There is a long tradition in the United States of municipal incorporation as a form of private appropriation of space and social exclusion (Keating, 1991a) and recently, this has extended to the erection of private governments, denying the public interest in space and appropriating it to private ends (McKenzie, 1994). Space also conditions the public domain, determining the scope of public goods like clean air, a healthy living space and access to the natural environment. It is space which conditions the non-excludability of these items, which can be denied to people in other places but not to anyone resident within a given place. Recent studies have pursued the idea of local public goods beyond these familiar categories, to include culture, social institutions and mechanisms for collective action, a theme discussed more fully later (Chapter 6).

Control of space also has a high symbolic content. This may take the benign form of the widespread European custom of flying four flags from town halls: the local, the regional, the national and the European. It is seen in more virulent form in the annual tradition of marching in Northern Ireland, a deliberately provocative assertion of rights in historic space and its appropriation for one community.

THE CREATION OF PLACE

Territory as a factor in social and political life cannot be appreciated simply as a two-dimensional variable, or inferred as the residual factor when other explanations have been exhausted. It is rather a complex of influences in physical space, which together shape the meaning of social life. The central factor is, of course, physical space, which itself influences economic activity, social interaction and ways of life. This is not to fall into the trap of geographical determinism. Physical space may condition social interactions but it does not determine them. Nor does physical space constitute the whole meaning of territory as a factor in politics. Its substantive meaning is provided by the activities which it encompasses, and by the sense of identity which it engenders (Agnew, 1987). In this broader sense, territory is a social, economic and political construction, not reducible to a single factor. The economic content of territory is given by patterns of territorial exchange, linkages between buyers and sellers and interdependencies in production, by labour markets and travel to work areas. It is also given by the activities of place-based development coalitions, defining the territory as the relevant unit for development and constituting territorial lobbies. As a social entity, a place is constituted by patterns of exchange in social life, by the constitution of civil society and by patterns of social solidarity. A sense of identity is a factor which builds on these processes and in turn reinforces their territorial basis. Finally, territories are constituted by institutions, notably the state, which defines territories both for the purposes of public policy and as the basis of representation, and more recently by international and supranational regimes, notably the European Union, which have moulded the sense of place and helped constitute territorial systems of action through their policy interventions.

As a construction, territories are the product of history but are continually being made and remade. French *annalistes* such as Braudel (1986) have documented the making of places and their evolution over time, and quantitative studies have revealed striking continuities in political and social patterns across wide time spans (Todd, 1990; Le Bras, 1995; Putnam, 1993). Rokkan (1980) and others have shown how critical events can shape patterns of territorial politics, which then become embedded for generations. Territories are the product of a complex interaction between their external environment, economic, political and institutional, on the one hand; and their internal life on the other. External influences are mediated by local factors and local influences in turn may impinge on the wider system. No place can be considered as a self-contained system. Boundaries are unstable and fluctuating, yet a sense of place often remains. Remarkably little is known at a general or theoretical level about the conditions of social reproduction of a sense of place, or of territorial systems of action. Rational actor-based explanations of territorial politics fail to account for the motivations of actors, the constitution of territorial spaces, or the assumptions and relationships that underlie the working of institutions. At the other extreme are path-dependency accounts, which show territorial politics as determined by the past experience. Todd (1990) assembles an impressive set of data on spatial continuities across Europe over centuries, but plumps for a reductionist explanation in attributing it all to family structures in the early modern period. Putnam (1993) similarly falls into the path-dependency trap, arbitrarily choosing one element of a long historical experience to explain present-day patterns, and then seeking to build a whole theory of social action on a limited case-study. A satisfactory account of territory in politics has to be historically sensitive, seeing history not as a process confined to the past but as something which is continually being lived. It must assess the relative contributions of past experience and present action, of social conditioning and political choice.

Territories as social systems are constituted at a variety of spatial levels. Conventionally, some six are recognized: the global; the continental; the state; the regional; the local, urban or municipal; and the neighbourhood. These, however, are simplifications and do not always correspond to recognizable units in given places. Territories as places are more than mere lines on the map. They are constituted by function, by culture and shared identity, by political mobilization and leadership, and by institutions. The resulting functional, cultural, political and institutional meanings of territory do not always coincide.

We cannot, for example, simply read off political restructuring from functional changes in the economy, or assume that a territorial culture will have political consequences. These spheres may coincide to a greater or lesser extent, or they may be quite distinct. Much of territorial politics is about the relationship among these various meanings of space, and an effort to bring them into line. This process of defining space is inherently conflictual since it affects the distribution of power and resources, defines the reference group for public policy, and frames the definition of social and economic issues. So territory is always contested, always being redefined and reframed in the politics, society and economics.

REGIONS – THE ELUSIVE SPACE

This book is about a specific type of territory, the region. Yet region is an elusive concept, covering a variety of territorial levels and a range of social contents (Beaufays, 1985). A minimal definition would present it as an intermediate territorial level, between the state and the locality, though this is broad enough and gives little idea of its territorial scope, since some regions in this sense are larger than some states. More positively, regions can be recognized according to geographical criteria, as physical spaces. These are either homogeneous regions defined by topography, climate or other fixed characteristics; or nodal regions, defined by a common central point (Wannop, 1995). An economic definition of a region would focus on common production patterns, interdependencies and market linkages, and labour markets. A broader functional definition would add patterns of social interaction, including leisure, recreation and travel patterns. Such functional regions are discernable in metropolitan areas, focused on large cities or conurbations but they may also be drawn more widely, on a provincial scale. However drawn, they are often unstable, changing their contours according to economic and social trends. Regions can be defined by cultural criteria, according to language, dialect or patterns of social communication, or delineated according to the sense of identity felt by citizens and political actors. Such a sense of regional identity may not exist at all in some places and, even where it does, its political implications may vary, from the constitution of regional lobbies in politics, through demands for autonomy, all the way to secession. Regions may also be seen as institutional divisions, historically constituted, or created more recently, and varying from bodies established for the convenience of state administrators, to political institutions built by political action on the ground. These varying definitions of the region not only do not always coincide, but they may be in conflict with each other, as the following illustrations show. Their relation with the state also varies. One conception sees the regions as nestled within national economic, social and political systems. Many analyses of regionalism have used a centre–periphery perspective to analyse this relationship, seeing regions as dependent or subordinate to a dominant central place. Other conceptions locate the region in a continental framework, or place it within the global market, or even see it as something that challenges the state itself as the framework of identity and action.

The first map (Figure 1.1) is a purely administrative one, the European Union's map of regions. While this is used for European purposes, it does not in practice challenge the state as the basis of territorial division and is less a European-wide set of regions than a collation of nationally-defined units, whose scale and significance varies not only among but within the states. These regions are defined by the European Commission for administrative convenience, but their political status varies considerably from one state to another. In Germany, Belgium and Austria, they are units in federal states, while in the Netherlands they are groupings of provinces. In Spain, Italy and France, there are elected regional governments, but of differing status and weight. In England, the regions are mere administrative divisions with no institutions of their own, while in Denmark and Ireland there are no regions at all. The second map (Figure 1.2) is one idea of a Europe of 'cultural nations', ignoring altogether the boundaries of states. Here we see a different pattern again, with culturally distinct regions appearing around the periphery of the state system and in the dense central belt from northern Italy through the Rhineland to the Low Countries. This belt, the shatter-zone between the large states, was a major trading route in mediaeval and early modern times and has re-emerged recently as a dynamic economic zone. This map, too, reflects a specific view of the social reality and collective identity. Other maps could be produced showing regions by economic criteria, or by patterns of functional dependency.

Regions, like other territorial units, are a construction of various elements with greater or lesser cohesion. Where the elements of geography, economic cohesion, cultural identity, administrative apparatus, popular identity, and territorial mobilization coincide in space, we have a strong regionalism. In other cases, the definition of regional space is contested or regionalism is expressed in different forms across the economic, cultural and political dimensions. In any case, because of the indeterminacy of regional boundaries and the

Figure 1.1 Regions of the European Union
Source: European Commission

differing types of system to which regions belong, regions must be
seen as open systems rather than self-contained societies. They are
partial social systems linked functionally to other levels, rather than
the global societies encompassing the totality of social relationships
which are the traditional aspiration of the nation state. For this
reason, regionalism is not an alternative principle of organization to
the state. Regions rarely seek to displace states or take over the state
functions of social regulation and legitimation. Yet their existence
does affect the workings of states and the emergence of strong
regions does modify the power and authority of the nation state.

Regions and regionalism have a long history in Europe. Regions
predated the rise of nation-states and helped shape the emergence of
the state system. They constituted an obstacle to centralized state and
nation building over centuries, and remained as an element in the
politics of states. Now that the nation-state is again being reconfigured
as a result of global processes, the changing relations between state
and market, and European integration, regions are again featuring in
political life. Yet it has proved difficult to give them their place in the

Figure 1.2 Cultural Nations of Europe
Source: CIEMEN (nova edició revisada, 1992), Barcelona. Adapted
by Mireya Folch Serra

history and politics of the European state. Social scientists have
often failed to find regions for want of looking for them. More
recently, enthusiasts for regions and regionalism have tended to see
them as something quite new, transforming a system of authority
hitherto based exclusively on the state. This is to ignore their historical
presence and the weight of history in conditioning regional identities
and behaviour. Regionalism is also prone to the reductionist treatment
so often used to dismiss territorial politics in general. A historical
reductionism, already mentioned, sees regions as fixed in their

formative characteristics at some point in the past, with history determined from that point on. Sociological reductionism presents regions as nothing more than the embodiment of class forces, either the working class struggling against a state which is allied to capital; or a bourgeoisie using regionalism to divide the workers and break social solidarity. Another form sees certain regionalisms as manifestations of 'ethnic' conflict, although the construction of ethnic identity is every bit as problematic as the construction of a regional identity. None of these captures the subtleties of territorial politics, or regions as systems of action. To appreciate the significance of regionalism, we must consider its relationships with other forms of social cleavage, and see how regional politics can draw upon other types of politics in the formation of a regional identity. At the same time, we need to appreciate the weight of historical tradition, without relegating the object of inquiry entirely to the past. Regions are often fragile formations, poorly defined and containing within them complex social divisions. There is a constant danger of reification, attributing to the region characteristics proper to its constituent elements. A related trap is that of anthropomorphism, in which regions are endowed with wishes, interests and strategies; again these are properties of regional actors and the definition of a regional interest is itself a complex political process.

Regions are seen in the remaining chapters as social constructions, within territorial boundaries. The territorial element in the definition of regions, if not its precise delineation, is fundamental; the social, economic and political content of regionalism varies according to the outcomes of political processes. It is a contested concept, both in its spatial limits and its social content, since these condition the distribution of power, the weight of social interests and the allocation of resources.

Contrary to the diffusion theorists who saw modernization as eroding the territorial principle, the definition of territory is of increased importance in the modern state. The intrusion of modernity, of the market and the state, forces people to confront their own identity. It is no longer enough to say, as did the Silesian peasants when confronted with the census question in the nineteenth century, that 'we are from here.' Now 'here' must be defined by reference to a 'there', giving people a sense of their place in a wider territorial framework. Modernity also replaces personalized authority by institutional authority and this is usually organized territorially. Not only is the state defined by reference to territory, but it organizes itself internally according to territorial principles. The increased scope of public action raises the stakes in the definition of authority and its spatial limits. For example, if the state undertakes universal education, then it matters a great deal to regions of minority culture whether it is organized nationally or locally. As states extended their scope and authority, they penetrated territorial societies, destabilizing old social relationships, redistributing resources, and undermining old practices. States themselves required a territorial basis for administration and either adapted to existing patterns or sought to impose their own. As territories were opened up to modernity, regions found themselves in competition for resources and favourable policies, both within the state and the market place. The next chapter examines these processes, tracing the dynamic of the relationship between the state and the regions in the process of state formation and consolidation.

The new state order emerging in the 1990s changes the stakes of territorial politics again. Some spatial constraints on economic, social and political life have been relaxed. Proximity to raw materials is not so important in a range of industrial activities. Communications technologies have broken the connection between distance and time. Yet in other respects, territorial influences have grown in importance. As the state is penetrated by the market and by international regimes, territories are remoulded and regional actors forced into a more direct relationship with the external world. Inter-regional competition for economic development is enhanced. The disintegrative effects of the market stimulate a search for new principles of territorial cohesion and responsible government. New forms of regionalism and new regional actors have emerged. The third chapter examines these processes and the emergence of the new regionalism.

There is a strong functional logic to the emergence of regions, as the needs of economic restructuring and the changing capacity and tasks of the state point to the regional level as the appropriate one at which to frame a response. The analysis that follows recognizes these functional tendencies, but rejects functionalist explanations for the rise of regions. Functional requirements are interpreted differently in different contexts and their effects are mediated by cultural values and political movements. In politics, it is rarely true that form follows function and teleological explanations (explaining phenomena by their effects rather than their antecedents) are quite inadequate. It follows that a general theory or regionalism driven by economic change, by the condition of post-modernity, or by the crisis of the nation-state, is not possible. The phenomenon is too diverse and conditioned by local circumstances. This is not to say that all we have is a series of local stories, each different from the others. There are general trends affecting the west European state and there is a revival of regionalism, but the forms which this takes are varied and ultimately driven by politics.

2. Regions and State-building in Western Europe

THE FORMATION OF THE NATION-STATE

The nation-state in western Europe is so familiar a category of analysis that it has until recently been taken for granted as the basis for political authority. A whole school in political science has examined its evolution and development as the culmination of political development. In recent years, as the nation-state has experienced strains arising from the simultaneous processes of international integration, regional decentralization, and the advance of the market, a new appreciation has come of the historical specificity of the nation state as we have known it (Agnew and Corbridge, 1995). With this has come an interest in forms of political authority which preceded it, as well as what might succeed it.

Europe before the rise of the modern nation-state was a highly differentiated political order. Power was fragmented territorially, among empires, kingdoms, principalities, cities and other self-governing places, as well as functionally, among the political, religious and economic spheres. Political authority itself was not absolute but divided among overlapping and shared jurisdictions. Territory was not the sole or even the main basis for political authority, as feudal relationships were personalized and complex, while city leagues provided a functionally specific form of political order based on common trading or military needs, but without any over-arching authority. The Roman Catholic Church claimed wide jurisdiction in ecclesiastical and secular matters without territorial limitation.

The nation-state differs from these pre-modern forms in its claims to absolute sovereignty over a given territory, with fixed boundaries, and to the unqualified allegiance of the citizens within that territory. Citizens share a defining identity, whether based upon cultural affinity or common

16

rights and duties. Scholars of international relations often date the establishment of the nation-state, as the unique basis for authority in Europe, to the Peace of Westphalia (1648). It is true that these treaties established the principle that ecclesiastical and secular authority should coincide in space. On the other hand, they did not inaugurate a system of sovereign states (Osiander, 1994) and explicitly maintained a balance in Germany between imperial and state power. Nor did they delineate the territorial pattern of European states, since the only state to keep its 1648 boundaries into the late twentieth century is Portugal. They certainly did not stipulate the substantive content of statehood, the scope of state authority or the principle of the unitary state.

The emergence of the state system was in fact a long and uneven process. Early examples of unified, but not necessarily unitary, states were France, England and Spain. The Scandinavian kingdoms also emerged in the middle ages, but were subject to mergers and secessions up to the twentieth century. In the late sixteenth century, the Netherlands joined the list of states. This left the eastern empires of Austria, Russia and the Ottoman Turks, Germany, and a swathe of territory from Italy, through the Rhone–Rhine corridor to Flanders, where political order took the form of city-states, duchies and bishoprics each with its own distinct status. These territories were not incorporated into nation-states until the nineteenth and twentieth centuries. Belgium and Greece emerged in the 1830s, while the period from the late nineteenth century to 1919 saw the break up of the three great empires, together with the emergence of Norway and Ireland. Unification of Italy and Germany into nation-states occurred quite rapidly between 1860 and 1870 while the Treaty of Versailles in 1919 finally put an end to the Ottoman and Austro-Hungarian empires.

A second process, closely connected with state-building, is that of nation-building. Nationalist historiography has tended to conflate the two, seeing states as the natural expression of primordial nations, which over time expanded to their natural frontiers or threw off alien rule. While these accounts are no longer taken seriously by scholars, many still see nations as primordial entities, based on ethnic affinities, and postulate these as the basis for state-building, usually with a core ethnic group gradually absorbing those around it (Smith, 1986). Other diffusionist accounts dispense with the ethnic principle, but still see national integration as a steady concentration of authority, combined with assimilation to common norms. States, starting from a core territory, extend their authority to the periphery, taxing and administering their subjects. Markets develop on a national basis, breaking down locally distinct economies. Social relationships assimilate to the dominant pattern of the centre as ascriptive roles are broken down under the pressures of modernization and market exchange and national loyalties are embraced by populations disoriented by change (Deutsch, 1969). The result is to produce 'sovereign governments which have no critical regional or community cleavages' (Deutsch, 1966). This approach, which Deutsch used to analyse the western European state, but which others stretched into a general theory of development, sees national integration as a one-way process whose results are generally irreversible. It has been falsified by the development of the European state and, notably, by the revival of territorial and community-based political movements since the 1960s.

Other theories see the process of state-building and national integration as uneven processes, whose outcome was not determined in advance and which produced states of different types, with a greater or lesser degree of territorial integration. Tilly (1990) presents state formation as based on two principles, coercion and capital, the combination of which leads to different paths. Large states emerged where rulers could mobilize coercion; city states survived where they could mobilize economic resources or exploit a key position in the international trading system. Where rulers of large states encountered cities with a strong economic position, they had to bargain with them, recognizing a degree of territorial autonomy (Tilly, 1994). Spruyt (1994) presents a more historically contingent view of state formation, arguing that the emergence of the nation state was not inevitable, and that city states and urban leagues represented formidable rivals. There is not one path of state formation but several, and any explanation must take account of the military, economic and cultural dimensions. These accounts help us understand the diversity of historical experience and the important legacy of the past, but do not explicitly address territorial dimensions in contemporary politics. Rokkan and his collaborators (Lipset and Rokkan, 1967; Rokkan and Urwin, 1983; Allardt, 1982) also traced the different patterns of state formation, with large consolidated states at the edges, where there was space for the assertion of centralized authority. In the dense central belt, the existence of trading cities and the infrastructure of the church left little room for state consolidation (Rokkan, 1980). Key events and processes, such as the Reformation, industrialization, and democratization, are presented as shaping politics and cleavage structures. Integration does not necessarily proceed at the same pace and to the same extent on the three dimensions of culture, economics and politics. The disjuncture among these three processes explains the varied patterns of territorial politics inherited by the modern state. This represents a major advance on diffusionist accounts of state and nation-building, but still tends to locate the production of territorial identities in the past, and to see it as an inheritance. Certainly, it is admitted that territorial political structures can change, but 'there has been a progressive freezing process in the territorial and group structure of Western Europe' (Rokkan and Urwin, 1983, p.120). Rokkan's (1980) later work recognized the persistence of ethnic configurations and migrations, but this does still not quite explain the continued production and reproduction of territory as an element in national and European politics.

At the opposite pole from the diffusionist and national integration schools are those who see territorial conflict as an inherent and persistent feature of the nation state. Lafont (1967), drawing ideas developed earlier by Gramsci for Italy (1978a,b), presented the formation of the French state as an example of 'internal colonialism', in which the core exploited the periphery and kept it in a state of continued subordination, preventing its full integration. Hechter's (1975) attempt to apply a similar idea to the United Kingdom, was marred by fundamental conceptual, factual and methodological errors, and few have taken up the theme since. The idea of internal colonialism itself was a rather questionable effort to extend an idea developed in one context to another completely different one, but the idea of uneven development, in which national integration sustains rather than eliminating territorial economic differences, has survived to feature in the political debate about territorial government, notably in Italy.

A historical analysis, in fact, shows a variety of forms of territorial domination and integration in the European state, together with a variety of territorial oppositions with which state elites have had to contend.

STATE AND NATION-BUILDING

The earliest states tended to be differentiated, economically, politically and institutionally within themselves. England was an early example of consolidated authority, with the merging of the power of the territorial elite with that of the monarchy in the institution of Parliament, although the English state was later to merge into a more complex multinational union. In Spain, the crowns of Castile and Aragon were united in a personal union in 1469 and then merged in 1516 but retained their own laws and customs until 1714. Within the kingdom of Aragon, Catalonia had its own self-governing institutions and privileges including exemption from military service or war taxation, except in defence of Catalonia itself. Within the kingdom of Castile, the Basque provinces retained foral privileges, which permitted them to raise their own taxes and negotiate a payment to the king. They were exempt from military service and enjoyed free trade with Europe and the world, the customs posts being placed at their boundary with the rest of Spain. The kings of Spain had on their accession to swear to uphold these inherent rights. From the seventeenth century, Spanish monarchical regimes sought to build a centralized state, reducing the privileges of the component territories, but with limited success. In 1714 the autonomy of Catalonia was suppressed, but Basque privileges survived until the 1870s and, in a modified form, to the present day.

Even in France, the archetypal nation state, an extraordinary array of territorial privileges and customs survived up to the Revolution (Braudel, 1986). There were *pays d'état* and *pays d'élection*. There were *parlements* in some regions and not in others, with the right to register royal decrees; and there was a variety of obstacles to free trade. In the Burgundian realm until the end of the fifteenth century there was a proto-state, under a duke some of whose lands were held under the vague feudal authority of the king of France while others were in the Empire. Institutional uniformity was not achieved until after the Revolution, but even then marked territorial differences remained. As late as the 1870s, local identities prevailed over national loyalties and large parts of the country did not speak the standard national language (Weber, 1977).

The Habsburg empire never evolved into anything like a national state and tensions between centralizing and decentralizing forces persisted through the nineteenth century (Sked, 1989). The component lands retained many of their historic institutions and privileges, usually based on the traditional ruling classes (Taylor, 1948) and these resisted the efforts both of eighteenth-century enlightened despotism and nineteenth-century liberalism to sweep them away. Before the failed revolution of 1848, administration in Hungary was largely in the hands of the county governments dominated by the Magyar gentry, while in the various lands of the Cislethenian part of the empire, local diets and assemblies held a variety of powers. These were abolished after 1848 but brought back in the 1860s as central government struggled with the management of territorial oppositions. By the latter part of the century, these territorial oppositions had given way to nationalist movements aiming for separate states, or at least a radical transformation of the system.

Monarchical states never succeeded in eradicating territorial distinctiveness, even in the age of absolutism. Rulers strove to exercise direct control by sending out commissary agents, like the French *intendants* or the Spanish *corregidores* (Page, 1995), but still had to compound with local interests. Such territorial diversity is quite compatible with monarchical authority, even absolutism, since what matters is the final authority of the monarch, not the relationship of the territories to each other. It is much more difficult to reconcile with the principle of popular sovereignty and republicanism. The doctrine of popular sovereignty, given expression in the French Revolution and fought out during the entire nineteenth century, required a definition of the people who were to enjoy this sovereignty. The chosen candidate was the national community, and this allowed no intermediate form of sovereign authority which might undermine it. As mass participation in politics developed in the later part of the nineteenth century, it was not easily accommodated by the old provincial institutions, representative of particular interests and dominated by traditional oligarchies. At the same time, construction of the modern, administrative and, later, interventionist state (Watkins, 1991), and the penetration of local societies by the norms of rational administration and efficiency served to break down old ways. The needs of unified markets in a time of economic and industrial expansion indicated administrative and regulatory uniformity. Rising national sentiment led governments to insist of cultural and linguistic unity.

One instrument of state-building was a centralized and uniform bureaucracy, achieved relatively early in Prussia and France, and later or not at all in other states. Another was military service, which removed young men from their home region and inculcated an ideology of nationalism. Universal education, from the late nineteenth century, was used to build national identity and national value systems as well as to standardize national languages. In the twentieth century, the welfare state both drew on and reinforced notions of national solidarity and shared values. States also promoted national economic markets, with policies of protection and promotion, especially after the 1870s. Railways and later roads linked national territories, often radiating from the national capital rather than linking the provinces among themselves.

Class alignments often followed as both capitalists and workers' movements abandoned their universalist and localist orientations and became national in scope and interest. This was not a smooth or uniform process. Local bourgeoisies retained distinct interests into the twentieth century, and often took a regional view of national issues like tariff protection. Labour organization typically began at the local level, where it was usually combined with a commitment to global class solidarity, leaving no special place for the nation-state. In time, labour movements were integrated into national systems of wage bargaining and sought dialogue with national governments, but strong traces of localism remained. Nineteenth-century liberalism, for its part, tended to regard regionalism as an obstacle to progress and modernization and a refuge for reaction.

THE STATE AND TERRITORIAL OPPOSITIONS

Both the historic states of Europe and the newly established ones faced territorial cleavages. These should be seen partially as a legacy from the process of state and nation-building, but also as a product of political exchange in the nineteenth-century phase of national consolidation. An important distinction in the process of state and nation-building is that between monocephalic and polycephalic states (Rokkan and Urwin, 1983). In the former, there is one dominant centre of political and cultural power and of higher-level economic activities involving information exchange; opposed to this are the peripheries. France is the archetype of the monocephalous state, the product of a long historic evolution. The late nineteenth century saw a strengthening of this dominance and a corresponding decline of rival southern centres. The United Kingdom was also dominated by the capital. London contained the seats of political power in Westminster and Whitehall and the financial nexus of the City; the intellectual centres of Oxford and Cambridge were extensions of this central elite, although Scotland retained its own university system and Trinity College, Dublin provided an intellectual centre for the Anglo-Irish Protestant Ascendancy. Germany, on the other hand, emerged as a polycephalous state, with multiple centres of economic activity, no dominant cultural centre, and a decentralized political and administrative system. The difference is starkly illustrated by the railway systems of the late nineteenth century. In France, the whole system converges on Paris, while in Germany there is a complex network with no dominant node. In other cases, there are centres of political, economic and cultural power, but these do not coincide. Spain's political capital, Madrid, was located in the centre of the country for strategic reasons, but never achieved the dominance of Paris or London and faced rival centres in Barcelona and Bilbao. In unified Italy, too, there was a disjuncture between the political power in Rome and financial centres in Turin and Milan, while cultural and intellectual dominance tended to lie with the North. The Netherlands, starting as a confederation of provinces, evolved into a unitary state (Daalder, 1981) and the early Belgian state was constructed on unitary lines with Brussels dominating in economics and culture. In Norway, on the other hand, a centre-periphery division of labour persisted, as the capital city never established social dominance.

Changing trading patterns and industrialization in the nineteenth century, however, followed a different pattern. These did not favour national capitals but cities with natural locational advantages, creating new territorial cleavages. In the United Kingdom, trade with the empire and the American continent boosted the western ports, such as Liverpool,

Glasgow and Belfast. In France, Marseille experienced a similar effect. Spanish port cities, by contrast, suffered from the loss of empire in the early part of the century and again in the catastrophe of 1898. The central trading belt of Europe, from northern Italy, through to Flanders, was eclipsed by the new trade patterns, though it recovered in the following century. Industrialization in the nineteenth century was concentrated on regions with natural advantages, notably water transport or access to coal, iron ore or hydro-electricity. This often dictated a peripheral rather than a central location. Lombardy, Vizcaya, the Pennine region of England, west-central Scotland, the Ruhr valley, the Lille area, extending into both France and Belgium, and eastern France, became new centres of economic might. Other regions, such as Brittany, were peripheralized. This created new tensions between growing and declining regions, as well as between the new industrial centres and the dominant political centres in Rome, Madrid, London and Paris. In Norway, the dominance of Oslo in politics, education and rail links was offset by the advantages of the coastal periphery in water transport, access to British markets and hydro-electric power (Aarebrot, 1982). In Bohemia, industrialization added to tensions with the imperial centre in Vienna. In some cases, as in France and the United Kingdom, industrialization was concentrated at the periphery, but financial services and banking at the centre, giving the tension between financial and industrial capital a territorial dimension.

The combination of changing economic realities with political state-building and policies of national integration also produced tensions. Emerging industrial classes generally favoured integrated national markets in order to facilitate the distribution of their products but had differing interests with regard to tariff protection. In the UK, industrialists were firmly committed to free trade until the First World War, and Manchester, often recognized as the spiritual centre of the Liberal Party, was both the centre of the export-oriented textile industry and a bastion of free trade (Schonhardt-Bailey, 1991). Industrialists elsewhere tended to define their own interests in relation to the threat of British competition and to support protectionism; but the national and regional context differed. The bourgeoisie of Catalonia, aware that they were the most efficient in Spain but unequal to north European competition, had an ambivalent set of interests. They wanted to escape the agrarian–military–clerical interests dominant in Madrid by a measure of regional self-government; but at the same time sought tariff protection to deliver them a captive Spanish market. In the north of Italy, industrialists faced a similar dilemma and also went for protection, but in alliance with the agrarian interests of the south. A similar protectionist alliance was forged between the German grain producers east of the Elbe and the industrialists of the Ruhr (Conze,

1962; Wilson, 1962). French northern industrialists were highly protectionist and were able to prevail in national politics, to the disadvantage of southern interests, which were trapped into existing modes of production (Brunstein, 1988). Wine producers in southern France used the political system to secure protection and support for the expansion of local viticulture, further discouraging diversification and rendering the region vulnerable to cyclical shocks. In Austria-Hungary, the lack of a national political system made a similar alliance impossible and the dominant aristocratic agrarian interests were able effectively to prevent the industrialization of Hungary, while in Bohemia an indigenous bourgeoisie developed an advanced industry. Belgian economic and political patterns of domination were mutually reinforcing, with industrialization benefiting Wallonia rather than the older commercial regions of Flanders.

In centralized states, there was a tendency for the provincial bourgeoisies to adopt the social values and cultural traits of the centre. They moved to the capital, adopted its accent and sent their children to the central schools and universities. This cultural deracination was notable in France and the UK, which lost their vigorous provincial bourgeoisies in the late nineteenth and early twentieth centuries. In Belgium, the French cultural pole had greater attraction than the Flemish one until the 1950s. This is a cultural effect, but one with economic and political consequences, reducing the status of regional identity and enhancing that of the centre. In Germany, the capital had less social and cultural pull and regional bourgeoisies retained their identities. In Spain, too, the centre failed to establish cultural hegemony and Catalonia and the Basque Country retained their indigenous bougeoisies, though some of these, especially in the Basque Country, did opt for identification with the centre. In Norway, regional dialects and culture remained a part of national identity and there was even less pressure for assimilation to the central norms as a mechanism for social advancement.

Territorial politics also moulded emerging peasant and working class movements. Agrarian discontent, perhaps because of the tie to the land and local structures of ownership, often assumed a regional form and in Ireland, Scotland, southern Spain and southern Italy was associated with territorial mobilization, of greater or less effectiveness. The industrial labour movement was usually local and regional in its origins, linked to locally dominant industrial sectors, only gradually extending to the whole national territory. This intense localism was allied with universalist doctrines of proletarian solidarity. Working class organizations, however, had to accommodate themselves to existing and developing national identities. In some cases, this led to identification with the central state;

in others with minority nationalism. In some areas, such as Catalonia and south Wales, labour movements were imbued with anarchist ideas hostile to the centralizing state and favourable to local action. Others were more tied to Marxism and revolutionary strategy. In the mining communities, local traditions of solidarity and struggle evolved into territorial solidarities. When not informed by Marxist or anarchist doctrine, labour movements tended to borrow much of their political ideology and strategy from radicals and advanced liberals and followed their Jacobin line of opposition to regional particularism and support for centralization; even the French Communist Party after 1920 strongly identified with republican and Jacobin principles. The intersection of class and territorial interests created further political cleavages. Unified Italy has often been presented as run by a coalition of the northern industrialists and southern landowners. In return for industrial tariff protection, the northern bourgeoisie agreed not to disturb the pattern of landholding in the south. In due course, the northern working class was taken into this coalition by the promise of industrial jobs, leaving the southern peasantry isolated and exploited.

Religious cleavages also had a strong territorial dimension. The division between Catholic and Protestant Europe was largely frozen after the Peace of Westphalia in 1648 and cut across several states, notably Germany, the Netherlands, Switzerland and the United Kingdom. The nineteenth century saw two further religious divisions. In Protestant countries, fundamentalist groups broke away to form their own factions or separate churches; this occurred in England, Wales and Scotland; in the Netherlands; and in Norway. Protestant fundamentalism tended to be strongest in peripheral regions and was associated with strong community norms, including regulation of sexual morals and prohibition of alcohol. In Catholic countries, a series of conflicts pitted the Church and the practising population against secularizing and anti-clerical movements. This also assumed a territorial dimension, since anti-clericals were usually republican and Jacobin and used the central state to challenge Church powers. Catholics, for their part, often took refuge in territorial defence and local tradition. This cleavage marked the politics of France under the Third Republic and was visible also in Spain, in Italy, where both state–church and class conflicts were moulded by region (Lyttleton, 1996) and in Belgium, where Flemish particularism rested on Catholicism, tradition and ruralism. In Germany, the challenge to the Catholic Church came from the political right, in the form of Bismarck's *Kulturkampf* of the 1870s but this also created territorial oppositions to the centralizing state (Urwin, 1982).

Language and culture were other markers of regional identity, which often collided with the policies of the centralizing and uniformizing state. Linguistic uniformity became an issue when nationalist ideology declared that it was a necessary element in national identity, with the corollary that minorities should be assimilated or secede. It became a crucial issue in public policy with the expansion of education, industrialization and economic change, the increased penetration of society by the state, and mass mobilization. This impetus for linguistic uniformity, transmitted through education and public administration, faced a complex linguistic reality in society. No state was linguistically homogeneous, with the possible exceptions of Denmark and Portugal, but the status of language groups varied. Some languages were quite distinct from the state language but indigenous, such as Basque or Gaelic. Others were distinct but exoglossic, that is they constituted the national language of another state, as with Flemish, the languages of Switzerland, or Swedish in Finland. Some belonged to the same language group as the dominant language, including the Iberian languages other than Basque, the Italian languages, Occitan, Norwegian and Scots. Exoglossic languages could never of course be extirpated by states and the existence of a written standard and literature allowed them to develop, to remain as bearers of regional identity, though there were usually arguments about accepting the exoglossic standard. Only in the 1950s did Flemish accept the written standard of Dutch and an argument continues about whether Galego should accept the written standard of Portuguese.

Languages without an external standard faced two dangers. One was extinction, the avowed policy of French policy makers towards Breton and Occitan and which found a reflection in the attitudes to Welsh of the 1847 British Blue Books. Another danger was represented by diglossia, in which the regional language is used in familiar situations but not in high status or official roles. In diglossia, the upper classes often abandon the language, which is reduced to the status of a *patois* and it comes to reflect as much as class as a regional identity. This was the fate even of languages with a previously flourishing literary tradition, such Occitan, Galego and Scots, much more so with lower status dialects. Such second-level regional dialects survived as a mark of identity over large parts of Europe until at least the 1960s. Education and the mass media then eroded them in the UK and France, but they survived more strongly in Italy, Switzerland, Norway and Germany.

In other cases, the language retained high status and the upper classes continued to use it, even while being forced to use the state language for official purposes. Regions with their own *koine*, or common dialect, could continue to use it as a medium of social communication in the modern age, while purely local dialects gave way to the national standard.

These issues were themselves part of the political and social struggle of the late nineteenth century. While in general only state languages thrived as a medium for advanced forms of communication, the work of philologists forged modern languages out of dialectical variants in some regions, where political movements supported and sustained the work. Hence Catalan survived and developed, while its neighbour Occitan declined. In Norway, the result was to produce not just one language distinct from the old Danish standard, but two, reinforcing a cultural cleavage within the emerging Norwegian state.

So territorial identity is not merely a legacy from the past but was reforged in the consolidation of the modern state. Territorial movements could be triggered by a number of events. The religious revivals sweeping large parts of Europe in the late nineteenth century provoked mass mobilizations around cultural distinctiveness. Local languages and cultures experienced a renaissance in Catalonia, Provence and elsewhere, but a separate language was not always necessary. In Ireland a literary revival took place in the English language. Economic shocks could provoke massive political change and a redefinition of identities, as happened in Vizcaya in the late nineteenth century (De La Granja, 1995). External shocks, such as Spanish defeat in the war of 1898 or Austrian defeat in 1866 could lead to a questioning of the territorial structure of the state itself. From these elements, territorial identities could be forged and reproduced.

State-building elites relied heavily on myths and invented history to legitimate their claims. Belgium, for example, was named after an ancient tribe who had struggled against Caesar but whose connection with the new state created in 1830 was tenuous, to say the least; after 1830 a Belgian history was created and provincial histories represented as a part of this (Erbe, 1994). In opposition, regionalists engaged in their own 'invention of tradition' (Hobsbawm and Ranger, 1983) as a means of legitimation through history, often helped by the contemporary Romantic movement. The Welsh Eisteddfod was an invention of the 1700s, a century which also saw the notorious Ossian forgeries of the Scot MacPherson. In 1822 Sir Walter Scott invented a pastiche of Highland ceremony to legitimize King George IV in Scotland, going so far as to dress the monarch in a kilt and pink tights for a parade through Edinburgh. Scott's historical romances stimulated a wave of imitation throughout Europe, though Scott himself was a firm believer in the progress of Britain through union and was more concerned to ease the transition to modernity than in returning to the past. In southern France, the late nineteenth century saw a cultural revival based on the local language and known as the *Félibrige*. While this was not explicitly political, its leading figures, such as the poet Mistral, stressed traditionalism and conservative values. The early Basque movement was steeped in romantic visions, as was that of Catalonia. Invention of tradition did not always reinforce conservatism and hierarchy. In Scotland and Wales, it was pressed into the service of radical and democratizing movements opposed to the British class system and structures in church and state which supported it. Democratic traditions were discovered in religious dissidence, such as the Scottish Covenanters and the Albigensian heretics of Languedoc. Erskine of Marr even managed to find a form of primitive communism in traditional Celtic clan society. One of the most blatant examples of historical invention was in the work of Sabino Arana, founding figure of Basque nationalism, who sustained the view that the Basque provinces had never been part of Spain, but merely shared the same monarch (De La Granja, 1995). His accounts of battles in the past were little more than inspired fiction. In Sicily, a mythologized past took the Sicilian Vespers as the foundation of a distinct nation, and promoted an ideology of *sicilitudine*, a romanticized view of Sicilian identity which is unchanging over time and resistant to the waves of foreigners who had conquered the island (Ganci, 1978). This was a consoling vision, enabling nineteenth-century Sicilians to deny responsibility for their own fate.

So tradition could be reinterpreted and invented to reproduce the contemporary self-image of the local society in a rather flexible way. This counter-history was of course merely the mirror-image of official histories transmitted either through a socializing state apparatus, as in France, or through the interpretation of a dominant class, as with the Whig version of history in Britain. These official histories consistently disparaged the peripheries and presented the movement towards national uniformity as synonymous with progress and civilization. In the Habsburg empire, the lack of state-building went along with a lack of official statist history. In the first half of the nineteenth century Metternich had even been prepared to invent provincial traditions to defuse opposition and sustain traditional order (Taylor, 1948).

The politicization of territorial opposition in the late nineteenth century took a variety of forms. Often these were rooted in conservative and traditionalist sectors, using territory as a protection against the encroaching state and social change. Traditional agrarian elites and the Catholic Church similarly emphasized the territorial theme in disputing the claims of the sovereign and secular state. The French Revolution had swept away the old provinces, replacing them with technocratically-designed departments in the name of uniformity and modernization. Opposition to the Revolution was concentrated in regions, notably in the west of France, and this territorial cleavage was reflected in the struggles over the republic versus monarchy throughout the nineteenth century. Regionalism became identified with traditionalism, conservatism and reaction; centralization with republicanism, democracy and secularization. So the Breton nobility, previously centralist and tied to the state, developed an ideology of localism after 1830 (Guillorel, 1981, 1991) and sought to insulate the province from the virus of modernity. In Spain, regionalism and defence of the *fueros*, or traditional territorial privileges, was associated with Carlism, a dynastic movement which provoked a series of civil wars and was particularly strong in Catalonia and the Basque Country. Carlism bears a striking similarity to Jacobitism, a movement in the British Isles which in the eighteenth century sought to restore the Stuart dynasty, appealing to traditional territories threatened with social change (Highland Scotland and parts of Ireland) and promising to respect or restore territorial institutions including the clan system and the Scottish parliament — it was not, contrary to a widespread belief, a movement of Irish or Scottish nationalism, which are essentially modern phenomena. Jacobitism was effectively killed off by the failed rebellion of 1745–6 and with it the alliance of regionalism and traditionalism in the British isles. In England, the last outbreak of traditionalist opposition was probably the Pilgrimage of Grace in 1536; thereafter the aristocracy and gentry had been taken into partnership in the development of the state. Regionalism and defence of territorial rights was also a theme played with greater success by landed elites in the Habsburg empire, where regionalism was regarded by liberals as generally backward (Taylor, 1948). The Hungarian gentry were able to carve out a position through control of local government before 1848 and, after the *Ausgleich* of 1867, held back social change and political development within their part of the empire. In imperial Germany, too, landed interests were successful in playing the territorial card and using decentralized government to protect their interests and they consistently upheld a federalist interpretation of the constitution (Mommsen, 1995). In southern Italy, traditionalist forces played a more complex game. They could call on regionalist and anti-Rome sentiment where it furthered their own interests, but never developed a regionally-based project of their own to counterpose to the unitary state, preferring instead to play the game of central politics to their own advantage by trading support with ruling coalitions in Rome. Nineteenth-century regionalisms tended not to be opposed to the unity of the state, but rather saw national identity as rooted in the regions and local communities rather than central institutions (Thiesse, 1994). This was a different and more traditional way of looking at authority.

Yet not all regionalisms were conservative. In Spain and Italy there was a liberal federalist tradition, but these failed to make headway. Spanish federalism was damaged fatally by the unhappy experience of the federal First Republic of 1873 and thereafter it was seen as a threat to the unity of the state. In Italy the needs of unification and pacification of the south left little scope for federalist ideas (Ciuffoletti, 1994). So the Jacobin element tended to predominate among Italian and Spanish liberals, modelled on France, where republicanism and liberalism were associated with centralization, albeit mediated by networks of clientelistic brokerage. In some regions, modernizing social classes used their territorial bases to seek reform in the state. This was the case of the dynamic Catalan bourgeoisie in the late nineteenth and early twentieth century, when the movement, in its 'regionalist' phase sought the 'catalanization' of Spain. In the UK, the energies of the thrusting industrial middle classes of Birmingham, Manchester and Glasgow were absorbed in municipal improvement. Liberals sometimes played the territorial card, notably in the UK and occasionally in Austria-Hungary before 1848 (Taylor, 1948). Generally, however, they favoured the central state, even when this was undemocratic as in Germany, seeing it as the best hope of progress (Urwin, 1982; Mommsen, 1995).

There were also radical/progressive regionalisms, for example in Scotland and Wales, where territorial politics was associated with the left more than the right, and which at this stage should probably be classified as regionalist rather than nationalist (Morgan, 1980; Keating and Bleiman, 1979). In France, the *Mouvement régionaliste français* gained support from politicians around the political centre, insisting, against the protests of reactionaries like Charles Maurass and radicals like Georges Clemenceau, that regionalism was indeed compatible with the republic (Flory, 1966). In Italy the *Meridionalismo* of Dorso and Salvemini (Galasso, 1978; Ciuffoletti, 1994) saw the answer to the underdevelopment of the south not in more centralization and dependency or centrally-managed solutions, but in social change through self-government. This theme, that modernization and reform of the Mezzogiorno could come only through reform and decentralization of the state, never quite died out and was to re-emerge in the 1940s, the 1960s and again in the 1990s. In France, the Occitan *Félibrige* , while generally traditionalist and leaning to reaction, had a left-wing element, the so-called *Félibrige rouge* (Touraine et al., 1981), though this proved weak and ephemeral. This linking of the left with regionalism was often merely the product of circumstance, left-wing strength in specific regions but weakness at the level of the state. As left-wing and progressive parties gained representation in national politics, they tended to abandon dreams of regional autonomy. This happened dramatically in Scotland after 1922

(Keating and Bleiman, 1979). In Norway, the early advances of the Labour Party in the north allowed a coalition of rural proletariat and urban working class which was to dominate national politics (Rokkan, 1966).

It is from these elements that regional politics emerged in the modern state. This was reflected in party structures and voting behaviour as states moved to universal suffrage, and in the political agenda. In some cases, territory dominated political life, producing parties based purely on territory and even separatist movements. In other cases, regional parties competed with state-wide ones. In yet others, territorial politics was conducted within a system of ostensibly state-wide parties, moulding patterns of support and shaping the nature of the parties themselves.

Politics in the Habsburg Empire revolved increasingly around ethnic and territorial alignments, forcing even the social democrats to follow by 1907, splitting into separate national parties. In Catalonia and the Basque Country, local parties broke the *cacique* system at the turn of the century and established a pattern of separate parties which have competed with the state-wide parties ever since. In Ireland, the secret ballot swept aside the landlord-dominated system of representation after 1867 and from then until 1918 the Irish Party acted as a territorial broker, while at the same time seeking home rule within the UK. Proposals for a similar party in Wales foundered as Welsh leaders found a home in the British Liberal Party, but the distinct pattern of Welsh politics, tied to non-conformist religion, communalism and a localist culture, survived to influence both the Labour Party and the nationalist Plaid Cymru. In Italy after the concession of universal male suffrage in 1913, the Popular Party of Sturzo preached a christian democratic message and supported regional autonomy in the south. After the First World War, a Sardinian party enjoyed a brief surge. For the most part, however, regionalism was subordinated to the manipulations of the power brokers who controlled the links with Rome. In imperial Germany, there were a few regional parties. Hannover had its own Guelph party which had refused to accept annexation to Germany, local parties in Alsace-Lorraine resisted successively France, Germany, then France again (Urwin, 1982) and in Silesia, the Polish fraction performed well (Conze, 1962). Generally, however, the state-wide parties formed alliances to share out seats regionally and locally. Under the Weimar Republic, regionalism increased. Bavaria developed its own dominant party, the right-wing Catholic Bavarian People's Party.

In many cases, ostensibly state-wide parties consisted of coalitions of locally-based formations. Until the early twentieth century, the German party system could be characterized as a loosely connected system of regional parties (Rohe, 1990a; Ritter, 1990). In France and Italy, politicians retained territorial bases and state-wide parties remained weak until after the Second World War. British parties were more centralized from the late nineteenth century, although Scotland retained many of its own structures, notably for the Conservative and Liberal parties.

Where territorial parties did not exist, territorial variations in voting were still often marked. Many of these variations corresponded to religious divisions or responses to critical events like regime changes; others may have reflected economic interests and patterns of interest intermediation. These influences were not randomly distributed across space but rather, patterns of religious affiliation and cultural norms were rooted in territorial societies. In the United Kingdom, religion and region were the dominant factors in voting behaviour before the First World War, only later giving way to class (Wald, 1983; Bogdanor and Field, 1993). French political cleavages under the Third Republic (1870–1940) reflected historical patterns forged in the revolutionary era as well as earlier religious and cultural patterns. The west was conservative and clerical, the Mediterranean south was republican and left, as were large parts of the centre (Dogan, 1967; Goguel, 1970). Nor did the advance of class voting eliminate regional patterns. While the move of the north and the Paris suburban ring to the left can be explained by industrialization and the arrival of a large working class, this cannot explain why eastern France, which was also industrializing, moved to the right, nor why the south-west, which was not, moved to the left (Goguel, 1970). Italian political behaviour was also strongly regionalized. In the former Papal States and in Tuscany, traditions of revolt and anti-clericalism favoured left-wing voting (Dogan, 1967), while in the more religious areas, there was support for conservative forces, especially after the lifting of the papal ban on participation in politics in 1913. In the south, a pattern of support for the governing party emerged, tied to the clientelist networks. So in the years 1892–1909, the *Ministeriali* gained between 73 per cent and 78 per cent of the vote in the south, against 48–60 per cent in the northern regions (SVIMEZ, 1954). Even in 1913, the Liberals, inheriting the client networks, gained markedly more in the south than in the north. This pattern was broken by the fragmentation of the party system in 1919 and the rise of Fascism but, as we shall, see, it re-established itself after the Second World War. In Belgium, the left consistently performed better in the Walloon areas than in the Flemish ones (De Smet et al., 1958). Norwegian voting behaviour was strongly regionalized, following local subcultures rooted in religious attachments and language (Hagen et al., 1991). In the south and west, a culture based on religious fundamentalism, temperance and the *Nynorsk* language survived the arrival of manhood suffrage in 1900 and left a strong legacy for future generations (Rokkan, 1967). In the united German Bundestag, universal male suffrage was established from the start. Among the national parties, the Social Democrats (SPD) won 30 per cent of the vote, but this reached over 60 per cent in Hamburg and only 16 per cent in Bavaria. They gained 56 per cent of the vote in Berlin in 1893, reaching 75 per cent in 1912, but only 11–22 per cent in the conservative heartlands of East and West Prussia (Ritter, 1980). The industrial heartland of the Ruhr was an electoral desert for the SPD up to the end of the century, because of the strong Catholic tradition and the social rooting of the Catholic *Zentrum*, which gained some 80 per cent of the Catholic votes there (Rohe, 1990a). While winning 60 per cent in the Rhine provinces and 53 per cent in Bavaria in 1893, the *Zentrum* barely registered in north eastern areas like Brandenburg, Pommerania and East and West Prussia. In the latter territories, the Conservatives dominated, but their support fell away sharply in the south (Specht, 1898).

Modernization, universal suffrage and the rise of class politics in the twentieth century did not obliterate these patterns. Rather, the rise of modern politics was shaped in large measure by these territorial influences. Working class and socialist movements were forged in specific contexts, drawing on local traditions and building varying coalitions depending on the balance of local forces. In some places, they drew on older traditions of dissent or religious alignments. In France, Italy and Spain, there was a strong anticlerical element, often geographically rooted. In Wales, and some parts of England and Scotland, socialism grew out of non-conformist religion, with its traditions of democratic equality and opposition to the gentry and established church. In some regions, the peasantry was won for radicalism and socialism or anarchism; in others it was a bastion of conservatism. In Ireland and Scotland, the class issue faced the competing question of nationalism, losing out in the former and subordinating nationalism in the latter.

Twentieth-century mass politics in some cases even accentuated the importance of place, by mobilizing people in subcultures rooted in local milieus. Working class subcultures were important in imperial and Weimar Germany, in the United Kingdom, in France, Italy and parts of Scandinavia, while Catholic subcultures flourished in other parts of Germany, France and Italy. In the Ruhr region of Germany, a Catholic subculture developed before the socialists got organized and, in this overwhelmingly industrial region, resisted the advance of the left until after the Second World War (Rohe, 1990a; 1992). In these regions, voting was part of a wider behavioural pattern. Parties complemented other institutions in civil society, including trade unions, cultural and sporting associations, youth and women's groups and, in religious areas, the churches. Far from being a relic of pre-state politics, these subcultures were precisely a way of coping with the presence of the modern state and mass politics since the political movements based in subcultures and territorial societies served in turn to reshape those societies themselves.

In the immediate aftermath of the First World War, there was a brief explosion of territorial discontent in many parts of western Europe. War and the destabilization of politics had upset old patterns, while democratization or the extension of the franchise brought in previously unmobilized electors. Disintegration of the central empires and the rhetoric of some of the victorious powers encouraged movements for self-determination or even separatism, fed often by discontents arising from wartime or postwar conditions. In Ireland, the home rule movements of the nineteenth century were eclipsed by the radical nationalism of Sinn Fein, leading to the establishment of the Irish Free State. Scottish nationalism experienced a briefer resurgence, before the state-wide parties re-established their dominance (Keating and Bleiman, 1979). In Spain, the Catalan and Basque regionalist movements reached their climax, before being stifled by the dictatorship of Primo de Rivera. When they re-emerged in the 1930s, they too had been transformed in a more radical and nationalist direction. Sardinian and Sicilian autonomist movements flourished briefly, drawing on the support of demobilized soldiers and accompanied by a spate of land occupations and extending in Sardinia to separatism (Caronna, 1970; Ganci, 1978; Mack Smith, 1986). There was a ephemeral independent state in Bavaria, and some rumblings elsewhere in Germany. In France, by contrast, the war had served to reinforce national identity and unity, and further delegitimize territorial politics, still regarded as somehow akin to separatism. Similarly, in Belgium the experience of war, and the collaboration by sections of the Flemish movement with the German occupation weakened the budding sense of Flemish particularism, and strengthened the sense of Belgian patriotism. By the late 1920s, regionalism and minority nationalism had generally been contained by the west European states, either through the reincorporation of territorial discontented populations into national systems of representation or, as in Spain, through overt repression. Regionalism and minority nationalism survived among opposition forces in Spain, and the experience of the Franco regime was to forge an alliance between these forces and democratic elements generally. In Nazi Germany, regionalism survived only in the form of folklore, presented as an integral part of the German nation, without political implications. Similarly in Fascist Italy, there were some official efforts to promote regionalism as tradition and folklore, in opposition to modernization and foreign influences (Bernardy, 1930). This passeist ideology was later taken up by the Vichy regime in France, forcing regionalism back into its old association with reaction.

THE TERRITORIAL STATE

Territorial diversity was thus an integral part of the national state, not merely a relic of pre-modern forms. Its management has been a feature of state practice ever since. This takes the form of institutional accommodation, political practice and policy concessions. Adapting the Rokkan and Urwin (1982, 1983) typology, we can recognize three types of state: the unitary state; the federal state; and the union state. In the unitary state, there is one source of sovereignty, a dominant centre and administrative centralization and standardization. There is a centralized bureaucracy and all territories are treated in the same way. France is usually seen as the archetype of the unitary state, in which the principles of unity and centralization laid down by the monarchy were made a reality by the Napoleonic regime. Republican regimes in the nineteenth century did not generally question Napoleonic centralization, but saw it as the appropriate framework for nation-building and citizenship. Italy on its unification in the 1860s also adopted the French model of the Napoleonic unitary state, as did Belgium in 1830 and the Netherlands in 1814. Successive Spanish regimes sought with less success to impose a unitary framework on the Spanish state. The smaller European states of Norway, Denmark, Sweden and Ireland also emerged as unitary states in the nineteenth and twentieth centuries. Few unitary states have concentrated power in the way Jacobin theory might suggest. In some northern European cases, political centralization is offset by traditions of municipal self-government and a degree of administrative decentralization. In the Napoleonic states of France, Italy, Spain and Belgium, formal centralization was balanced by intricate central–local linkages which permitted local elites to extract resources and policy exceptions. These were not the traditional territorial elites who so often formed the social basis for regionalist movements, but a new middle class of lawyers, educators and other professionals. Their power resided in their control of the central–local nexus, through the accumulation of office and the capture of the territorial officials of the central bureaucracy. Secure in local power bases, they displaced territorial politics into bargaining in the national arena through loosely-structured and largely unprincipled political parties. Such were the *notables* of France, the *notabili* of Italy and the *caciques* of Spain.

The federal state divides sovereignty between the centre and the regions, with constitutionally entrenched power at each level. There is typically a second legislative chamber at the federal level to represent the federated units. Federal systems may further be divided into mechanical federalism, imposed from above and in which there is a hierarchical system with one centre; and organic federalism, constructed from below, in which divergent territories come together but retain their own individuality, and there is no dominant centre (Rokkan and Urwin, 1983). Germany was the principal example of a federal state in the late nineteenth century, composed of the old states which had been brought together in the course of unification. Unlike France, where a dominant urban centre had subdued the periphery, Germany was unified from the rural periphery, in the form of the militarized Prussian state. The empire was therefore forced to concede autonomy to the advanced urban heartland (Rokkan, 1980) as well as the culturally distinct south, and the traditional rulers elsewhere. There was some confusion about the theoretical status of the federation and locus of sovereignty under the Empire between 1871 and 1918 (Emerson, 1928) but in practice power was centralized in the imperial government and chancellor, while the weight of Prussia, with 62 per cent of the population, effectively dominated the whole. In the Bundesrat, representing the federated states, Prussia's vote was enough to block constitutional changes and the imperial chancellor was, at least until the later years of the regime, able to operate through the Prussian government (Mommsen, 1995). Nonetheless, the states did have substantial powers in police, education, judicial affairs and several fields of taxation (Urwin, 1982). Bavaria and Württemberg had special privileges, especially in military and postal affairs (Conze, 1962). Federalism had been employed by the Bismarckian regime as a means of limiting democratic influence, a factor which hardened opposition among democrats and the left. After a struggle between unitarists and federalists, the Weimar Republic retained the federal principle, but the federation was strengthened by taking over most of taxation and giving legislative predominance to the federal Reichstag over the Reichsrat, which represented the states. The unbalanced pattern of states was unchanged but Prussian predominance was reduced (Heiber, 1993).

Switzerland is the prime example of an organic federation, though it is usually described as a confederation, an association of equal states with a weak central government. The federal principle was invoked by republicans in Spain in the nineteenth century but was discredited with the failure of the first republic in the 1870s. Thereafter, it had limited appeal to conservative Basque and Catalan nationalists, who were more interested in their distinct needs and were suspicious of the association of federalism with republicanism. The principle was retained by some of the Spanish left, and became the official policy of the socialist party in 1918. It was also taken up by left-wing Catalans from the 1920s, who dreamed of a free Catalonia in an Iberian confederation. Federalism was also urged as a way of managing the Austro-Hungarian empire towards its end, but these ideas made little headway given the discredit into which the regime had fallen.

The union state possesses a single centre of authority but this does not enjoy identical relations with each of the constituent territories. These have been incorporated over time by treaty and agreement and their status continues to be governed by written or unwritten pacts. There is administrative standardization over most of the territory, but various territories retain their own institutions, laws and customs. This was the characteristic state form of the pre-modern era, as we have seen, but was often swept away by Napoleonic and Jacobin reformers in favour of unity and control. Some states, however, preserved union features. The most complex example was the Austro-Hungarian empire. From 1867 this was divided into two parts, united by a shared monarchy and common defence and foreign policy. In the Hungarian part, the dominant Magyars sought to build a unitary state, with little room for minorities. In the other part, which did not even have an official name but is usually known as Cislethenia, a complex system of provincial diets, varied laws and privileges applied in the various territories. Since Cislethenia did not have a government of its own, it relied on the imperial government and the local diets for its administration. The United Kingdom is also a union state (Mitchell, 1996; Brockliss and Eastwood, 1997). Wales was largely assimilated administratively into England after 1536, though from the late nineteenth century it was able to obtain some legislative and administrative exceptions. Scotland was brought into Great Britain by a negotiated pact, which stipulated the preservation of many of its institutions and practices. Thereafter, it was managed apart from England, under the control of its local elites and, as long as these were true to the union, they were left alone for most of the nineteenth century (Fry, 1987; Harvie, 1995; Paterson, 1994; Dicey and Rait, 1920). Ireland had a different status again. Its parliament, representing the Protestant minority, survived until the union of 1800. Thereafter Ireland was not assimilated administratively to England, but nor was it managed by its own elites. Rather it was governed by representatives of the central power in London. A whole series of exceptional measures was applied there to manage dissent, by concessions, as in the land reform of the late nineteenth century, or by repression. Spain, too, retained features typical of the union state in the Basque *fueros*, which were not attacked until

1839 and finally suppressed in the 1870s, following Carlist revolts. Even then, a special fiscal regime, the *concierto económico*, was put in place, allowing the Basque provinces to collect their own taxes and negotiate a contribution with Madrid.

In their various ways, then, European states continued to recognize the importance of territory, incorporating mechanisms for managing it even within ostensibly unitary states. There is rather little to say about the inter-war years. In the face of resurgent nationalism, insecurity and the collapse of the international trading order, states tended to strengthen themselves and territorial politics was quiescent, with the notable exception of Spain. After the Second Word War, however, a new challenge was posed by the rise of the welfare state, the extension of social citizenship and the assumption by government of broad responsibilities in economic management. While these, too, were often thought to involve the suppression of territorial politics and the final stage in national integration and homogenization, they too needed to take account of the territorial dimension.

3. Regions in the Welfare State

THE POSTWAR SETTLEMENT

In the aftermath of the Second World War, western European states reacted to the regional question in contrasting ways. In the post-authoritarian regimes of Germany and Italy, regional decentralization was associated with democratization, pluralism and stability, and was written into their new constitutions. For the established democracies, by contrast, modernization was associated with centralized government and regions were downgraded. Some countries which had experienced German occupation had a further reason to reject regionalism since elements of regionalist movements had collaborated with the occupying power. The two remaining authoritarian regimes, in Spain and Portugal, were run on rigidly centralist lines.

In Germany, the regional dimension in politics had been weakened under Nazism, which had destroyed regional institutions and undermined regional subcultures and civil societies. Massive population movements after the war further weakened regional and local attachments, though these remained strong in the south. Political activity started at a local and regional level, which was all that was initially permitted under the occupation but soon a national party system emerged. The Social Democratic Party (SPD) was a revival of the pre-war party and was national in orientation, though strongly entrenched in certain parts of the country. The Christian Democratic Party was new and was the first conservative party in Germany to unite both Catholics and Protestants, giving it a broader geographical as well as social appeal than its predecessors. As a 'catch-all' party with a broadly-defined set of principles, it gradually absorbed its rivals on the centre-right, including local and regional parties. The only one of these to hold out was the Christian Social Union (CSU) of Bavaria, which formed a close alliance with the CDU under which they did not contest elections in each others' territory. The third party, the liberal FDP, was also new, and nationally-based.

Allied policy in the western zone was based on the principles of the 'four ds' — denazification, demilitarization, democratization, and decentralization. German political activity was permitted first at a local and regional level, with eleven new Länder carved out of the occupation zones. Only three of these had a solid historic basis, the former kingdom of Bavaria and the Hanseatic city-states of Hamburg and Bremen. Particular care was taken to break up the former Prussia, seen as the seat of German militarism. The result was a very unbalanced set of regions. The largest, North Rhine-Westphalia, has a population of 17 million and contained the heart of German heavy industrial production, while the city-state of Bremen, by contrast, contains just 600,000 people. Some adjustments were made to the system in the 1950s. After the French withdrawal in 1957, the coal-producing region of the Saar became a Land, and in 1952 three Länder were merged to produce Baden-Württemberg. West Berlin, although not formally part of the Federal Republic, was treated in many respects as a separate Land. Otherwise, the Land boundaries, as they came to provide power bases for political elites, have remained unchanged. Only in 1949 did the allied powers permit the Land governments to come together to form a national government. The Basic Law, which was intended as a provisional constitution, was drawn up and adopted by the Länder without a national referendum and reflects the traditions of German federalism in its division of responsibilities and provisions for cooperation.

Italy had experienced rigid centralization under the Fascist regime, though this was less effective than in Germany and the Fascists had been obliged to leave many of the local and regional power structures, notably of the Church and the big landowners, intact. Regional development focused on grandiose civil engineering projects, but schemes for land reform proposed by the more radical elements of the regime came to little and the social and economic structures of the underdeveloped south survived little changed. The fall of the Fascist regime produced an outbreak of regionalist movements in the periphery. In Sicily, occupied by the Allies in 1943, there was a short-lived separatist movement linked to Mafia elements who had helped the Allied takeover, but this was a tactical manoeuvre. Both the Mafia and the Americans, fearing a long war and a left-wing government in Rome at its end, saw Sicily as a safe base, positioned strategically in the Mediterranean. When these fears proved ill-founded, both dropped the Sicilian secessionist option. The movement had been powerful enough in the meantime to force the acceptance of a special autonomy statute for the island, which was only later incorporated into the new Italian constitution. In Sardinia, there was a weaker repetition of the regionalist agitation which had followed the First World War and a special statute was conceded here too. Other special statutes were provided for the northern border regions of Val d'Aosta and Trentino-Alto Adige, to satisfy the demands of linguistic minorities and stave off irredentist forces from France and Austria respectively. A fifth special statute was conceded in 1963 to Friuli-Venezia-Guilia, another ethnically-mixed border region where there was a dispute with Yugoslavia.

In principle, there was a broad commitment to decentralization on the part of the anti-Fascist parties in the post-war coalition emerging from the Committee of National Liberation (CLN), which itself had operated at a local and regional level under the German occupation (Bonora, 1984). The principal components of this were the Christian Democrats, the Communists and Socialists, and a short-lived liberal democratic party known the *Partito d'Azione*. Italian Christian Democracy was the heir of Sturzo's *Partito Popolare* (Popular Party) and inherited its commitment to decentralization, subsidiarity and traditionalism. Regionalism was both a means to deepen democracy and a way of keeping communism and fascism at bay. The *Partito d'Azione* was committed to administrative decentralization and contained a number of southern autonomists who saw it as the best vehicle for their ambitions (Caronna, 1970). The left was more circumspect, seeing regions as bastions of conservatism and an obstacle to the ambitions of a radical government in Rome. It supported the establishment of regions, but sought to limit their powers and autonomy as far as possible. So the 1946 constitution stipulated that Italy was a regionalized state, but left the structure and powers of regional governments for a later stage.

These positions underwent a radical reversal after 1948. With the outbreak of the Cold War, the Christian Democrats broke their coalition with the Communists and went into the election on an uncompromising platform of anti-communism, supported strongly by the Church. The result was an electoral triumph, but especially in the Catholic regions of the north and in the south. Immediately, they abandoned the constitutional commitment to regional government, which was to remain a dead letter until 1970. The Communists for their part, excluded from central government, became ardent regionalists, demanding the activation of the regional clauses in the constitution, and throwing themselves into the campaign for land reform to break the power of the established classes in the south. In the following years, the Christian Democrats entrenched themselves further as the old *notabili*, especially in the south, attached themselves to the party and recreated the former system of clientelistic dependency. During the early 1950s, a new generation of Christian Democrats under Amintore Fanfani came to power, with the aim of breaking the power of the *notabili* and establishing a modern and efficient administration. The outcome of their efforts was indeed to break the old political class, but to substitute for it the political party and a new, professionalized and modernized version of clientelism, fed with the resources of the expanding state (Chubb, 1982).

Regional divisions remained marked in Italy, in religion, culture, economic structures and politics. The most religious regions were in the far north, while in the south deference to the Church was part of the respect for traditional authority. Central Italy was more secularized, and more egalitarian in culture. Economic divisions were as wide as at the time of unification. The south remained agrarian and poor, while the northern regions contained heavy industries and the centre sustained a small business culture. Political divisions were illustrated in the postwar referendum on the monarchy in which the south voted two to one in favour of the king, while in the north and centre the proportions were reversed. The Christian Democratic regime's strategy of territorial management was to exploit these regional differences, while directing all demands for redress and, indeed, all political activity towards the centre.

In France, the traditional association of regionalism with reaction and anti-republicanism was reinforced by the experience of the Vichy regime which used provincialism as part of its strategy of consolidation and stabilization. This was not, of course, a democratic form of regionalism, but an attempt to bolster traditional authority and continue the fight against the republic. Regionalism was further discredited by the collaboration of some Breton regionalists with the Germans. Accordingly, the Liberation regime swept away all forms of regional administration and reverted to the classic republican forms of the commune and the *département*. *Commissaires de la république* briefly replaced the regional prefects of Vichy, but were soon eliminated. As in Italy, there was a tripartite governing coalition until 1948, consisting of the Gaullists, the Socialist and Communist left, and the *Mouvement Républicain Populaire* (MRP), a Christian Democratic party. Although, like its counterparts in Germany and Italy, the MRP had inherited a vaguely regionalist philosophy, it did not pursue this (Schmidt, 1990); rather as the first Catholic party with a specifically republican stance, it largely adopted the Jacobin ideals of centralization. The Gaullists were resolutely centralist, while the left-wing parties clung to their Jacobin traditions.

In the United Kingdom, the postwar Labour government was committed to centralized planning and the nationalization of major industries. Although the party was theoretically committed to Scottish home rule, it resisted pressures from the Scottish Convention movement and confined itself to administrative decentralization (Keating and Bleiman, 1979). Ambitious regional plans and development schemes were launched for Greater London and the Clyde Valley (Wannop, 1995), but without any element of political devolution. There was some consolidation of regional administration and the Treasury attempted, with limited success, to ensure that all central government departments used the same regional boundaries. By the late 1940s, however, the impetus for regional planning had been lost and the incoming Conservative government of 1951 downgraded regions further. The requirement for uniform boundaries was abandoned and regional offices were in many cases closed. Although the Conservatives had attacked Labour's centralizing policies in the 1940s and noted that nationalization of industry represented a loss of regional control, this was a tactical stance and they never showed the interest which some of their continental counterparts had in regionalism as a form of politics.

In Spain, the Franco regime regarded all expressions of regionalism as abhorrent, a threat to the unity of the nation. The only exceptions were the retention of the fiscal privileges of Navarre and the Basque province of Alava, which had supported the Francoist side in the civil war. Francoist suppression proved counter–productive in the longer term since it was to force regionalists and other opposition forces together and forge an identification of regionalism with democratic change, especially towards the end of the regime.

In Belgium, as in France, Flemish regionalism was regarded as tainted with collaboration and there was a centralizing reaction. Flemish–Walloon divisions, however, re-emerged over the return of the monarchy, massively supported in Flanders and rejected in Wallonia. Linguistic divisions soon re-emerged and deepened, compounded by widening economic differences between the two halves of the country.

REGIONS AND POLITICS

During the 1940s and 1950s, there was some evidence of the 'nationalization' of voting behaviour, as regional differences were attenuated, but this evidence needs to be treated carefully. Party competition in the age of mass politics meant that parties needed to establish a presence throughout the national territory. This could come about through a homogenization of political attitudes, culture and behaviour; but it could also be the result of parties adopting differentiated strategies to appeal to distinct territorial constituencies. If more uniform party voting is the result of the former, we would expect the change to be permanent, and that any political realignments should similarly be national in scope. If what we are seeing is the assembly of territorial coalitions into national parties, or the use of differentiated strategies by national parties, then changes in the national party system should have direct effects on territorial patterns of politics. It seems, in fact, that both effects were at work, but most interpretations until recently ignored the second possibility, assuming that nation states were becoming more homogeneous.

In postwar Italy, there was a continued electoral cleavage between the north and south. While the Christian Democrats did equally well in both parts of Italy, the left remained weaker in the Mezzogiorno, gaining 48 per cent in the north and just 20 per cent in the south. By 1953, this difference had disappeared, but this is not to be interpreted as a simple process of homogenization. Rather it reflects a decision on the part of the Communists to adopt a distinct southern strategy (Tarrow, 1967), taking up the cause of land reform and supporting peasant ownership, a policy which the left had rejected in the past (Gramsci, 1978), relying on the *vento del nord*, or the leadership of the northern workers to liberate the south (Zagarrio, 1981). This coexisted with the traditional strategy of mobilizing the industrial proletariat in the north and, later, an appeal to the modernizing middle classes. Meanwhile, the Christian Democrats had also increased their penetration of the south by taking over the client networks of the old Liberal *notabili* and, after the Fanfani seizure of the party in the 1950s, modernizing and professionalizing them. The Christian Democratic hegemony in the most northern parts of Italy, by contrast, was based on a strong subculture rooted in Catholic domination of civil society. Regional subcultures were also marked in the central areas of Italy, dominated by the left. So the more even spread of votes reflected specific factors in the different parts of Italy, a fact which became even more apparent when the party system entered its crisis in the 1980s.

It is difficult to trace continuities and discontinuities in the territorial implantation of French parties, since the system itself has been unstable, with parties changing names, reconstituting themselves and forming alliances. It does appear, however, that under the Fourth Republic and in the early years of the Fifth Republic, traditional territorial political orientations changed little (Ysmal, 1989; Le Bras, 1995), though the Massif Central moved from the left to the right (Goguel, 1970). After 1970, the refounded Socialist Party was able to penetrate new regions, appealing to Catholic voters who had traditionally rejected the left, and including local and regional appeals in its message, and decentralization, building on its base in local government, in its programme. It extended its influence, notably, into the far west, including Brittany. Later, it suffered in its traditional strongholds in the Mediterranean south and then in the north, with the rise of the extreme right National Front.

British political behaviour also presented a more territorially homogenized appearance in the 1940s and 1950s as the two main parties consolidated their position and class came to replace other bases of voting. Class voting appears to have reached its peak around 1951–55 (Bogdanor and Field, 1993; Pattie and Johnston, 1995) and thereafter regional effects began to reappear. Even during the heyday of class voting, however, detailed ecological analysis shows the continued presence of territorial factors (Welhofer, 1986) which were to come to the fore with the decline of class alignments. Study of individual regions also shows the parties positioning themselves to take advantage of local and regional peculiarities. Scottish Conservatives, known until 1965 as Unionists, represented a coalition of rural Tories and Liberal Unionists, which was able to break out of the minority position in which the Conservatives had been since 1832, marrying rural deference to urban Protestantism and populism (Mitchell, 1990; Fry, 1987; Brown, McCrone and Paterson, 1995). By the 1940s, they were doing better in Scotland than in England, but after 1959 the pattern was reversed. Scottish Unionists had never operated in local government, only entering the field in the late 1960s, after changing their name to Conservatives. A formerly dynamic Scottish industrial bourgeoisie had almost died out with the loss of control to the south, the Conservative parliamentary presence was increasingly dominated by anglicized aristocrats and military officers (Keating, 1975a) and, as it lost its distinct Scottish image, the Conservative Party faded. In Wales, the Labour Party built a hegemonic position by taking over the old Liberal networks, rooted in nonconformist religion, radicalism and defence of Welsh values. In southwest England, the Scottish borders and parts of Wales and the Scottish Highlands, the Liberals maintained a presence, which they could build on during their revival from the 1960s. Regional issues were played on by politicians. Conservatives would attack the nationalization policies of the postwar Labour government and a form of centralization arguing that, for Scotland, nationalization meant denationalization. In opposition in the 1950s and early 1960s, Labour exploited regional discontent, but never carried this to the point of arguing for regional autonomy. Rather, it insisted that centralized government was all the more necessary in order to redistribute resources back to the needy areas. Within Parliament, a disciplined two-party system coexisted with elaborate patterns of territorial interest articulation which in no way undermined it (Keating, 1975a).

West Germany provides another example of greater territorial homogeneity in voting. Social change, the turbulence of the Nazi era and massive migration after the war undermined the old local subcultures, while the political system of the Federal Republic encouraged parties with a broad geographical appeal. Yet this system itself was, at least partly, built from local and regional elements. The Christian Democratic Party (CDU) emerged as a coalition of local forces, only gradually displacing its competitors on the centre-right, and continued to adapt its message to the needs of individual places (Rohe, 1990a). In Bavaria, it had to deal with an independent partner, the CSU, which was imposing itself as the dominant regional party. Under CSU leadership, a new Bavarian identity was forged, rooted in the myths of an independent kingdom, though this had dated only from the Napoleonic era. Modernization was managed in a specific way so as to incorporate elements of the traditional Catholic culture and, later to include Protestants as well (Mintzel, 1990). On the left, the Social Democrats (SPD) never succeeded in establishing their Bavarian credentials and declined drastically from the 1970s. By contrast, the SPD progressed in the Ruhr area, formerly hostile to them despite the existence of a large industrial proletariat. After the war, the SPD gained the support of the Protestant workers and, from the 1960s, made inroads into the Catholic vote. Gaining firm control of the Land government of North Rhine-Westphalia after 1966, it established its own milieu based in the trade unions, local government, and a political machine (Rohe, 1990b). So even at a time of greater social homogenization, parties were able to use the instruments of government in order to build up their own bases regionally.

Even in the smaller European states, some regional influences persisted. Norwegian voting behaviour was marked by spatial variations (Hagen et al., 1991), as was that of Belgium (De Smet et al., 1958).

Overall, national political systems were cohering and national parties penetrating all parts of their respective states. There is also some evidence for the breakdown of older patterns of cultural distinctiveness and the political behaviour associated with them. At the same time, parties had to adapt themselves to distinct milieus as the cost of penetrating the national territory, while at the same time moulding local societies in the process of building their own bases. This recognition of the territorial dimension of the political process became more explicit with the advent of regional policy in the 1960s and this in turn served to forge new forms of territorial politics.

THE POLITICS OF REGIONAL DEVELOPMENT

Regional questions came back onto the political agenda from the late 1950s in the form of regional development policies, largely managed by central governments. In a context of generally full employment and growth, regional economic problems were seen as a marginal issue which would be addressed by specific policies aimed at integrating depressed regions fully into national economies. The problem regions were generally those whose industrial development had lagged and which possessed large reserves of agricultural labour, for which a more productive and modernized farm sector would have no use. In the United Kingdom, on the other hand, the main problem lay in regions of traditional heavy industry where obsolescence and overseas competition had led to economic decline. Regional development theory and policy gained in technical sophistication over the years but a key feature of early policies was the diversion of industrial activity from one region of the state to another. From a political perspective this had the advantage of addressing several constituencies at the same time. For the problem regions, diversionary policies brought jobs and investment. For regions of full employment, they relieved pressures on infrastructures, labour markets and housing, and limited in-migration. For the national economy as a whole, the policy could be presented as a way of utilizing under-employed resources in the regions and expanding national output in a non-inflationary manner. There was also a social dimension, as territorial equity comprised part of the postwar social settlement, along with the integration of the working class. Finally, there was a political rationale, as regional policy was seen as a mechanism for consolidating the nation state in regions where dissent was likely, as well as boosting the fortunes of governing parties. This form of regionalism was therefore driven by functional considerations, but the technocratic rationale for the policy covered a series of potential political conflicts over the definition of the regional problem and the strategies to pursue, as well as over the control of the policy instruments.

There were several instruments of regional development policy. Governments provided grants and tax allowances for firms investing in priority regions. Public investments and infrastructure projects were steered into development regions and nationalized industries were instructed to place their investments in the regions. Private firms dependent on government sponsorship were also sent to the regions.

Key industries were established in regions to act as 'growth poles', attracting complementary activities and so generating a take-off into self-sustaining growth. Originally developed in relation to industrial sectors, the idea was adapted in the 1960s to apply to regions, tying in with the earlier Marshallian theory of industrial districts (Thomas, 1972). The automobile industry, seen as an industry of the future and one with a high potential for local spin-offs, was used as an instrument of regional development in France, where Citroën successfully established itself in Brittany, and in the UK, where car plants in Scotland and Merseyside ultimately failed. So was the steel industry, in which economies of scale could increase efficiencies and attract other steel-using industries to the region. Large-scale steel plants were established at Fos in southern France and at Taranto in southern Italy, though plans for a British equivalent failed when the Macmillan government, under pressure from both Scottish and Welsh lobbies, exercised the judgement of Solomon and split the project in two.

Another strand of regional thinking in the 1960s concerned physical land-use planning and focused on metropolitan urban regions. The need to accommodate population growth, to develop modern infrastructure and to expand public services indicated planning over wider areas than the municipal level. In some cases, too, national governments were distrustful of municipal politicians, seeing them as too closely tied to traditional distributive politics and not sufficiently committed to development and change. There was a series of initiatives in Britain, in the 1940s and again in the 1960s (Wannop, 1995). In France, planning for metropolitan regions started in earnest in the 1960s. Regional planning in the Netherlands was focused on the metropolitan level within a national physical planning framework. Germany also engaged in regional planning exercises, organized jointly between the federal and Land governments, though intergovernmental rivalry hampered strong action. Under a 1965 law, Länder had to allow regional planning associations among local governments (Wannop, 1995); in the Ruhr, an older body, the *Siedlungsverband Ruhrkohlenbezirk* (SVR) gave way in 1975 to the *Kommunalverband Ruhr*. Many saw the metropolitan region as a potentially important tier of government and there were initiatives to reorganize local government along these lines (discussed below) although, in the event, it proved difficult to institutionalize a politically significant tier of government at this level (Keating, 1995a).

Regional development policies were more or less closely associated with regional planning. The most elaborate linkages were in France, where national economic planning had been introduced under the Fourth Republic and strengthened under the Gaullist regime as a way of modernizing the economy and equipping it for European competition. The DATAR (*Délégation à l'aménagement du territoire et à l'action régionale*) was responsible for the spatial dimensions of the national plan, which became more important from the early 1960s. *Aménagement du territoire*, a term untranslatable into English, encompasses an integrated view of spatial development, incorporating economic development, land use planning and infrastructure provision, although in France this integration was less complete than in small countries like the Netherlands (Drevet, 1991) or in Sweden. In the United Kingdom, on the other hand, there was a notorious lack of coordination between regional economic policy and land use planning. In the early 1960s, there was a brief experience with national economic planning on French lines. The Conservative government started in 1962 with the National Economic Development Council and the Labour government, taking office in 1964, elaborated it with the National Plan and the Department of Economic Affairs. Despite the commitment to produce regional plans to complement the National Plan, however, land use planning was never integrated with regional policy. After the death of the National Plan in 1967 and the subsequent demise of the Department of Economic Affairs, regional planning was confined to land-use guidance for local governments, and had little connection with regional policy, which was run by a different department of government.

Regional economic development policies from the 1960s tended to be rather centralized in conception and administration. They were conceived of as an integral part of national policy and, concerned with ensuring balanced regional development, not easily transferable to regions themselves. States also tended to be rather suspicious of existing territorial elites, seeing them as insufficiently modernizing in their outlook and tied to distributive politics and the maintenance of the status quo. Regional development was entrusted, instead, to specialized agencies at one remove from political influence. Italy provided an early example with the *Cassa per il Mezzogiorno*, set up in 1950 to develop the south of the country. It was initially only supposed to operate for ten years (Galasso, 1978) but became an essential part of the political landscape, along with an array of special agencies for smaller areas. In its early years, the Cassa focused on 'pre-industrialization', building infrastructure to attract investment. After 1957 more attention was given to industrialization through the provision of incentives and the diversion of state industry; then from the 1960s a policy of selective industrialization, focused on growth poles, was pursued. Originally established under the impetus of modernizing elites in industry and the technical bureaucracy, the Cassa and other agencies had by the 1960s fallen under the control of the Christian Democratic machine, used as a means of distributing patronage (Tarrow, 1967; Allum, 1973; Caciagli, 1977); later the Socialist Party came to share in the spoils. Policy was bent to the clientelistic needs of the machine rather than being used to promote self-sustaining growth. Credits were distributed for political effect rather than economic efficacy and corruption grew. In France, the DATAR, staffed by modernizing technocrats, was used to bypass not only the political *notables* entrenched in local government but also the central field bureaucracies such as the corps of *Ponts et Chaussées*. In the UK, the Highlands and Islands Development Board was set up in 1965 by a Labour government intent on bypassing the influence of the landowning class entrenched in the local government system. It was followed ten years later by a Scottish Development Agency, part of whose rationale was to bypass the clientelistic municipal political machine in Glasgow.

As regional policy became more sophisticated and as governments sought to integrate it with regional planning, they needed partners on the ground. In Britain and France, incorporation of local interests took the form of consultative regional planning councils, alongside a strengthened and more integrated regional arm of central government. The French *régions de programme*, first delineated in 1959, were in 1964 given consultative organs known as CODER (*commission de développement économique régionale*) and regional prefects were appointed, each assisted by a *conférence administrative régionale* grouping the main central government departments in the region. This was intended to focus central government's efforts, while at the same time co-opting potentially disruptive regionalist elements in a functionally-driven system (Hayward, 1969). In England, Regional Economic Planning Councils included representatives of local government, industry, trade unions and independent experts, while parallel Regional Economic Planning Boards brought together the regional offices of central departments under the leadership of the Department of Economic Affairs (later the Department of the Environment). Similar arrangements in Scotland and Wales came under the Scottish and Welsh Offices respectively. In Italy, CPRE were established with a similar remit and, in Belgium, Regional Economic Councils were set up in 1970 (Houthaeve, 1996). The experiment with consultative bodies for regional planning was not a success. It was never made clear whether their role was to represent the regions to central government, or to implement central policy in the regions. Their representativity and therefore legitimacy was always in question, since they were appointed by central government. Local government was suspicious of bodies which might undermine its claims to territorial representation. Members were unsure of their role and, lacking real powers, many resigned in disillusion. The British planning councils never recovered from the failure of the National Plan in 1967, though they remained in existence in England until they were abolished by the incoming Conservative government in 1979. In Scotland and Wales, where they had a territorial interlocutor in the person of the Secretary of State, they survived to play a low-key role in keeping open channels of communication between government and business and trade unions. In France and Italy, the consultative machinery evolved into a system of elected regional government, an idea which some in Britain had also favoured in the 1960s. So while starting from a largely functionalist impetus, regional reform opened up a range of institutional and political questions but the political and constitutional implications of all this remained unclear.

In Germany, the political and institutional strength of the Länder meant that they were essential partners in federal regional policies and could not be displaced by consultative machinery. In 1969, the *Gemeinschaftsaufgabe Verbesserung der regionalen Wirtschafts-struktur*, or joint task framework, was introduced (Anderson, 1992). This replaced a series of federal grant programmes with a planning framework in which the federal and Land governments jointly decided on priorities and allocations.

As in Fascist Italy, the Franco regime in Spain at first saw regional development as a matter of massive public works projects managed by the state with the participation of the big banks. Following the economic modernization strategies adopted under the influence of the new technocratic elites in the 1960s, Spain experienced the same functional needs as other European countries for a regional level of planning and intervention (Cuadrado Roura, 1981; García, 1979). Yet such was the paranoia of the Franco regime about the political implications of regionalism that it was impossible to get the issue of regional machinery onto the agenda.

The intervention of the central state into the regions through planning and modernization initiatives had the effect of destabilizing existing patterns of territorial representation since the old intermediaries no longer controlled the new resources and programmes. French *notables*, who initially saw regional policy spending as 'manna' descending on them without any effort on their own part, began to resent their exclusion from the details of its distribution. In Italy, by contrast, the political class had by the early 1960s largely managed to gain control of the resources in question. More generally, centralized interventions had redefined economic issues in a territorial perspective and raised expectations which could not always be fulfilled. The result was a politicization of what had begun as a rather technical set of initiatives, managed by the modernizing state bureaucracy. Efforts at co-opting local and regional actors into the elaboration and implementation of development and planning policies had the effect of further politicizing the field and introducing new actors and new perspectives. Meanwhile, centralized direction of regional development was increasingly challenged by the emergence of new regionalist movements on the ground, with their own ideas on the appropriate shape of development.

REGIONS FROM THE BOTTOM-UP

By the early 1970s, a critique of conventional regional development policy had developed. The emphasis on industrialization as the instrument of modernization was questioned. In the Highlands of Scotland, this strategy implied a transformation of the economy into one approximating to that of the central Lowlands and a shift within the Highlands from traditional activities into manufacturing industry, and from the dispersal of population to its concentration in growth poles in the east of the region. Tensions between these two had been identified at an early stage. In France, the transformation of Languedoc from dependence on viticulture to tourism implied a sectoral shift as well as a territorial movement of activity from the hinterland to the coast. This was undertaken by centralized state agencies which, with ruthless efficiency, eliminated the mosquitos, opened up the coast and established a series of tourist resorts, carefully calibrated to match the various income groups. Resistance to rural depopulation and to what was seen as a move from independent farming to the dependent, even servile, activity of servicing tourists, fed into a strategy of regional resistance. Of course, the independent wine growers of Languedoc had themselves long been dependent on state support and protection, obtained by the mediation of local politicians; but this had not prevented them, like farmers elsewhere, from developing an ideology of sturdy independence. Along the coast at Fos, a massive steel project had been built with public subsidies. Although the official rationalization of the project was based on regional policy, local politicians were excluded, and the plan was really designed to fit a national policy of moving the steel industry from the coalfields to the coast (Tarrow, 1978). So the plan sparked off a movement of territorial protest. In Italy, the growth pole strategy was undermined as *cosorzi*, intended to focus growth, were allowed to proliferate in response to political needs, while the large funding went to a few big projects tied into the needs of large industry (Dunford, 1988). As in France, the relocation of the steel industry to the coast, at Taranto, was dressed up as regional policy. Critics derided the big oil, steel and petrochemical plants established in the south with state money as 'cathedrals in the desert' for their failure to stimulate self-sustaining growth (Clark, 1996). Even where transplanted industries were successful, large scale capital-intensive industry was no longer a major generator of jobs, yet development incentives tended to focus on investment rather than job creation. This model of development, already under considerable pressure, was further undermined by the oil crises of the 1970s, with the consequent pressures on public expenditure.

In some regions, resistance to national development policies took the form of opposition and defence of the status quo. Elsewhere, new elites were emerging in local society, in business, in agriculture, in trade unions and in politics, committed to growth and change. In France, the rather general term *forces vives* was used to describe these new actors, especially in Brittany, where the CELIB (*Comité d'études et de liaison des intérêts bretons*) dated from 1950. In southern Italy, SVIMEZ (*Associazione per lo sviluppo dell'industria nel Mezzogiorno*) was formed in 1947, bringing together industrialists, including many from the north, with technical people. Supporting a strategy of industrialization and social modernization, it hoped to break with the passeist preoccupations of the old meridionalist tradition (Barucci, 1974; Galasso, 1978). The Scottish Council (Development and Industry) dating from the 1930s and bringing together industrialists, government and local authorities, was active in promoting new ideas in regional development, including the 1962 Toothill Report on the Scottish Economy. All these represented a re-emergence of dynamic forces in regions of decline. In Germany, local bourgeoisies had not declined in the same way, nor was the economy or political system so centralized, and the dispersal of economic activities ensured a more dynamic economic life in the regions.

The 1960s also saw the emergence of a left-wing regionalism, associated with the libertarian left and the 1968 generation, rather than the main social democratic or communist parties. Drawing on anarchist and communitarian traditions, these movements saw the centralized state as oppressive and compromised by its association with large-scale capitalism. The anti-colonial movements of the period also provided inspiration and led some regionalists in France to talk of 'internal colonialism' (Lafont, 1967), seeing their predicament as analogous to that of the imperial dependencies. These movements made common cause with coalitions of territorial defence organized to resist plant closures and centrally-imposed regional development strategies. From the 1970s, the environmentalist movement, also committed to small-scale government and localism, provided further support. Gradually, this affected the parties of the mainstream left and even the trade unions, which came to incorporate the defence of regions and not merely of social groups in their prospectus.

There was also a revalorization of regional cultures, dialect and accents, previously held in disdain by metropolitan elites. Minority languages in the UK, France and Spain enjoyed a revival. The use of regional dialects became more acceptable in high status uses in those countries where they still survived in daily use, as in Italy, Norway and southern Germany. Non-metropolitan accents were heard on the BBC and in Parisian society. The use of accent and dialect represented a symbolically important shift in the relationship between centres and peripheries, a rejection of central cultural domination and the values which it often incorporated. The expansion of universities both increased the size of the educated population and dispersed it away from the old centres. Regional cultures began to shed their archaic and folkloristic character, to become vehicles for looking at contemporary society and issues. Folk music traditions were revived and modernized, and flowed into the youth culture; even the German *Heimat* theme, traditionally associated with reaction, was incorporated into the emerging new left (Morton and Robins, 1995).

In regions with historic national identities, there was a revival of nationalist movements. The most prominent were in Scotland, Wales, Catalonia and the Basque Country. In France, there was a weaker Breton nationalist movement, caught between rival groups, and an ephemeral Occitan movement, which drew on the regional language, rural discontent, and opposition to central regional development policies (Touraine et al., 1981; Keating, 1986). In Belgium, language issues became a political flash-point. A Flemish nationalist movement, protesting against the domination of the state by French-speaking interests, challenged the old consociational mechanisms in the name of self-government. In Wallonia, economic crises prompted a movement of regional defence. This was to produce an asymmetrical and complex set of regional demands.

The various strands flowed into a set of revived regionalist movements and transformed the idea of regionalism. While a traditionalist regionalism still existed, associated with rural defence, another regionalism emerged, linked with modernization and change (Ruffilli, 1980). Politically, it moved from an association with the right towards the left, although right wing forms of regionalism did continue to exist. This is not to say that regionalism became a coherent ideology or movement from the late 1960s. There were still tensions between traditionalists and modernizers. There was an inherent conflict between the politics of territorial defence, wanting to preserve threatened sectors at all costs, and the politics of modernization and change, although short-term alliances against centrally-imposed regional development strategies were easily forged. There was a tension between a form of regionalism which sought to integrate the region more closely into the national economy and political system, merely removing the obstacles to territorial equality, and regionalisms which sought autonomy and a distinct path of development. Defenders of industrialization differed in their ultimate goals from environmentalists and agrarianists, though again tactical alliances could be forged on the basis of territory.

The definition of territory was also contentious. Top-down visions of the state technical bureaucracy, based on functional criteria, or in some cases a desire to discourage territorial mobilization, did not correspond to the territories imagined by regional social movements. Even among the latter, the definition of territory was contested. In a historic nation like Scotland, there was little argument about territorial boundaries but a lot of resistance to the idea that Scotland should be a political unit and fear on the part of the left that Scottish identity could undermine class solidarity. In Brittany, there was argument about the boundaries of the region and what it meant to be Breton. The Occitan movement was quite unable to define just how far Occitania extended, let alone its social, economic and political significance. In Brittany and Wales, culture and language proved divisive rather than uniting factors, since only a minority in the territories concerned still spoke the historic language. Elsewhere, regionalism was an even more diffuse philosophy, unable to provide a unifying set of ideas or establish a secure social basis. This facilitated the task of states in managing the new territorial politics and reestablishing equilibrium, albeit temporarily, in the spatial design of government.

THE MOVE TO REGIONAL GOVERNMENT

By the 1960s, regions had become an important basis for administration and for political mobilization in many countries. Establishing them as a level of government was another matter and there was a wide variety of experiences. Three conceptions of regions as a level of government competed. The first was the functional conception of the metropolitan region, usually seen as a means of consolidating local governments and some of their functions. The second was the larger, provincial level of region, seen as the appropriate level for consolidating existing regional activities under political control, and for devolving functions from the central state. A third conception was the cultural region, or minority nation, defined by sentiment and history, which could vary greatly in geographical scale, from the Åland islands or the Val d'Aosta, to a vast, amorphous entity like Occitania.

The argument for metropolitan government hinged on issues of efficiency, democracy and representation, though technical questions tended to dominate over the political ones. It was widely believed that larger units of local government could exploit economies of scale in service delivery, though evidence for this is elusive and inconclusive and the case often rested on assertion rather than proof (Keating, 1995a; Dearlove, 1979). Perhaps a more important motivation was the desire to extend modern services to rural and suburban areas which had been reluctant to invest in modern infrastructure. A dominant argument concerned the needs of physical planning which, it was believed, needed to be long term and broad in scope. This in turn required the extension of cities to their functional boundaries as determined by economic linkages, travel to work patterns or infrastructure needs. The arguments for planning, like those about economies of scale, had a strong technocratic bias, influenced by the growing self-confidence of the planning profession. Many planners saw good planning as a matter of technical competence but gradually it was accepted that, if plans are to be implemented effectively, they need the backing of a politically elected body possessing functional competences and financial powers. In due course, it was recognized that planning is itself a political process.

More delicate politically was a series of distributional questions. Local government fragmentation was widely used to sustain social segregation, as the middle classes congregated in their own neighbourhoods, whether these were the suburbs as in the UK, or the city centres, as in France. The location of new, subsidized housing for the working class became a divisive issue, which could be resolved only on a metropolitan scale. More generally, fiscal equalization among neighbourhoods could be facilitated by consolidating local governments but this too was a highly politically charged question.

States were also interested in changing the composition of the local political elite, replacing the old notables, concerned with distribution and support-building, with new types who would be more policy-minded and committed to development and change. Partisan considerations also featured here, in the UK, where local politics was increasingly dominated by the national parties; in France, where the Gaullists sought in the 1960s to increase their local implantation at the expense of the old conservative elites; and in Italy where the Christian Democrats sought to contain the Communists, while being forced to share the spoils of office with the Socialists and lay parties. Left-wing observers saw in consolidation a plot to dilute working class representation in those institutions which they had conquered (Dearlove, 1979; Giard and Scheibling, 1981; Clément, 1988) while conservatives feared domination by a statist and technocratic elite. Political parties were divided internally. On the left, social democratic and communist parties coveted the large tax base which metropolitan government could provide but feared the weakening of their political base through incorporating more middle-class voters. Parties of the right were divided between technically-minded modernizers and defenders of traditional communities and middle-class interests. National governments stressed the need for strong local government, but glossed over the question of whether it should be functionally strong, able to undertake the new plans for development or change, or politically strong, in the sense of being able to stand up to the central state itself.

Metropolitan reorganization was thus fraught with political conflicts, since it raised important questions of power and distribution and threatened the power bases of existing elites. Where it emerged, it represented a compromise among competing ideas and interests. The most common form was a two-tier system, in which a metropolitan level was superimposed on the existing local governments and functions divided between them. The upper tier was typically given strategic planning and some infrastructure functions, leaving most service delivery in the hands of the lower tier. Political pressure served to ensure that the lower tier was not subordinate to the metropolitan level, which tended to create difficulties in ensuring the implementation of strategic planning. For the same reason, the upper tier was often indirectly elected, or constituted as a federation of municipalities, as with the French *communautés urbaines*. Political considerations also led to boundaries being drawn rather conservatively around urban areas rather than taking in cities with their whole hinterlands. This inhibited broad scale planning and often did little to control development taking place beyond the urban boundary. There is in any case something inherently unstable and temporary about the idea of a planning region, which changes in scale and shape in response to economic and social changes over quite short periods (Wannop, 1995). This makes it a rather poor basis for a level of politicized government which could engage the loyalties and encourage the participation of citizens.

There has been variety of types of metropolitan government in western Europe. Perhaps the strongest was in the Strathclyde region of Scotland, where an elected council was established covering a wide area taking in Glasgow and its entire functional area, with a strategic planning role, powers over the detailed plans of the lower tier municipalities, and major infrastructure and service provision responsibilities. Its birth in the early 1970s can be attributed to an unusual constellation of conditions. The ruling Conservative Party was weakly represented in Scottish local government and left the question of reorganization to the planning-minded officials of the Scottish Office who were committed to radical change and the creation of a body able to cooperate in strategic planning and make its decisions stick (Keating, 1975b). Elsewhere, metropolitan governments were weaker, as entrenched local elites were able to resist change. Usually, the upper tier was given only weak powers, often it was indirectly elected and in many cases metropolitan boundaries were tightly drawn. All this weakened the potential of the metropolitan model and made it an easy target for opposition.

By the 1980s the impetus had gone from the creation of metropolitan governments. Strategic planning had been weakened in the wake of the economic instability provoked by the oil crises of the 1970s, and by the rise of neo-liberal ideology. Central governments had never resolved the question of whether they really wanted strong subnational governments, which might take on a political life of their own, and municipal politicians in many countries resented the intrusion of another layer above them. So metropolitan consolidation was halted and even reversed, with the abolition of the English metropolitan counties, the Rijnmond and the Metropolitan Barcelona authority. By the 1990s, however, the tide was turning again as governments reacted to the rapid urban expansion of the late 1980s and the need to plan major infrastructure projects. The opening of European markets and the increased competition among metropolitan regions in the new Europe focused attention on the need for stronger units to control wasteful intra-metropolitan competition and encourage collaboration in infrastructure development and capital attraction. These considerations stimulated a return to metropolitan issues. A new French law provided for the establishment of *communautés de villes* in those places where urban communities had not already been established. A new strategic authority was introduced in the Greater Rotterdam area, replacing the defunct Rijnmond. New provisions encouraged Italian cities to form metropolitan governments. In the UK, opposition parties were pressing for a strategic authority, at least in Greater London.

Regional government, however, more commonly refers to the creation of larger, provincial scale regions which can assume some of the powers of national governments. The main pressure for this came in the larger, unitary states of the United Kingdom, France, Spain and Italy, and in Belgium. This reflected a variety of functional and political considerations. As regional planning and development policies became more ambitious and more politicized, there was an argument that they could only effectively be carried through by multi-functional authorities with the political weight provided by direct election. It was also argued that functional imperatives were leading to the creation of a range of government agencies at the regional level, which needed to be brought together in the interests both of efficiency and of democratic accountability. Within the regions, there was a gradual shift in attitudes and strategies. In the postwar era, regional politicians and leaders of organized interests had often taken a centralist stance, since centralized government could be used to divert resources to the regions, as long as regional interests were well represented at the centre. From the 1970s, this began to evolve into a demand for regional autonomy. Some regionalist politicians were aware of the contradiction between supporting a strong centre for redistribution, and supporting regional autonomy and clung to the centralist view; this explains the centralism of British regional Labour politicians. Others played the two themes together, with little concern for inconsistency; this was the strategy of the French Communist Party in the 1970s and of some Spanish socialists during the confusion of the transition years. In those territories with a cultural, linguistic or national identity, pressures for autonomy strengthened noticeably in the 1970s. Basque and Catalan nationalists played a key role in the opposition to late Francoism and the transition to democracy there was closely associated with regional autonomy. Scottish and, to a much lesser extent, Welsh, demands for autonomy began to compete with the traditional strategy of playing within the centralized state. In France, regional autonomy was taken up by the new left movements which came into the reconstituted Socialist Party after 1971. Belgium's linguistic divisions deepened and the strategy of resolving them at the centre through consociational accommodation gave way to one of decentralization, to territorial and cultural communities.

National governments, while reluctant to concede power, in some cases could see the logic of decentralization as a strategy to enhance functional efficiency and to diminish the administrative and political burden on the centralized state. This was particularly true in France and Italy where regional devolution was seen as an important contribution to social and economic modernization. Devolution could also push down to the regional level difficult questions of distribution and priorities. Where national unity was threatened by regional agitation, it could conciliate local feeling and help accommodate distinctive territories into the national community. Regional government, freed of its connotations of conservatism and defensiveness, was now seen as a contribution to administrative and political modernization.

ESTABLISHING REGIONAL GOVERNMENT

Establishing regional governments has proved to be a difficult process, usually proceeding by small steps rather than through revolutionary change. Regions have to be inserted into systems of government which are already rather institutionally crowded, in which existing political and administrative elites seek to maintain their power and status, and interest groups try to protect their established channels of influence. It might seem obvious that central governments should be reluctant to surrender power but, within them, individual departments and political tendencies might have different attitudes and interests. For example, ministries of the interior, or of local government, might take a proprietorial interest in the existing system of municipal administration, while ministries and agencies for economic planning might see them as an obstacle to modernization and change. Local governments themselves will generally be rather hostile to regional government, seeing it as a competitor and even as a centralizing force, more likely than a remote central administration to interfere in the details of local affairs. Territorial intermediaries, including members of parliament, field administrators of the state and party apparatuses, might also feel threatened by the emergence of a new tier which by-passes them and undercuts their role in distributing resources, negotiating detailed policy exceptions and political management. On the other side are new and emerging political forces and social movements, who see in regional government enhanced opportunities for influence and for changing policy priorities and criteria of allocation.

Creating a new tier of regional government requires not merely that there should be a functional logic to justify it, but also that the political conditions be present for a broad coalition in support of it. One favourable condition is a regime change at the centre, undermining the old elites and their territorial power system and providing an opportunity space for new actors and new policies. A change of government at the centre, while less drastic, can also create, at least temporarily, the conditions for radical reform, particularly where the new governing party or coalition has built up a base in the periphery prior to conquering power at the centre. Unless change is put through rapidly, however, a governing party is likely to get used to power at the centre and lose its appetite for decentralization. It may happen, in extreme cases, that the central parties themselves effectively agree to divide power on a territorial basis, emptying the central state of functional capacity, rather than reinforcing the centre against the regions. Another favourable condition is the existence of a local demand, and of organized movements pressing for change and ready to take advantage of it. This may be provided by the emergence of new social movements at the regional level, or by a change of attitude on the part of municipal politicians, and an appreciation of the advantages of regional government as a more effective safeguard against central interference, or for its functional benefits. Business interests tend to favour a functional regionalism, focused on economic development issues and depoliticized as far as possible. This implies support for functionally-specific agencies but opposition to elected regional governments, which might reflect broader social interests and provide a platform for anti-business forces. If regional government is to be established, this opposition must be over-ridden, or business persuaded that elected regional government is in its own interest. These conditions are rather difficult to meet, hence regional government has moved forward slowly and hesitatingly, and has been institutionalized in diverse ways and to very different extents in the countries of western Europe. Leaving aside Germany, which was federalized after the Second World War, the most important examples are from Italy, France, Spain, Belgium and the United Kingdom.

ITALY

Italy's 1946 constitution had made provision for regional governments but this remained a dead letter following the triumph of the Christian Democrats in the 1948 elections and the consequent polarization of national politics. It was not until the 1960s that the issue came back on the agenda and only in the 1970s did the conditions exist to put the constitutional provision into effect. Rapid economic growth and migration, from south to north and from the countryside to the cities had raised the issue of regional planning among administrative and political leaders and even in the business community (Indovina, 1973; Rotelli, 1973), while the failure to solve the problem of the south continued to put a strain on national unity. Initial responses were to try and rationalize the system without radical political change, so protecting the position of the central administration and reassuring the business elites who feared left wing influence in a more decentralized regime. CPREs set up in 1964–5 were advisory bodies appointed by the Ministry of Economic Planning and included representatives of local government, business and trade unions. Very similar to the bodies set up at the same time in France and the United Kingdom, their role was to draw up regional plans to complement the 1966-70 National Economic Plan (King, 1987).

Political forces were moving towards the idea of regional government following the arrival of the centre-left coalition which brought the Socialists back into government with the Christian Democrats in 1962. The Socialists had abandoned their previous opposition to regions (Good, 1976) and the Communists had also moved in favour, as they began their 'march through the institutions', building their support base in territorial government (Modica, 1972; Ingrao, 1973; Flogatis, 1979). Progressive and left-leaning Christian Democrats saw in regions a mechanism for reforming the state, drawing on the old regionalist tradition of Sturzo, as well as on newer ideas of economic planning and modernization. Business interests still favoured the tripartite formula of the CPREs, but industrialists, especially in the north, were gradually coming round to the idea of reform, and by the early 1970s the Confindustria had come out in support of regions as a necessary component of reform of the state (Rotelli, 1973). These modernizing impulses were stronger in the north than in the south, which remained beholden to the centralist–clientelist politics inherited from the unification era.

Political opposition meant that the first regional elections were not held until 1970, and the legislation providing for their functions was passed only in 1977. Meanwhile, a 1953 law had ensured that their powers would be very limited (Gourevitch, 1978) and the ordinary status regions which emerged were an example of functional decentralization rather than being a general level of political government (Zariski, 1972). Although in theory they were endowed with wide legislative powers, their functions were rather carefully specified, and in many areas were limited by national legislation (King, 1987), while court decisions further restricted their scope. In 1978, the regions were given responsibility for managing the national health service, but this involved managing national programmes and passing through money received from the centre. More than 90 per cent of their funds came from central transfers and some 70 per cent of this was tied to specific programmes, notably health service moneys which were passed on down the local health agencies (Buglione and France, 1984). Instead of passing framework laws, allowing the regions to fill in the details, Parliament continued to pass detailed laws even on matters of regional competence (Ministro per gli affari regionali, 1982). National ministries were not dismantled, even in areas transferred to the regions; it took a referendum in the 1990s to start this process. Nor did the political parties reorganize themselves on a regional basis, retaining the province as the basis for their machinery (Dente, 1985). The result was described as 'regions without regionalism' (Pastori, 1980), a manoeuvre by the political parties to retain control rather than a response to democratizing pressures from below, or a real will to modernize and reform the state.

FRANCE

Regionalization in France involved a similar interplay of functional and political considerations. The CODER of 1964 were intended to provide coherence for regional planning, to integrate it with national plans, and to tap the energies of new social actors, or *forces vives*. In the regions, a number of territorial social movements agitated for a more bottom-up approach, but made little impact until the political circumstances were favourable. Sections of the new left, and of the *autogestionnaire* (self-management) movements of the 1960s adopted regionalism and these in due course flowed into the reconstituted Socialist Party put together by François Mitterrand in the 1970s. The first initiative, however, came from President de Gaulle, in the aftermath of the turbulent events of 1968. The Gaullist movement by this stage was in control of the presidency and national assembly, but was still very weak in the localities, where the old notables of the Fourth Republic had their power base (Schmidt, 1990). Regional government thus presented an opportunity to by-pass them and forge an alliance with modernizing forces. Reform of the Senate, which is indirectly elected from local governments, would have the same effect of marginalizing the old political class. De Gaulle's proposals of 1969 envisaged regional councils, 60 per cent of which would be composed of deputies in the national parliament and local councillors, and 40 per cent elected on a socio-professional basis. The Senate would be transformed into a chamber of socio-professional representation. Despite the concession of generous representation in the new regional councils, this was a threat to the power base of the territorial political class and to their intermediary role between the state and the localities, and it attracted their massive opposition. Although there is evidence that public opinion was broadly favourable to regional reform, de Gaulle's insistence on holding a referendum and making it a test of confidence in himself and his government backfired and the proposals were defeated.

Following de Gaulle's resignation, his successor, Georges Pompidou, proceeded more circumspectly. In 1972, he set up *Etablissements Publics Régionaux*, a form of indirectly elected regional government composed exclusively of national deputies and members of local governments, with tightly restricted powers. Regions would not have their own administration but, as in the *départements*, the centrally-appointed prefect would be the executive. The principal functions of the regions were in economic planning and investment programming and their financial powers were extremely limited. This gave them considerably less formal status and power than their Italian counterparts but, in contrast to Italy, there was a tendency to push these powers to, and beyond, their formal limits. So, in defiance on the prohibition on maintaining their own administrations, several regional presidents ran large *cabinets* of advisors. Semi-autonomous agencies were used to the same effect. Like big city mayors and presidents of the *conseils généraux* (of the *départements*) before them, politically influential regional bosses could constrain the prefect to work with them rather than against them. Investment funds, while limited, could be used strategically to lever resources from other local governments and agencies, so expanding the region's scope of influence. This kept the question of regionalism alive, especially among the parties of the left, who were conducting their own 'march through the institutions', building on their territorial power bases in order to mount a convincing national challenge.

By the late 1970s, the Socialists had been converted to regionalism under the influence of the new left, who had come into the party under leaders like Michel Rocard, and the experience of regional presidents like Pierre Mauroy in Nord Pas-de-Calais. Yet defenders of the *département* and the commune remained a strong presence in the party and the programme ended up as a compromise. Regional councils would be directly elected and become fully-fledged local authorities (*collectivités territoriales*) but the *départements* and the communes would also be strengthened. Mitterrand's victory in the presidential elections of 1981 provided the opportunity for change and the new Minister of the Interior and Decentralization, Gaston Defferre, determined to move quickly to take advantage of the transition, before the new government became too entrenched in its powers. A first law on the rights and liberties of local government was followed by a series of acts removing central controls, devolving powers, and transferring parts of the administration to local control (Keating and Hainsworth, 1986; Schmidt, 1990). Regions were to be directly elected, to have their own functions, and to have an executive president in place of the prefect. They were also to enjoy the enhanced status of local authorities, but only after direct elections had taken place. In the event, the weight of local notables in government, the national parliament and the Socialist Party was such that regions lost out to *départements* and cities, which were the big winners of the reform. Direct elections were postponed repeatedly, as the Socialists feared an adverse mid-term swing and eventually took place only in 1986, at the same time as the national legislative elections. Regional competences in economic development and planning were spelled out more formally, and they took over responsibility for vocational training and some educational building and maintenance. This did not fundamentally alter their role as functionally-specific bodies engaged in planning and investment programming. There was no question of giving them legislative powers, and national programmes tended to limit their discretion in those areas they did manage. Most of their funding was provided by central government and was earmarked, notably for the vocational training programmes.

THE UNITED KINGDOM

In the United Kingdom, a similar interplay of functional and political considerations brought regionalism onto the agenda, but without, in the end, achieving regional government. The Regional Economic Planning Councils set up by the Labour Government in 1964 bore great similarities to their French and Italian counterparts and there were those, notably in the Department of Economic Affairs, who hoped that they might evolve into a new tier of government (Lindley, 1982). The councils were composed of representatives of local government, of business and trade unions, and independent experts. A parallel system of Regional Economic Planning Boards brought together regionally-based civil servants from the departments with economic and planning functions. From the beginning, the Councils and Boards were regarded with suspicion by the Ministry of Housing and Local Government, and local government interests were hostile to anything which might encroach on their powers or endanger their direct links to the centre. At the same time, their raison d'être was based in the National Plan, whose custodian was the Department of Economic Affairs, engaged in what was to prove a losing struggle for control of economic policy with the Treasury. The abandonment of the Plan following the devaluation of 1967 left them without a clear role, although they continued in an advisory capacity until being abolished by the incoming Thatcher government in 1979. In Scotland, where the Council had a more powerful interlocutor in the form of the Scottish Office, it continued as the Scottish Economic Council.

Notwithstanding this failure, the debate on regional government continued, impelled by both functional and political considerations (Garside and Hebbert, 1989). Functional needs led governments to put in place regionally-based agencies in health, water, the arts and various other matters, and to use a variety of improvisations to achieve regional coordination in land-use planning. In Scotland and Wales, administrative devolution continued to progress, notably in the 1970s and the 1990s, to the point at which most domestic policy, with the notable exceptions of the taxation and social security systems, was handled by the Scottish and Welsh Offices. By the 1990s, even the anti-regionalist Conservative government set up Integrated Regional Offices in England in an effort to coordinate central government's own initiatives in planning, infrastructure and development (Hogwood, 1995).

The main political impetus for change came from Scotland, where the Scottish National Party posed an increasing challenge to the main British parties from the late 1960s. After nationalist by-election victories in both Scotland and Wales, Prime Minister Harold Wilson set up a Royal

Commission on the Constitution, to examine the case for reform. Conservative leader Edward Heath pre-empted this with his own commitment to a Scottish assembly, although when the detailed plans for this emerged from Conservatives' Constitutional Commission, they promised only a weak body to take the committee stage of Scottish bills in Parliament. In 1970 the issue appeared to die away but it returned in force in 1974 when the Scottish and Welsh nationalists returned eleven and three Members of Parliament respectively. With the fall of the Heath government, Harold Wilson came back to office in a minority administration, just after the Royal Commission on the Constitution (the Kilbrandon Commission) reported. Labour went back to its historic policy of home rule for Scotland and Wales but opposition in Parliament, not least within Labour's own ranks, hobbled the legislation. Eventually, bills were passed to provide for assemblies in Scotland and Wales, subject to support in a referendum, provided that the majority in favour amounted to at least 40 per cent of the entire electorate. In Wales, the proposals were defeated by five to one, while in Scotland they passed, but not by the qualified margin required. The Labour government fell and the incoming Conservative administration of Margaret Thatcher repealed both the Scotland and the Wales bills. This was the end of one episode in the devolution saga, but the issue lived on, especially in Scotland, where the Labour Party became increasingly convinced of the need for change, though still facing an unenthusiastic party at the UK level.

In England, there was even less progress. Proposals for a regional level of government were floated in the report of the Redcliffe-Maud commission on local government, and more strongly in the minority report by Derek Senior. The Kilbrandon Report also recommended a regional tier in England, though the commission was split several ways on the issue. In the 1970s, the Labour Party adopted the idea of English regional government in principle, but every attempt to make a concrete scheme was squashed by a combination of traditional centralists, the local government lobby and public sector trade unions who favoured corporatist institutions in which they would have a guaranteed place (Keating, 1984). By the mid-1980s, the long experience in opposition and initiatives being taken in local government led to a revived interest in subnational politics within the Labour Party, an interest intensified by the repeated assaults on local government autonomy on the part of the governing Conservatives. Labour politicians in the north of England, who had previously opposed Scottish devolution as a threat to their interests, began to consider the possibilities of devolution for their own region as an alternative to mere opposition. In the late 1990s, as the party again had a realistic prospect of returning to power, enthusiasm for devolution within the leadership waned. The commitment to devolution for Scotland and Wales was accompanied by a requirement for new referendums, and a scheme for the English regions was produced which was designed to make anything more than a mere coordinating committee of local governments extremely difficult. Nonetheless, the election of a new Labour Government in May 1997 did bring the issue back onto the political agenda and action soon followed. White Papers in July 1997 provided for a parliament for Scotland on quasi-federalist lines, with legislative powers and a general competence over all matters not expressly reserved for the centre. Wales was offered a weaker assembly, without legislative powers and whose administrative competences would be specified rather minutely. This was followed by referendums in September 1997. In Scotland, the proposals were overwhelmingly supported on a turnout of 60.1 per cent, with 74.3 per cent voting in favour of the parliament, and 63.5 per cent agreeing with a second question to give it tax-varying powers. There was a positive vote in all regions of Scotland, demonstrating a high degree of consensus and shared identity around a project for political and economic modernization in Europe. The Welsh proposals fared less well. Turnout was barely 50 per cent and the YES side won with only 50.03 per cent of the vote. The breakdown of the vote showed Wales still divided on traditional lines, into a Welsh-speaking heartland, an 'old Labour' industrial belt in the valleys, and a modern urban centre focused on Cardiff. While the first two voted YES, Cardiff returned a negative vote, indicating that the reforged Welsh identity of the 1990s has not yet captured the modernizing middle classes of the south. This setback in Wales served to halt, at least for the time being, the regionalizing momentum of the new government and deputy prime minister John Prescott, associated closely with the issue of regionalism, indicated that, apart from London, there was unlikely to be further movement on English regional government in this parliament.

SPAIN

In Spain, the same functional impetus for regionalism was felt in the 1960s but the rigid centralization of the Franco dictatorship prevented any concession, even of an administrative type. With the transition to democracy in the late 1970s, there was both a political impetus for decentralization and an opportunity for institutional change. One of the principal challenges in the transition to democracy was that of accommodating the historic nationalities, in Catalonia, the Basque Country and to a lesser extent Galicia, since it was clear that without a commitment to autonomy, no regime would command legitimacy in these regions. After complex negotiations, the 1978 constitution incorporated a solution whose unstated objective was to allow the three historic nationalities to proceed rapidly to home rule, while making it extremely difficult for other regions to follow. In this way, the dominant parties, notably the governing *Unión de Centro Democrático* (UCD) and the opposition socialists (*Partido Socialista Obrero Español*, PSOE) hoped to conciliate the historic nationalities, without sacrificing the principle of the unitary state, or federalizing Spain as a whole. In contrast to the Italian and French systems, the initiative is left to the regions themselves, and there is no requirement for the whole country to be covered by regional governments. Three routes were provided. Under article 151, those regions which had already voted for autonomy in a referendum could proceed directly to a statute of autonomy with extensive powers, which then could be approved in a referendum. In practice, this was limited to Catalonia, the Basque Country and Galicia, which had voted statutes of autonomy under the Second Republic in the 1930s. Other regions wishing to take this route had to go through a lengthy procedure involving an initiative by three quarters of the municipalities, a referendum with approval by an absolute majority of voters in each province of the region, followed by another referendum to approve the final statute. The second route to autonomy was by article 143. This required an initiative by half the provincial councils and two-thirds of the municipalities, provided that these covered the majority of the population; in some territories where pre-autonomous institutions had been set up, their assent could substitute for that of the provinces (Aja et al., 1985). Autonomous communities set up under these provisions could accede to full powers only slowly (*por vía lenta*) but in principle could eventually become the equals of the historic nationalities. A third route allowed those territories with traditional foral rights to convert themselves into autonomous communities without a special statute.

In the event, the three historic nationalities proceeded by article 151 and Andalucia sought to join them but fell short of the absolute majority of voters in one province, albeit gaining an absolute majority overall. Other regions moved quickly to take advantage of article 143 and it was soon apparent that the system of autonomous governments would cover the whole country. The only foral community to convert itself was Navarre, the Basque provinces having come together to form the Basque autonomous community. The spread of the autonomy movement alarmed the governing UCD which did everything in its power to sabotage the 1979 Andalucian referendum. PSOE, for its part, supported the Andalucian movement for tactical reasons but, once the referendum was over, moved in conjunction with UCD to try and draw the line. An attempted military coup in February 1981 alarmed the parties of the transition further and a pact was agreed whereby Andalucia could proceed under article 151, while autonomous governments would be set up for the other regions under article 143. Two laws on the harmonization of autonomy statutes, LOAPA (*Ley Orgánica de Armonización del Proceso Autonómico*) and LOFCA (*Ley Orgánica de Financiación de las Comunidades Autónomas*) attempted to bring the various statutes into line, effectively reducing the powers of regions which had proceeded under article 151. After a challenge by the Catalan and Basque governments, large parts of LOAPA were struck down by the Constitutional Court but the PSOE government in power after 1982 continued its efforts to bring the autonomy statutes into line, this time by transferring additional functions to the slow-route regions. Valencia and the Canaries were given more or less the same powers as Andalucia in 1982, while other regions had to wait for five years. Throughout the 1980s, conflicts pitted the autonomous communities, especially Catalonia and the Basque Country against the central government in the Constitutional Court, but by the 1990s this had given way to political negotiation as the nationalist parties used their position in Spanish politics to negotiate autonomy for their own communities.

Provisions for transferring competences as specified in the constitution are rather complex. There is a list of competences which are reserved exclusively for the central government, and another list of competences which can be transferred to the autonomous communities. Another clause stipulates that matters not expressly reserved to the central government can be devolved to the autonomous communities. Each individual statute of autonomy contains the lists of competences, which can be amended by agreement of the national parliament. Pacts of 1992 between the national parties PSOE and PP provided for the transfer of most competences except health to all autonomous communities within five years (Agranoff, 1993) and further pacts with the nationalist parties in 1993 and 1996 provided for extended financial powers and participation in European Union matters.

Regional government in Spain is rooted more in a political than a purely functional dynamic and a window of opportunity was provided by a regime transition. Autonomous governments have established themselves more strongly than in France or Italy, not merely in the historic nationalities but in other regions as well. There are still powerful forces of resistance in the national administration on both the political and bureaucratic sides, but many observers see Spain as on the way to a federal constitution (Agranoff, 1993; Moreno, 1997).

BELGIUM

In Belgium, there was a dual impetus for the move to regional government, from linguistic conflict and territorial regionalism, and this influenced the unique form of the solution, combining territorial and non-territorial devolution. Linguistic tensions in the 1950s and 1960s had undermined the old consociational procedures whereby Flemish and French-speakers managed their joint affairs within the Belgian state, and produced a militant Flemish movement seeking autonomy in cultural matters. At the same time, a Walloon regionalism developed, based more on a sense of economic grievance, given the loss of the region's former industrial dominance (Hooghe, 1991). A law of 1962 sought to stabilize matters by establishing homogeneous Flemish and French linguistic regions, with unalterable boundaries, leaving Brussels as a bilingual zone (Senelle, 1990). Over the next thirty years, a series of deals managed by the national political class, itself fracturing into separate Flemish and Francophone segments, separated out most of the domestic functions of government and finally converted Belgium into a federal state. The basic principles of the reform were territorial, but pure territorial regionalism was ruled out because of the difficulties of Brussels, a majority francophone city but surrounded by Flemish-speaking areas. Flemish politicians could not abandon the Flemish minority in Brussels by handing them over to a Francophone government, whether this was the government of Wallonia or a special Brussels government. Nor could they surrender their historic claims to the city, which is the main economic centre of their region and was until this century a majority Flemish-speaking area. The German-speaking minority, located physically within Wallonia, posed another problem.

A dual form of devolution was thus adopted. A constitutional reform of 1970 set up three language communities, the Flemish, the French and the German, and three territorial regions, Flanders, Wallonia and Brussels but gave these little standing or competences. In 1980 they were given their own councils, except for Brussels; these were indirectly elected and consisted of the national parliamentarians from the respective regions and communities, except for the German community, which was elected. A further reform in 1988 transferred significant functions to the regions and communities and gave Brussels its own council. Finally, in 1993 a new constitution was put into effect, making Belgium a federal state, and providing for the direct election of the regions and communities as of the next national election - in the event, 1995. This represented a radical transformation of the state, of much greater significance than the regional reforms of France, Italy or even Spain, and introduced a major complexity in the form of territorial as well as community devolution. The basic principle was that matters pertaining to physical space, including planning, urban issues, regional development and transport, would be entrusted to the three regional councils. Culture, education and 'personalizable matters' including social services, would be given to the three communities. The Flemish community has responsibility for the population of Flanders and the Flemish-speakers of Brussels; the Walloon community for the population of Wallonia, less the German-speaking area, and for the French-speaking population of Brussels; and the German community for the German-speaking cantons located in the east of Wallonia. The Brussels regional council has Flemish and French commissions and complex provisions for dealing with matters affecting each language group in areas of regional competence. In practice, the territorial principle has become more important than the communitarian one, especially on the Flemish side, where the regional and community institutions are effectively merged into a single Flemish Council and executive (with more complex arrangements for Brussels) and the Flemish political elite engages in a purposive strategy of region or even nation-building. In Wallonia, the institutions are separate, although the French community has tended to act through the territorial institutions rather than maintaining its own administrative system.

THE MODERNIZATION OF REGIONS

Across Europe, regionalism thus moved from a movement of territorial defence, through a strategy for economic modernization, to a movement for constitutional change and transformation of the state. The region is a contested territory and there is continuing tension between the strategy of regionalization as state policy, and regionalism as a movement from below (Loughlin, 1994). During the era of Keynesian economic management and an expanding welfare state, in which active spatial policies were used to counterbalance territorial disparities, compromises could be reached and embodied in institutional reforms. An emerging regional level could be discerned across much of western Europe, but its form differed according to the institutional, cultural and political characteristics of each state. In the 1990s, these contexts have themselves been radically altered by changes in the state and market, producing a new regionalism, which escapes the boundaries of traditional territorial management and which puts regions in competition with each other in the European and global market.

4. The New Regionalism

THE CHANGING CONTEXT

After the intense regional activity of the late 1960s and 1970s, there were signs of a stabilization of territorial politics in western Europe in the 1980s. The French regions set up in 1972 were weakly institutionalized and, despite the regionalist element in the Socialist Party programme, they did not become fully fledged governments, directly elected, until the very end of the Socialists' term in 1986. The institutional development of the Italian regions, after the law of 1977 expanding their functions, was disappointing. Proposals for devolution in Scotland and Wales failed in 1979 and regional administration in England was run down with the abolition of the Regional Economic Planning Councils and downgrading of regional offices of central government. Only in Belgium and Spain, in response to pressures from linguistic and nationalist movements, was there a continued evolution towards a regionalized state. Yet even in Spain, the LOAPA of 1981 represented an attempt on the part of the state and the central parties to recover lost powers. Metropolitan consolidation had been halted and in some cases reversed.

From the late 1980s, however, there was a new wave of regionalism. Once again, it was impelled by a functional pressure combined with new forms of political mobilization and a redefinition of the social and economic meaning of territory, but this time the context was provided not just by the state as in the past, but also by the changing international market and the emerging continental regime. Regionalism is no longer manageable through the old mechanisms of territorial accommodation and exchange, nor can it easily be fitted into an overall design of spatial planning. The state itself was being transformed and in the process was losing its former ability to manage spatial change and development. Its power and authority has been

72

eroded from three directions: from above by internationalization; from below by regional and local assertion; and laterally by the advance of the market and civil society, eroding its capacities in economic management, in social solidarity, in culture and identity formation, as well as its institutional configuration. This has produced a new regionalism marked by two linked features: it is not contained within the framework of the nation-state; and it pits regions against each other in a competitive mode, rather than providing complementary roles for them in a national division of labour. The new regionalism is modernizing and forward-looking, in contrast to an older provincialism, which represented resistance to change and defence of tradition. Yet both old and new regionalism continue to coexist in uneasy partnership, seeking a new synthesis of the universal and the particular.

National economic management is made more difficult by the increased mobility of capital and the rise of transnational corporations. Speculative capital flows constrain governments' freedom in macroeconomic policy, forcing them often to maintain higher interest rates than the domestic situation would indicate. The ability of transnational companies to move their investments intensifies competition to attract them, while states are hesitant to try and push firms into development regions, since they might then choose to leave the country altogether. Fiscal pressures have restricted the scope for regional spending and intensified international competition has led governments to favour their most competitive sectors and regions, rather than the most needy. Regional subsidies have further been restricted by international trading rules and the competition policies of the European Union, while the convergence criteria for qualification for the single currency further constrain governments' ability to pursue expansionist policies. All this has undermined diversionary regional policy and the panoply of instruments used by states to manage their spatial economies. Yet this has not reduced the importance of territory. On the contrary, it is widely recognized that economic restructuring depends on specific combinations of factors in particular places. Since the state is unable to play the mediating role which it did in the past, the impact of global capital on territories is more direct. A tension is created between the global logic of capital, seeking out the most profitable locations, and the spatially-bound logic of regions, which seek to tie capital down. There is an imbalance here, since places have become more dependent on mobile capital than capital, able to choose among competing locations, is dependent upon any specific place. So, while states are no longer able to manage their spatial economies as in the past, the question of spatial development is more salient than ever.

Hence there is a search for new mechanisms for managing the impact of economic change on territories, focused more on the contribution of regions themselves and less on the directing and planning policies of the state. Policies now put less emphasis on investment incentives provided by the central state and more emphasis on endogenous growth, or the attraction of investment by qualities linked to the region, like the environment, the quality of life or the labour force (Gore, 1984; Stöhr, 1990; Storper, 1995). Policy has also shifted from infrastructure provision to human capital and business development, tasks requiring a more refined capacity for intervention on the ground. Influenced by the classic notion of the industrial district, scholars have examined regional economic systems, characterized by networks of territorial interdependence (Dunford and Kafkalas, 1992; Morgan, 1992). Drawing on this, a new development paradigm gives an important role to the construction of identities, territorial solidarities and of territorially-based systems of action, which are now placed more directly in confrontation with the international market, rather than being mediated by the state (this is discussed more fully in Chapter 6).

The state's role in defining and reproducing a national culture has also been eroded by internationalization and the rise of global culture, although arguably this represents an American cultural hegemony rather than a transcultural product. At the same time, there is a revalorization of local and minority cultures visible in the reassertion of Catalan as a language of education and government or the revival of Welsh among sections of the middle class. Technology has mixed effects here. It facilitates the dissemination of American culture and makes it almost impossible for states to retain barriers to it; yet it may also lower the cost of cultural production and diffusion and so enhance the viability of minority cultures.

Social solidarity remains a key responsibility of the European nation state. Yet global competition and the need to reduce the social costs of production have put it under great strain. Identities too are changing, and becoming more complex and multiple, shaped by region, ethnicity and gender as well as the traditional factors of nation and class. The weakening of class consciousness undermines the class compromises at the base of the postwar welfare settlement, and in some places territory may itself constitute a new form of social solidarity, or a line for the defence of the welfare state. New social movements and struggles over plant closures and public service provision give some evidence of this.

Institutionally, the state is also challenged from three directions. From above, it shares powers with international and supranational regimes, notably the European Union. There is a debate in international relations theory as to what constitutes an international regime and what are its features, which we will not get into here (see Haggard and Simmons, 1987; Keohane, 1989; Strange, 1982). For these purposes, the term refers merely to an institutional political structure above the level of the nation state. The debate over whether the EU represents an erosion of national sovereignty, or a mechanism whereby states can more effectively exercise their sovereignty is similarly unconcluded. Yet in both accounts, the supranationalist and the intergovernmentalist, the locus of decision making is shifted from the domestic political arena. This undermines the old links between states and regions and the compromises which were possible in the past. States are also challenged institutionally from below by the rise of regional governments as institutional competitors and by regionalist and minority nationalist movements demanding a restructuring of the state. Laterally, their power is eroded by the advance of the market, itself a response to global capital mobility and to the rise of neo-liberal ideology. Hence the move to privatization and deregulation.

Much has been written on the crisis of the state and the end of sovereignty (Camilleri and Falk, 1992). It would be a mistake to exaggerate the decline of the European state, since it retains a formidable arsenal of powers and resources. It is also important to avoid falling into the analytical trap of contrasting a mythical past state, all-powerful, monopolistic and sovereign, to a modern state which is weakened, pluralist and forced to share its powers with supranational, subnational and private sector agencies. As already noted, these tendencies have always been present. Nonetheless, there has been an important transformation in the state and a disarticulation of the various spheres of social, economic and political action which it formerly encompassed. There is a gap between the system of representation, through state institutions, and decision-making, which has retreated into territorial and social networks. Consequently, the divorce between politics, understood as public debate and competition for office, and public policy is growing. This division of the social reality can have serious effects, not only for governmental efficiency but also for democracy and social cohesion (Touraine, 1992 a, b).

The international market, modern communications technology which breaks the link between space and time, and the individualization of social life, are sometimes presented as destroyers of territory as a principle of organization (Badie, 1995). This may be true if we identify territory with the classic nation-state. If we take a broader view of territory, however, it would be more accurate to say that space is being reconstituted. This has been extensively studied in relation to the geography of production. New spatial systems of production are emerging, which have been characterized as regional complexes with their own internal dynamics and connected to others on a global scale (Scott, 1996). Some observers have extrapolated from the new spatial organization of production directly into politics and government, predicting a 'borderless world' or a future of 'regional states' (Ohmae, 1995). There are three problems with extrapolating from the emergence of regions as economic dynamos to the downgrading of states in favour of a regional world. First, it is not clear that functional restructuring is producing a single territorial hierarchy. Much of the literature on industrial districts refers to small areas which do not correspond to regions in other senses, notably the cultural and the political. Second, not all regions are affected by this functional/spatial restructuring; the literature has tended to focus on the easiest cases to the neglect of those in which the territorial principle is weakly articulated. Third, functionalist analyses neglect the autonomous role of politics (Pintarits, 1995) in shaping territorial systems of action. Political and institutional form does not necessarily follow function, whatever Marxists, neo-liberals or exponents of 'post-Fordism' or regulation theory might argue. Political responses can seek to accommodate the new functional logic, they can oppose it, or they can bend it, but in all cases the functional logic is mediated by politics. People are rarely content to be ruled by mechanical principles and the erosion of the state as a domain of action may stimulate a search for new forms of public space. This new public space, however, has now to be constructed at various territorial levels, and not merely that of the state. Where states contain existing territorial fault lines inherited from the historical process of state-building, contemporary global changes may impact along these lines, encouraging territorial fragmentation. New forms of territorial politics then emerge out of the old, as in Catalonia, Scotland or the Basque Country. In other cases, a tradition of territorial politics is bent to new forms and uses, as in the regions of Belgium, where Flanders and Wallonia, relatively new political creations based on territorial–linguistic criteria, have emerged to occupy the old political space, at the expense of the old provincial and urban units. Elsewhere, a territorial politics is constructed anew,

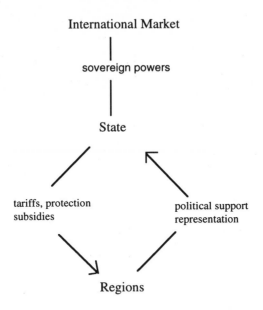

Figure 4.1 States and regions. The traditional order

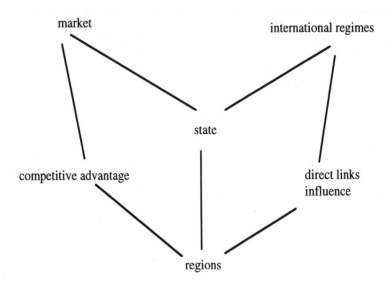

Figure 4.2 Regions, state and market

as in the case of the Italian Northern Leagues (Schmidtke, 1995). Here, there was little by way of regionalism to build on initially, but Italy is the western European country whose governing regime was perhaps most destabilized by the end of the Cold War and the rise of the new Europe. These influences in different contexts produce different forms of regionalism and territorial politics.

Regions have emerged from this process in two senses. On the one hand, they are political arenas in which issues are framed, policies debated, decisions taken and resources allocated. This is facilitated by a tendency to decentralization in politics and social movements and a consequent tendency to adopt a territorial frame of reference for policy debates. On the other hand, the increase of place-based competition for investment, markets and other opportunities may lead to the displacement of intra-regional political competition by inter-regional competition. In this game, the regions constitute themselves as actors within the new systems of decision making.

In the traditional mode of territorial management, the relationship of regions to the global market and to international regimes was mediated by the state, as indicated in Figure 4.1. Regions provided political support for states and governments and were represented in state politics. States in exchange provided protection and subsidies. This dyadic exchange has now been destabilized by globalization, European integration and the advance of the market. Regions have now emerged as new places for the construction of policies, as systems of action, and as actors themselves in the global order, as illustrated by Figure 4.2. This is a more complex order, in which states have lost their monopoly of mediation and their ability to control their own spatial economies. Regions still engage in exchange with their respective states, but are also in direct contact with international regimes, and with the global market. Their positioning within these new systems of action is not governed in the same way as their relations with the state. Within regimes such as the European Union, influence is exercised in multiple ways, through divers channels (Chapter 6). Regions' position in the international market place is governed, not by political channels of representation, but by their competitive advantages and their success in exploiting these. States, it must be emphasized, have not disappeared and are not likely to, but they no longer monopolize the external links of regions.

THE CONSTRUCTION OF REGIONS

There has thus been a reconfiguration of territorial politics, in which regions have come to feature more prominently, but these regions are so varied that the term almost escapes descriptive definition. As Anderson (1994, p.6) puts it:

> From the outset, the term was highly indeterminate – floating between the specifically territorial and the generically sectoral, and lending itself to any number of metaphorical applications or extensions.

The need for regions to find a place within a varied set of national and supranational socio-political structures further differentiates the phenomenon. We can most usefully conceptualize regions as spaces, but extending the notion of space beyond the purely territorial to include functional space; political space; and social space. A region is constituted from a territory, whose significance is given by its functional and political content. It is also an institutional system, in the form of a regional government, or a set of administrative institutions operating in the territory. It may contain its own institutions, practices and relationships to constitute a distinct civil society. Finally, it may have constituted itself as an actor, able to articulate and pursue a common interest in the state and global systems.

TERRITORIAL SPACE

One way to define the regional space is negatively, as intermediate between the state and municipal government, although even here there are exceptions, since in some cases the term region has been applied to units of local government. There are differences between metropolitan regions, built around big cities with their hinterlands, unified by economic linkages, transport, and systems of functional interdependence; and provincial-scale regions, drawn on the map of the whole state. These vary among themselves; some cover vast areas while others are drawn on the basis of smaller historic units and others again are the leftovers from the construction of neighbouring regions. Even in the same country, regions may exist at different levels. In Germany, there are the *Flächenstaaten* (which themselves range from North Rhine-Westphalia to the Saar) and the *Stadtstaaten* of Hamburg, Bremen and Berlin. In Spain, there are large regions like Catalonia and Andalucia, and simple provinces turned into autonomous communities, like La Rioja and Cantabria. In the smaller European countries there are no regions at all, but this is perhaps a trivial point, since these states are themselves the size of regions. Even at the European level, there is no consistent territorial definition of a region. The EU Commission uses the NUTS system, with three levels, but these are mere aggregations of national units and in the implementation of its own regional policies it uses a whole range of territorial units according to the task at hand (Hooghe and Keating, 1994). So regions cannot be delineated simply by topographical criteria. Their extent and shape will depend on what functions they are to fulfill, and on patterns of political mobilization which give them a political meaning. Territorial delineation thus becomes a political issue in itself, since the drawing of the boundaries can alter not only the social content of regionalism, but the political power balance in regional institutions.

FUNCTIONAL SPACE

One of the most powerful forces behind the new regionalism is the functional dynamic of economic restructuring. This has produced a new territorial hierarchy and new systems of action, which may escape the control of nation states (Scott, 1996). As already noted, it does not follow that government will recompose itself on this functional basis, but a link can be traced between functional needs and political restructuring, where there is a political will to make it. Global economic restructuring and technological change have eroded the old spatial division of labour based on factor attributes such as raw materials, access to transportation links or proximity to markets. Comparative advantage, an essentially static concept in which regions concentrate on those activities at which, because of their factor endowments, they are best, has given way to the more dynamic concept of competitive advantage (Scott, 1996). In this vision, policy makers seek to maximize the capacity of their territory to compete by endowing it with the resources, notably in human capital, which are critical in the global economy, and by mobilizing local energies. This implies an active policy stance, and a complex network of public-private linkages to engage local synergies. Regions have emerged as an important level for this type of mobilization but with strategies which are shaped by political dynamics (Chapter 6).

Regions may provide an appropriate level for overcoming the

destructive tendencies to competition among local governments to attract investment (Le Galès, 1997). In highly fragmented systems of local government, the political incentive to local politicians to engage in policies to attract investment often leads to sub-optimal outcomes for metropolitan areas or regions as a whole (Keating, 1995b). Industrial sites are over-provided and infrastructure duplicated. Confusion rules in the marketing of the area. Incentives (whether financial where these are allowed, or in kind) proliferate, allowing firms to play municipalities off against each other without affecting the overall level of investment in the region. Yet, while everyone might gain from cooperation, no-one has an incentive to do so as long as others have the opportunity to free-ride. A regional approach can overcome these problems, by imposing cooperation. Regions may also be the best level to manage various aspects of labour markets. It is notable that manpower training is a function which has recently been regionalized or localized in several states.

Regionalism is still closely connected with planning, especially for large infrastructure projects which, in the absence of regional decision-making, could be under-provided (because of an unwillingness to share external benefits) or over-provided (because of competition to attract complementary investment). Ports, airports, major highways, railways, universities and research centres and major industrial sites, would be examples. Regions are also seen as an appropriate level for determining priorities and programming in capital investments which have repercussions for wide areas. So a regional level of planning has often been introduced within sectorally-defined functions, such as education or health, even where the primary policy responsibility lies at another level.

Regions are the site of many of the interdependencies which have been identified as an important feature of contemporary government (Balme, 1996). These interdependencies are both functional, where one function is closely connected with another, and institutional. So regions have an important function as intermediaries, both in the territorial and functional sense, as a place where central and local government can meet, and as a level of integration of functionally-differentiated government policies. This was an important theme in the regional initiatives of the 1960s, such as the French CODER and the British REPBs. Similarly, the French regional prefects and the English regional offices emerged to fill a perceived functional need for integration. In Scotland and Wales the decentralized ministries have long performed this role. The political requirements for the roles of territorial and functional intermediaries may differ. The territorial intermediary role could be fulfilled by a regional level without its own political base, serving as a meeting place and forum for negotiation between centre and locality. This could consist of consultative bodies and multipartite institutions. Functional integration, on the other hand, implies giving power to regional bodies in order to pull together the strands of policy and impose priorities. It implies not mere brokerage among interests but the redefinition of problems from a regional perspective and the bending of programmes in accordance with it. This is a political role and one which multipartite bodies, responding to different constituencies, or bodies which represent one of the interests, are ill-equipped to fulfil.

Social solidarity is not generally an important regional function but one located at the national and local levels. The sense of identity and solidarity necessary to underpin social redistribution is linked to national identity and to community feeling, and tends to be felt more weakly at regional level, perhaps with the exception of those stateless nations with a strong historic identity. There has been a tendency over the decades to centralize social transfers, since the state has a larger tax base and uniform provision can discourage people migrating to take advantage of higher welfare provision. At the same time, social integration at the community level has devolved upon municipal government, with its local knowledge and powers. Proposals to decentralize social welfare spending to regions have been made in Belgium by Flemish interests, in Germany by neoliberals in the Christian Democratic and Free Democratic Parties and by a few voices in Spain, but raise fears of a 'race to the bottom' as regions seek to attract investment by reducing the social costs of production while cutting back welfare provision.

Regions may also provide a space for the resolution of cultural and linguistic conflicts, through a territorial demarcation of language areas. Most western European countries contain zones in which minority languages have a special status which they do not possess elsewhere. It has proved difficult, however, to territorialize the management of linguistic and cultural issues, since language zones rarely correspond to regions for other purposes. Even in Wales, a territory with a strong historic identity, the language is spoken only by a minority; the same is true of Brittany and the Basque Country. In Belgium the lack of fit between territory and language has led to a dual model of devolution, with the establishment of three regions (Flanders, Wallonia and Brussels capital) and of three linguistic communities (Flemish, French and German), which overlap territorially in rather complex ways.

Regions have arisen as the functional meaning of territory has changed. In the past, territorial politics revolved around the mediating role of local political elites, and issues of distribution. These were the key elements in territorial exchange and accommodation. The rise of regions betokens a different type of territorial politics, geared to the management of change and to modernization in the new market conditions. Yet it would be a mistake to derive the existence of a regional political dynamic or the evolution of regional institutions by reference purely to functional necessities. These functional criteria are interpreted and given meaning by social and political factors. These include culture, identity, politics and the institutions and traditions rooted in regional civil society.

REGIONAL CULTURE

The nation-state has been a powerful force for cultural uniformity, through universal education, official language policy and administration, and since the Second World War mass media, especially television, have served to reinforce these national patterns. In most countries, there is considerable social pressure to adopt the dominant form of speech and manners and at least a mild contempt for the cultures and languages of the periphery. Modernization has been associated with nationalization and regional culture has often been regarded as backward, reactionary or 'provincial', where provincial is seen as the opposite not only of national, but also of the universal values of the Enlightenment and progress.

In recent years, all this has been changing. Minority languages have been given new status in the historic nationalities of Spain, where they now have a central role in the education system. This process of linguistic normalization has been uneven and has gone much further in Catalonia, where the local language has always enjoyed high status and social extension, than in Galicia, where it is still widely regarded by the urban middle classes as a mark of backwardness and peasant conservatism. In Wales, the language has received institutional support in public administration, the media and education so that it is now an asset to aspiring professionals, rather than the mark of a pre-modern rural society — hence its dramatic expansion among the anglicized middle classes of south Wales who are increasingly sending their children to Welsh schools. A similar phenomenon is visible among the non-Basque-speaking population of Bilbao. Minority languages have fared less well in France, where there is only minimal provision for teaching them, and none for teaching *in* them, in the schools, where the curriculum is still centrally controlled and uniform.

A less easily measurable phenomenon is the enhanced social status of dialect in Scandinavia, Germany and German-speaking Switzerland, where politicians will use dialect to stress their local roots and identity and send subtle signals to their electors. In Italy, dialect is still used regularly by about a third of the population in informal settings, reflecting the intense localism of culture, although its use has been declining over the last 30 years (Lepschy et al., 1996); in 1955 only some 11 to 12 per cent of the population spoke Italian regularly (Salvi, 1996). The *Lega Lombarda* in its early days tried to make the dialect a vehicle of political mobilization, but with little success. In France, by contrast, use of dialect denotes the 'old regionalism' of affective attachment, tradition and even resistance to modernity (Parisot, 1996) and it is never used in political communication. Dialect use in the United Kingdom has fallen sharply since the Second World War but since the 1970s there has been an enhancement of the status of regional accents, which are now acceptable on radio and television and from national politicians.

Interpretation of the past is a key element in the cultural representation of a region and there has been something of a boom in regional history. Sometimes this has taken the form of the 'heritage industry', an effort to exploit a real or imagined past as a tourist attraction; the proliferation of theme parks in the former industrial regions of the United Kingdom is a good example. In other cases, regional culture is romanticized or stereotyped — in this way industrial Europe or rural ways of life can be quietly put to sleep in much the same way that the romantic novels of the nineteenth century managed the passing of an earlier era. There is also, however, a search for a 'usable past', a set of historical referents which can guide a regional society on its distinct road to modernization, bridging the past, via the present, with the future. The revival of serious regional history and the challenging of dominant national interpretations of the past then becomes an instrument in guiding a regional society to its own future.

Regionalism has revived in art, music and literature, reflecting the declining prestige of officially-sanctioned national cultures. The local and regional novel has enjoyed a renaissance (Agnew, 1997a) as has dialect writing, though this tends to be confined to poetry. This new regional writing and associated film production is less inclined to present nostalgic and sentimental views of the local society, but tends often to social realism and the representation of cultural pluralism, diversity and social conflict.

Cultural production is not in itself necessarily political and can easily be divorced from other dimensions of regionalism, but the revalorization of regional culture is an important part of the creation of a modern regional identity. It tells a different story from the nationalist accounts of identity and development, and one which is arguably more consistent with other trends in politics and economics (Agnew, 1997b). Regionalism is divorced from its provincialist and antiquarian connotations and presented as a path to modernization and globalization that is as valid as that presented by the national state.

REGIONAL IDENTITY

It is easy to note that regional identity is a key element in the construction of regions as social and political spaces and systems of action. It is more difficult to define just what this identity consists of, or how it affects collective action and politics. One measure of a regional specificity is provided by the existence of different values, norms and behaviour among regions within the same state. Such a map of values can be superimposed on that of the states, tracing underlying values, which may predate the state system, or be independent of it. The most common sources of such values and patterns of social communication are religion and language. In general, these follow state boundaries, since following the Reformation states determined the religious affiliation of their citizens, while state-imposed language policies were a force for national integration from the nineteenth century and, in some cases, earlier. Yet, in some cases, notably Germany, the state was formed after the Reformation, and religious divisions became identified with regions within it; other states, notably Belgium and Switzerland, were bilingual or multilingual. In the twentieth-century, secularization and the revalorization of minority languages have had an uneven incidence. The European Values Study shows that northern states are generally homogeneous in values, with Spain, Portugal and Italy showing more variation (Chauvel, 1995). The homogeneity of Western Germany appears to be the product of post-war mingling of population and the destruction of old local and regional subcultures. Belgium comes out as surprisingly homogeneous on various measures, a fact attributable to its common religious heritage, distinct both from the Protestant Netherlands and secular France. Britain, despite its multinational character, comes out as quite homogeneous in values. The variations within the southern countries are also attributable to religious factors, the degree of secularization and the anti-clerical traditions of different regions. On the other hand, there is a certain spillover across national boundaries, with Catalonia showing similarities to Midi-Pyrénées, Bavaria displaying some affinity with north-west Italy and Schleswig-Holstein with Denmark (Chauvel, 1995). Wallonia shows many commonalities with France, although Flanders does not share values with the Netherlands; the homogeneity of Belgium thus still pulls it closer to the French pole, which was historically dominant. In the late twentieth-century, these religious factors may be giving way to others, notably language, as in a modern society social communication requires a common language. In this case, we would expect the rise of Flemish consciousness and political activism, together with the internalization of social communication within Flanders and the reduction of Francophone influence there, to lead to an increasing distance between the two parts of the country. Similarly, the values that have united Switzerland are giving way to divisive linguistic quarrels in the context of the modern state.

Regional identity, however, is still more complex and not always linked to differences in values. There are three elements in analysing regional identity and its relationship to political action (Frankenberg and Schuhbauer, 1994). The first element is the cognitive one, that is people must be aware of such a thing as a region, and of its geographical limits. This in turn requires a knowledge of other regions, with which the home region can be compared and from which it can be differentiated. People must also be aware of the region's characteristics, although they may differ on which ones are salient— for one the region may be the scenery and landscape, for another the cuisine or the folklore, for a third, it might be a language, a historical legacy, or a political disposition, while others may emphasize economic structures. A second element is the affective one, that is how people feel about the region and the degree to which it provides a framework for common identity and solidarity, possibly in competition with other forms of solidarity, including class and nation. This provides a form of interpretation of the cognitive element, and links to the third element, the instrumental one, whether the region is used as a basis for mobilization and collective action in pursuit of social, economic and political goals. These goals may include the attainment of regional autonomy, or they may be focused on more immediate social and economic policies, to be achieved through the existing structures.

A series of difficult issues arise in analysing these identities and appreciating their significance. Survey techniques are the easiest way of finding out how people identify themselves, but the survey instrument is essentially about individual experience largely devoid of context (Jacquemain et al., 1990, 1994) while collective identity is something experienced and lived collectively. Reading off collective identity from individual, isolated responses thus risks falling into the individualist fallacy, which arises when units of observation are smaller than the units for which inferences are made (Rose and Urwin, 1975). This is why surveys often fail to capture collective mobilizations or to explain collective behaviour by reference to individual motivation. A political crisis, a traumatic event, an emotional anniversary, can mobilize collective identities which for most of the time are a dormant element in the mindset of individuals or lack immediate saliency. So evidence from surveys must be complemented with evidence from behaviour and political action.

Another issue concerns the creation and reproduction of identities. Regional identity may be rooted in historical traditions and myths but, in its contemporary form, it is a social construction, forged in a specific context under the influence of social, economic and political pressures. As with other identities, scholars debate how far these identities are rooted in individuals' formative experiences, and how far they are created to meet short-term needs, how far they emerge from the bottom-up and how far they are invented by elites for their own purposes. Local identities, which predominate in many parts of Europe, are typically based on personal experience, individual contact and the events of everyday life. Regional identity is another matter, since it requires citizens to relate to people whom they only know at second hand, through the media, political parties or broader social institutions. Like national identities, therefore, it rests upon 'imagined communities' (Anderson, 1983) rather than lived experience. Such imagined communities are the product of social mobilization and political leadership. Political leaders certainly engage in region-building in much the way that an earlier generation engaged in state and nation-building, although the success which they have in this varies greatly. Although Catalonia is an ancient nation, its leaders can speak of the need to *fer país*, to create the country in the modern era. French regional presidents and the minister-presidents of German Länder have used policy initiatives and communications in order to build a regional image, coincidentally bolstering their own personal status in the process. Italy's *Lega Nord* has engaged in an elaborate exercise in region-building, proceeding in a few years from the idea of an economically exploited region to the construction of an alternative 'national' identity. It has established its own social institutions in the localities and in 1996 launched a daily paper, *La Padana*, giving its own version of the news, with even the weather forecasts confined to northern Italy. Outsiders have scoffed at this as a purely artificial exercise, yet the invented history of Padania is little more misleading than the official accounts of many of the established nations, and there is evidence that the message has begun to find an audience and a social base within the region (Biorcio, 1997). The new state context facilitates this construction of alternative identities, both by weakening the prestige of the established states, and by providing opportunities for regional leaders to project their regions and themselves in the international and European arenas. In other cases, a depoliticized form of cultural identity or folklore is encouraged, in order to minimize the disruptive potential of territorial politics. Like nation-builders, region-builders take liberties with history, seeking legitimation in an imagined past. Flanders has been given a historic unity, transcending the provincial and local divisions of its real past; Occitania was reinvented by nineteenth century historians out of a tradition of revolt and dissent (Martel, 1994); Padania has been invented as the 'oldest community in Europe' (Oneto, 1997).

Another question concerns the political significance and uses of identity. The existence of a shared regional identity, in both its cognitive and affective dimensions, does not necessarily have political consequences. It depends on whether this identity is used as a framework for perception and judgement of political issues, notably in voting at elections and referendums. A further stage is reached with the demand for regional autonomy. These represent successive steps in political regionalism, since the second (politicization of identity) is not possible without the first, nor the third (demand for autonomy) without the second. On the other hand, regionalism may well stop at the first or second without proceeding to the third. Matters are complicated by the emergence of the phenomenon of multiple identities, encouraged by the changing state and European order, which have broken the monopoly of states in forging identity. This allows people to assume a regional identity without, in general, giving up their national identity or even weakening it greatly. It also affects politics in another important way, by giving a premium to those individuals able to bridge differing spheres of action and operate in multiple arenas, territorial as well a social.

There is a lot of evidence on regional identities in Europe, but the surveys tend to measure different things in different contexts and it is difficult to compare the importance of regional identities across countries or at different times. Surveys are highly sensitive to the wording and context. There are French surveys asking to which level people feel closest whose results suggest that people are taking the question quite literally, indicating that they are closest to the town or village, followed by the region, the nation and then Europe (Dupoirier, 1994). Eurobarometer surveys show high and similar levels of attachment to the town or village, the region and the country, with Europe coming a considerable way behind (Eurobarometer, 1991,1995). There is much evidence, too, that a sense of attachment to a region more generally is strongest among the least geographically and socially mobile and among older people (Eurobarometer, 1995; Lilli and Hartig, 1995). This provides evidence for the modernist thesis, that territorial identities are a feature of traditional society, and will disappear with secularization, modernization and mobility. Closer inspection, however, shows that this generally involves the traditional sense of the region, as a place, a culture and way of life rather than the modern sense of the region as an actor in the political life of the nation and in Europe. This is surely the meaning of the Eurobarometer surveys which show that among the countries with the highest level of strong regional identification are Portugal, Greece and Ireland, three states without any form of regional government or regionalist political movements (except in the Portuguese islands). The modern regionalism tends to be found among upwardly mobile, young, urbanized and politically efficacious people (Jiménez Blanco et al., 1977; Lilli and Hartig, 1995; Dupoirier and Roy, 1995; OIP, 1997) or in modernizing, more prosperous and more socially integrated regions (this is one interpretation of the data in Putnam et al., 1985, though they emphasise historic legacies). Regionalist parties also appeal to middle-class professional elements (Urwin, 1983). We can therefore make a tentative distinction between 'regional traditionalists', largely depoliticized or conservative in orientation and resembling nineteenth-century conservative regionalisms, and new or modern regionalists found in the more educated sections of the population, and interested in the region as an element in modernization and the construction of Europe. Regional traditionalists may be uninterested in regional autonomy, seeing the region in a purely cultural or topographic perspective, and preferring traditional mechanisms of representation in central and local government, including partisan and clientelistic networks. Modern regionalists will be more outward-looking and see the region as a dynamic force for economic and social change. These are generalizations, since the meaning of regionalism is shaped by the historical and contemporary politics of individual states, and by the character of regional institutions.

In some places, there is a conflict of identities, where historically the region (or stateless nation) has been pitted against an integrative state. Elsewhere, regionalism has historically been compatible with belonging to the nation, and may even be an important component of this. In some places, regionalism is merely an extension of localism. The Eurobarometer surveys show strongest regional attachment in those countries where there is also the strongest local attachment, suggesting that it is tapping a more diffuse territorial sentiment rather than a mature regionalism. In other places, the regional level is identified quite distinctly. This accounts for paradoxes like the findings of surveys conducted for the British Kilbrandon Commission in the early 1970s, which apparently showed equal degrees of identification and as much support for self-government in some English regions as in Scotland (Kilbrandon, 1973). The problem is that they were not measuring the same thing, since in the English regions there are no institutions and the survey tapped no more than a vague agreement with the idea that local people should have more say, while in Scotland it related to a specific proposal, with which people were reasonably familiar and which had been subject to a political debate in which both benefits and costs had been rehearsed. Here being Scottish was in some senses opposed to being British, whereas in the English case, this question did not arise. In the multinational states of Spain and Belgium, similarly, regional identity is often juxtaposed to national identity while in France (OIP, 1997) and Germany, being a regionalist does not imply being any less French or German.

The 'new regionalism' is predicated on a link between the region and the international or European order, with regions seeking their own place in the state, Europe and the international market. Surveys show little evidence that this link is being made at the grassroots level. Certainly, surveys do show a growth of multiple identity, with the region, the state and even Europe (Grivel, 1994), above all in the most educated sections of the population, but the region-Europe or region-global link is not always evident. This is not surprising if we think of regions, like states, as creations rather than spontaneous or primordial entities. The question is not so much whether citizens are of their own accord starting to think regionally and internationally, but whether they provide the raw material for political elites to make such a link. As we shall see in Chapter 7, regional elites are in many instances making the connection. This depends not just on the strength of regional attachments, but on the weakness of national identities and the ability of states to provide a counter-pole of attraction. The European Values Study shows some rather high levels of dentity with the nation-state in southern Europe, where the state is the incarnation of the nation and of collective identity, but it is precisely in these states that the state is weakest and challenged most by globalization and European integration. Confidence in state institutions is also lower in these societies, preventing them from being agents of socialization in the manner of the nineteenth-century early twentieth-century state. In Belgium, similarly, confidence in the state and feelings of pride in the nation are rather low (Eurobarometer, 1991, 1995). There is also a tendency for attachment to the state to be stronger in central than peripheral regions of states, and to be weakest in places of historical, cultural or linguistic specificity, such as Scotland, Northern Ireland, the Basque Country, Bavaria, Schleswig-Holstein or the regions of Belgium (Chauvel, 1995).

It is also apparent that a differentiation of values is not necessary for a region to develop its own identity. What is required is that it become the framework for appraising political and social issues. Indeed, it may be that territorial identity increases precisely as value differentiation declines, with the sub-state level taking over as the framework for expressing and operationalizing universal values (Keating, 1996). This new, modern or secular identity may be less constraining than the old cultural values, functioning as a mechanism for collective action in the face of changing political and market conditions and based more on rational calculation than affective community (Keating, 1992b).

When regional identity is matched to specific regions, Spain emerges as a country of strong and rather politicized identities. At the time of the transition to democracy in the 1970s, regionalist sentiments were quite strong around the periphery and dominated over Spanish identity in the historic nationalities (Jiménez Blanco et al., 1977). In historically-defined regions such as these, together with Aragon, Andalucia, Extremadura and Valencia, regional identity was stronger than provincial identity. Support for regional autonomy was less certain, but soon spread as the transition proceeded. By the 1990s, dual identity was the majority sentiment almost everywhere, with only around 20 per cent, mostly in the central regions around Madrid, having exclusively national identity (Moreno, 1997; CIRES, 1996). This regional identity has several dimensions — cultural, economic and political — but there is a tendency for the more politicized forms of regional identity, implying support for autonomy, to correlate with higher education and social status (Lopez-Aranguren, 1982). In Galicia, a poor region noted for its lack of social modernization, a strong sense of identity and almost universal command of the regional language coexists with rather weak support for autonomy and a clientelistic style of governing; in a 1988–89 survey it came out as the least autonomist of all regions (Montero and Torcal, 1990). This can be considered an example of traditionalist regionalism, a phenomenon also reflected to a degree in Andalucia. In Catalonia, by contrast, support for autonomist options is high and especially high among the better-educated, the young and the professional classes (Institut de Ciènces Politiques i Socials, 1995). Here autonomism both taps a historic sense of national identity, reforged in the struggle against dictatorship, and ties into a modernizing project in the context of Europe.

In Belgium, the construction of regions and of regional identities is rather recent, since historically attachments to provinces, towns or the broad linguistic group predominated. The regionalization process was largely undertaken in response to linguistic conflict but the resulting institutions have since developed their own dynamic, especially in Flanders where the tendency has been to the establishment of an integrated regional/community institution. This has been accompanied by a nation-building project on the part of Flemish political elites dedicated to constructing a new political space (Kerremans, 1997). Surveys show that regional identity did indeed tend to displace linguistic identity in the 1980s, especially in Flanders (Collinge, 1987) as the linguistic issue was regulated, and economic issues came to the fore. There regional identity was slightly higher than Belgian national identity by the end of the 1970s (De Winter and Frognier, 1997), while local identities were also very marked. This is explicable by the traditional localism of Flemish society, by the struggle of Flemings for recognition in the Belgian state, and by the strategy of Flemish elites. Walloons, by contrast, identified with the state in which they had traditionally been dominant. Regionalism was strongest among the better educated sections of the populace (De Winter and Frognier, 1997), although this is complicated by a number of other factors. Flemish strong regionalists tend to be found among the better off sections of the society while, since the late 1980s the reverse has been true in Wallonia, reflecting the relative economic positions of the two regions. The most striking tendency of the 1990s, however, has been towards a revalorization of Belgian identity, which has been strengthening at the expense both of regions and communities (De Winter and Frognier, 1997). There is a generational effect here, with both regional identity and support for regional government strongest among the middle-aged population who had come of age in the struggles of the 1960s and weaker among the older and the youngest cohorts. Flanders is generally seen, even by Flemish identifiers, as a region of Belgium, perhaps reflecting the advances of Flemish interests in the politics of the state. This all shows once again that regional identity is highly contextual, is moulded by events and political strategies, and can be mobilized for different purposes, which does not mean that it can be dismissed, since national identities have the same characteristic. Belgian national identity can be mobilized on emotive occasions like the death of the king, or the child-abuse scandals of the mid-1990s, but this too is an ephemeral phenomenon since, for the rest of the time, Belgians have the weakest sense of national identity in Europe (Eurobarometer, 1991). There is therefore little countervailing pressure against the regionalization of political life and a tendency for political issues to fall rapidly into a Flemish/Walloon context, even where their origins have nothing to do with the territorial/ linguistic conflict.

German regional identity can be strong, but it does not in general coincide with the Länder (Benz, 1997), except perhaps in Bavaria and the three city-states. Elswhere, the region is situated somewhere between the

Land and the city (Lilli and Hartig, 1995). There is a homogeneity of values, reflecting the experience of migration and the destruction of local subcultures after the war, but some distinctiveness does remain in Bavaria and Schleswig-Holstein (Chauvel, 1995)

France remains a country with weak regional identities. In a 1994 survey, only 61 per cent of respondents could name their region, concentrated in the most highly education strata of the population (Dupoirier and Roy, 1995). Most saw the region as a historic and cultural place or simply a 'territory'. Of those giving it a functional meaning, most saw it as a space for economic development, and only three per cent primarily as a space for political debate (with seven per cent putting this as second choice). This reflects the state of French regions themselves, defined by their cultural/historic features and the functionally-specific role of the regional councils; it indicates a lack of strong political pressure to make the regions real rivals to the state. When asked to rank the various levels of government on the basis of closeness to them, respondents have consistently placed them in their territorial hierarchy, commune, department, region, state, Europe (OIP, 1995). Surveys have shown that people believe that the regions are the level of the future, but this has not translated into mass political mobilization to achieve it.

In Italy, local identities remain strong, rooted in civic cultures and practices, and there is a marked variation in social values between the south and the centre and north (Chauvel, 1995). Yet this has largely failed to crystalize into a political regionalism. Surveys in 1986 and 1992 showed an increase in those identifying with their region, against the state, the locality or Europe/the world, from 10.3 per cent to 12.4 per cent, rising to 15.1 per cent in the north. Local identity, on the other hand, scored 49.6 and 35 per cent respectively in the two years (Biorcio, 1997). Yet there is also evidence that the *Lega Nord* has made an impact on its own supporters, with over 30 per cent of them identifying first with the region (Biorcio, 1997).

The United Kingdom is a multinational state, with Scotland and Northern Ireland and, to a lesser extent, Wales, differentiating themselves from England (Keating, 1996; Chauvel, 1995). In the regions of England, on the other hand, regional identity is rather weak. Identity in the historic nations of the United Kingdom rests less on a sharp distinction of values, since in this respect the state is rather homogeneous (Chauvel, 1995) than on their institutional differentiation and historic status. Here, as in the historic nationalities of Spain or in Flanders, the sub-state level competes directly with state as the frame of perception of issues and the basis for political mobilization. Scotland, as it has gradually acquired institutions of administration if not until now self-government, has internalized political debate and interaction to become the primary frame of reference for many issues. In a longer perspective, as a historic nationality, Scotland does not have to be 'different' to exist (McCrone, 1992), but can mould the way in common issues of modern society are addressed and debated.

It would be easy to conclude from these examples that regional identity, in the sense of popular identification with regional units of government or administration, is rather weak except in historic nationalities like Scotland, Wales, Catalonia or the Basque Country. This certainly presents an obstacle to projects for a Europe of the regions, in which the old 'artificial' states would dissolve in favour of supposedly more 'natural' units beneath them. A more sophisticated analysis, however, shows that territorial identities are part of citizens' mind-sets but that they are malleable and change in accordance with circumstances. They do not necessarily displace national identities but are supplementary to them. Territorial identities often represent weak ties (Granovetter, 1973) rather than binding ones, and are often nested within wider ones (Marks, 1997). Individual surveys tap people's immediate identification and aspirations but often provide poor guides to behaviour in specific circumstances and in response to specific stimuli. Regions can become a frame of reference for political judgement and action in so far as political issues are regionalized and social institutions present politics in a regional frame. Regionalist sentiment and the demand for self-government comes, if at all, at a later stage, when regional policy demands are frustrated. Then old identities are politicized, as in the UK in the 1980s, or new identities are forged and pressed into service, as may be happening in the 1990s in Italy. Some writers (for example Chauvel, 1995) continue to see regionalism as evidence of retarded modernization, a transitional stage from a premodern society of faith to the modern world of the nation-state. This may have been true in the nineteenth-century, but in the late twentieth-century the nation-state is often too weak to forge a unitary national culture and identity. As religion fades as a mark of identity, it may leave behind residues of values and behaviour that differentiate one region from another, while language becomes ever more important. At the same time, new issues arise to distinguish regional values, behaviour and identity, notably linked to their position in the global economy.

REGIONS, PARTIES AND VOTING

One measure of the regionalization of politics is the existence of regional
political parties, or regional branches of national parties. It might be
expected that regional parties would be more important in regional
elections than in state-wide ones, but this proves not to be the case, except
to some extent in the historic nationalities of Spain. Elsewhere, both
national and regional parties contest both regional and national elections
with results for the one generally reflecting those for the other. Once
again, however, this appearance of homogeneity can be deceptive, since
national parties may have to adapt themselves to regional milieus,
exploiting distinct bases of support and specific issues.

In Belgium, the party system is completely regionalized, so that no
elector has the opportunity to vote for a Belgian-wide party, a factor
which increases the incentives for politicians to make specific regional
or community appeals and ensures that issues are framed in a regional
context. This regionalization of the national party system has undercut
the principal regionalist or minority nationalist parties, the *Volksunie* and
Rassemblement Wallon, and the latter disappeared from the political
spectrum in the 1980s, although the extreme-right *Vlaams Blok* has made
progress with its virulent anti-immigrant platform. Regional parties are
common in Spain, where at the 1996 elections, eight non-state-wide
parties gained seats, depriving either of the major contestants of a
majority. They were most important in Catalonia and the Basque Country,
where they gained about half the vote, but also made gains in Galicia,
Valencia, the Canaries and Aragon. Overall, non-state-wide parties
gained some 12 per cent of the vote. For elections to the autonomous
communities, the party systems in Catalonia and the Basque Country are
entirely distinct and have been dominated by the nationalist options. In
the United Kingdom, the party system of Northern Ireland is distinct
from that of the rest of the state, with none of the mainland parties
presenting candidates there. Scotland and Wales have partially distinct
systems, with nationalist parties gaining around 20 per cent and ten per
cent of the vote respectively in recent elections while the Conservative
Party has been very weak, finally losing all its seats in 1997. This has
ensured a distinct pattern of competition, with issues framed in a local
context, and the dominant Labour Party facing little effective competition
on its right. In Germany, the two regionalized parties are the Christian
Social Union, based in Bavaria but allied with the Christian Democratic
Party, which does not run candidates in Bavaria, and the Party of
Democratic Socialism (PDS), a post-communist party which effectively
operates only in eastern Germany, where it won enough constituency

seats (four) in 1994 to entitle it to representation in the national parliament. Land elections in eastern Germany and Bavaria take on a distinctive pattern as a result, though elsewhere local issues are less salient. In Italy, regionalist parties dominate politics in the peripheries of Val d'Aosta and Trentino-Alto Adige and made a sporadic impact in Sardinia, but elsewhere were not important before the 1980s when the *Lega Lombarda*, later expanded into the *Lega Nord* made its breakthrough. The collapse of the national party system allowed it to consolidate its support, campaigning on a platform of opposition to the old regime and autonomy for northern Italy. For some years, it was unable to make a reality of its imagined region of Padania and was highly ambivalent on its constitutional demands, oscillating between threatening separatism and demanding the federalization of the country. Consequently, its regionalist message tended to give way to a generalized populism and anti-statism (Schmidtke, 1993; Savelli, 1992). In the late 1990s, it experienced a rather suprising revival, putting down roots in communities in northern Italy adopting an openly separatist line. By 1996 it was gaining 20 per cent of the vote in northern Italy on this uncompromising line. Regionalist parties have made little progress in France, except to a minor extent in Corsica, despite a series of efforts since the 1960s. In Brittany, regionalist movements have arisen sporadically but have usually been coopted by the mainstream parties. So some Breton regionalists have been able to come into local governments on socialist-led tickets.

Regional branches of national parties may have a greater or lesser degree of autonomy. In Italy, the regional structures of the parties in the former regime of the *partitocrazia* were weak compared to the provincial structures (Dente, 1985). In Spain, by contrast, regional political elites are strengthening their influence within the national parties and a regionally-based political class may be emerging. Where state-wide parties compete with minority nationalist or regionalist forces, they must give their regional branches more autonomy to insert themselves into the distinctive political space, and so the Catalan and Basque Socialist parties are technically independent, albeit affiliated to the state-wide party. The post-communist *Izquierda Unida* (United Left) takes the form in Catalonia of *Iniciativa per Catalunya*, with a more liberal as well as a more decentralist and Catalanist policy line. In France, regional structures of the parties are not a significant level, but local leaders in practice can often take their own line on political strategy, including deciding on where to stand down on the second ballot of parliamentary and local elections, as well as opening local electoral lists to other political formations. This was used in the 1970s and 1980s to co-opt regionalist forces into the main parties, notably the Socialist Party.

	no state wide parties	local parties more than 20%	local parties less than 20%	regional allies of state parties
UK	N. Ireland	Scotland	Wales	
Germany				Bavaria
Belgium	Flanders, Wallonia			
Spain		Basque Country, Catalonia, Canaries	Galicia, Valencia, Andalucia	Aragon
Italy		Lombardy, Veneto, Piedmont, Fruili-Venezia-Guilia, Val d'Aosta	Other northern regions, Sardinia.	
France			Corsica	

Figure 4.3 Regional party systems

Figure 4.3 shows the main regional parties in western Europe.

Even in the absence of regional parties, territorial distinctiveness can emerge in patterns of voting for the national formations. Analysis of the importance of territory in voting behaviour comes up against a methodological problem similar to that encountered in the previous section. If we rely on survey data correlating voting behaviour with various socio-economic characteristics, it is easy to define territory out of the picture; at best we get a 'geographical infraction' of social and cultural factors (Agnew, 1990, 1996). This has been the predominant approach to electoral studies since the 1960s in English-speaking countries (Pelling, 1967; Johnston, 1985) and in Germany. If we take the ecological approach, which has predominated in France, starting with territory and mapping cultural and social factors onto this, we get a very different result, with territorial factors appearing to be a major influence. Since the

1980s, there has been a new appreciation of territorially-focused approaches, as territorial differentiation in voting has appeared to increase, and new syntheses of survey and ecological methods have emerged. The new approaches focus on the way in which the territorial context shapes behaviour and the interpretation of signals given by political parties even when these are nationally-based and organized.

The United Kingdom saw an increased spatial polarization of the vote from the mid-1960s (Fieldhouse, 1995), a trend reinforced in the 1980s and only partially reversed in 1992 (Pattie et al., 1994). In the latter year the Conservative distribution of the vote so closely resembled that of 1910 (Bogdanor and Field, 1993) as to suggest that the phase of nationalized class voting was the historical aberration. The factors shaping these regionalized patterns are still under-explored (Heath et al., 1991), but Pattie and Johnston (1995) show that differing perceptions of the economic well-being of their region played a role in electors' choices, at least when they held government responsible, and that there is also an independent regional factor (Johnston and Pattie, 1997). Changing electoral fortunes in turn helped reshape local and regional political agendas. Conservative decline in Scotland and Wales after 1983 was an important factor in bringing the devolution issue back into political debate there, and even in spurring a renewed interest in regional government in the north of England.

Spanish voting behaviour has always been regionalized. From the transition to democracy until 1996, conservative parties were unable to win national majorities because they could not penetrate Catalonia and the Basque Country, dominated as these were by indigenous centre-right parties combining christian democracy and moderate nationalism. The Socialists, for their part, were able to win national elections in Catalonia, even as the nationalist *Convergència i Unió* (CiU) continued to triumph in voting for the autonomous community. Socialists also found it easier — though not unproblematic — to accommodate the nationalist dimension there than did the conservative parties with their centralist heritage. By the 1990s, however, the conservative *Partido Popular* was making some advances in Catalonia and the Basque Country, exploiting nationalists' links to the Socialist central government and offering a moderate conservative alternative to the regional middle classes, a strategy culminating in their pact with the Basque nationalist *Partido Nacionalista Vasco* (PNV) and Catalan CiU after the 1996 Spanish elections. The Socialists' main stronghold continued to be in the south, notably in Andalucia, where strong patronage networks allowed them to survive the conservative swing of the mid-1990s. Elections to the Spanish autonomous communities follow two patterns. For the regions with ordinary statutes, they are all held on the same day, and tend to be seen as referendums on national issues. Catalonia, the Basque Country, Galicia and Andalucia have their own electoral calendars and here elections focus on regional issues, moulded except in Andalucia by the distinctive party systems.

In Italy, elections for the regional councils were dominated by national issues and used by the national parties as part of their state-wide strategy, but regional factors did play a role in voting at both levels. The geographical polarization of the vote after the Second World War gave way to a more even pattern of competition between 1963 and 1976 (Agnew, 1996) as the Communists repositioned themselves ideologically and extended their influence. Thereafter, as both main parties declined, regional variation reappeared. By the 1990s, the Christian Democrats had retreated to the 'white belt' in the far north and their patronage fiefs in the south, while the Communists (renamed the *Partito Democratico della Sinistra* or PDS) were forced back more to the 'red belt' of the centre. The collapse of the old party system after 1992 produced more polarization, as the new parties used different strategies to penetrate the various regions (Agnew, 1994). Silvio Berlusconi's *Forza Italia* pitched its appeal nationally, with a centralist message, while the PDS pursued a moderate regionalism, consolidating its hold in the centre. The post-fascist *Aleanza Nazionale* dug in in the south, where the anti-fascist heritage is weaker and it was able to take over some of the old Christian Democratic client networks with a centralist discourse linked to a distributive policy line. The *Lega Nord* retained its strength in the north, despite regular predictions of its decline.

In Germany, as we have seen, the tendency to homogenization in voting in the 1950s and 1960s followed the breakdown of the old subcultures, but this apparent homogenization itself disguised a series of regional processes. From the 1980s, a small gap in voting behaviour opened up between the north and the south as the Social Democratic vote held up better in the north (Ritter and Niehuss, 1991). The penetration of the Greens and the extreme right was also uneven. The neo-fascist Republicans, based in Bavaria with its rightist heritage, were able to exploit the gap provided by the decline of the CSU following the death of its dominant leader Franz-Josef Strauss, gaining Land seats there and in Baden-Württemberg. In the 1990s, the major difference is between the eastern and western Länder. At the time of unification in 1990 the CDU rather surprisingly won both the last East German and the first all-German elections in the east and has consolidated its position both nationally and at Land level. The post-communist PDS presented a serious challenge on the left, preventing the Social Democrats from making much headway. While voting in Land elections in Germany is generally seen as following national trends, the emergence of a five-party system has made the competitive context very different from one to another and coalition formation varies greatly, with the Social Democrats showing themselves willing to coalesce with, or (in the case of the PDS) accept external support from, all of the other parties depending on the local circumstances.

It is perhaps less necessary to insist on the importance of territory in French electoral behaviour, since electoral studies in France have always given it prominence. The 1980s and 1990s saw a more competitive party system in France, as alternation in power took place on a regular basis. This itself partly reflected the ability of the two major formations, the Socialists and the conservative alliance of RPR (*Rassemblement pour la République*) and UDF (*Union pour la Démocratie Française*) to extend themselves across the national territory. In the 1990s, both Socialists and Communists have steadily fallen back in their former strongholds in the south, with the latter now largely confined to the 'red belt' around Paris. The conservative parties, for their part, have been able to compete on more equal terms everywhere. On the extreme right, the National Front has traditionally been strongest along the Mediterranean coast but in the 1980s it extended its influence into eastern France and in the 1990s made considerable progress in the industrial areas of the north, formerly a fief of the left. Regional elections in France tend to be dominated by national issues and the national parties (Garaud, 1992) and, although a territorial basis is important for the party notables who head the lists, this tends to be local rather than regional. Regionalists have sometimes been able to participate on joint lists with ecologists and occasionally have been taken into the left-wing lists, but generally regional parties have played a negligible role even in regions with a strong historic identity like Brittany (Bonenfant, 1992). The fragmentation of the French party system, however, prevents a simple national confrontation at regional level between the main formations, and requires complicated games of coalition-building within each region, taking into account the relative weight of parties and personalities. Legal restrictions on the accumulation of mandates have reduced the role of national personalities in regional politics and may be assisting in the emergence of a new regional political class and, despite the focus on national issues in the campaign, two exit polls after the 1990 elections showed 36 per cent and 44 per cent respectively of the electorate voting on the basis of regional issues (Gerstlé, 1992; Perrineau, 1992) while 38 per cent voted differently at the regional and the cantonal elections held at the same time (Laurent and Wallon-Leducq, 1992).

The absence of national parties makes it more difficult to trace regional differences in voting behaviour in Belgium and, until 1995, the regional and community councils were composed of deputies in the national parliament. There has been a divergence in the swings among the main political families in the various parts of the country since 1971 (De Wachter, 1996). When the first separate elections occurred in 1995 they coincided with the national elections and the campaigns were dominated by national issues and personalities rather than programmes to be put in place by the regional and community councils (Versmessen, 1995). On the other hand, the national issues, as usual, were regionalized; notably the debate over the future of the social security system, which transfers resources from Flanders to Wallonia and which many Flemish politicians, as well as some market liberals, want to see regionalized.

Territory has always been an important factor in voting behaviour in the Nordic countries, and this remains true, as shown in the 1994 referendums of membership of the European Union. Support for membership was concentrated in the south, with massive opposition in the north and interior of Norway, Sweden and Finland (Tema Nord, 1995; Hansen and Bjørklund, 1997). Indeed, the regional distribution of the Norwegian vote closely followed not only the 1972 European referendum, but also the referendums in the early part of the century on the monarchy and alcohol prohibition, giving clear evidence of the survival of strong regional political cultures (Hansen and Bjørklund, 1997).

It remains true, then, that voting behaviour in western Europe is shaped by regional contexts, which serve to interpret national issues and frame local ones. There may have been a trend to homogenization in the post-war era, although some of this was more apparent than real, as parties sought to adapt themselves to national-level competition by extending their appeal across the entire state with subtly differentiated messages. Since the 1980s, this trend has been halted and, to some extent, reversed. Parties are forced increasingly to take account of differing conditions and issues, themselves forged by the changing social construction of regions.

SOCIAL SPACE

An important element in the construction of regions is the pattern of social relationships and the degree to which associative life takes a regional form.

The main economic interest groups of capital and labour emerged in the context of the nation-state and their organization and orientation tends to reflect this. Yet both are affected by the restructuring of the economic and political systems. Globalization, European integration and free trade tend to favour capital over labour, since it is more mobile. Big firms have thus been able to reduce their dependence on specific places, sometimes by deliberate strategy (Plan Urbain, 1986) or by relocating constantly (Piore and Sabel, 1984). Small firms, on the other hand, tend to be more bound to local markets and less able to relocate, giving them a more local or regional outlook. Labour interests have found themselves using territory as the basis for social mobilization, given weakening class loyalties and the impact of closures and downsizing on communities. On the other hand, trade unions are committed to broader forms of social solidarity and are suspicious of decentralization projects which would make it easier for firms to play one region off against another.

These conflicting motivations are generally reflected in the attitudes of business organizations and trade unions to regionalism. Business tends to resist anything that might threaten to divide the market, but small business groups are more inclined to support regional decentralization. Trade unions, where they take an interest in such matters, have increasingly favoured regional government, but insisted on assurances that this would not affect national labour market regulation. All this is mediated by the characteristics of individual states and regions. German business and trade federations are organized by Land as well as by sector, giving a strong regional structure. In Belgium, which has few large corporations, business interests are regionalized and Flemish employers have been adopting very decentralist stances, seeking to free the dynamic economy of Flanders from what they see as the burden of Wallonia. Trade unions are divided on confessional/partisan lines but so far not by region or language, although this may gradually be changing. While the structures of the society are gradually pulling apart into Flemish and Walloon segements, wage negotiations still take place at national level (De Wachter, 1996). The Spanish employers federation CEOE (*Confederación Española de Organizaciones Empresariales*) is organized on a state-wide basis, although there are also regional bodies, notably in Catalonia. Catalan employers are, at the same time, closely integrated into the CEOE, which they were largely instrumental in founding in the 1970s. The two principal trade union federations, the UGT (*Unión General de Trabajadores*) and CCOO (*Comisiones Obreras*), formerly linked to the Socialist and Communist parties respectively, are also state-wide in scope, although CCOO operates in Catalonia as CONC (*Comisió Obrera Nacional de Catalunya*). In Galicia and the Basque Country there are regional unions, which are nationalist or christian democrat in inspiration.

Regional levels of organization for employers and unions are very weak in Italy (Ritaine, 1994) and France, although local chambers of commerce are of some importance in the cities. In the United Kingdom, the CBI (Confederation of British Industry) is state-wide, with a regional structure which, even in Scotland and Wales, has little autonomy, although small business does have its own Scottish federation. The TUC (Trades Union Congress) is also UK-based, although it has a regional structure in England and operates a Wales TUC. The STUC (Scottish Trades Union Congress) is quite separate, with unions operating in Scotland affiliating both to it and to the TUC. Separate trade unions did once exist in Scotland, but mostly merged with their UK counterparts between the wars, with the last important ones disappearing in the 1960s. The STUC has been of some importance since the 1970s in articulating a Scottish economic interest and in pursuing political devolution.

Regional business and labour groupings both shape and are shaped by the regional political context. As the region has gained in importance as a level of economic intervention and restructuring, they have sought institutions which will enhance their own role in this and have contributed to the wider debate on the subject of the region. In this way, they provide a link from economic restructuring to policy and politics, helping to create and sustain the region. Where there is already a strong sense of territorial identity and political mobilization, as in the historic nationalities, they are forced to take this into account, adapting their own structures to it, while seeking at the same time to operate within the institutions of the state. Other bodies in civil society, from churches to sports clubs, to cultural societies, also help create a regional social space, reinforcing identity and co-operation in pursuit of common goals. Territorialized civil societies are found in the historic nationalities and in strongly defined regions like Bavaria, and in much of Scandinavia. In France, Italy and many parts of Spain, civil society is more localized, based in cities or even in rural communes. These localized activities may themselves be part of regional groupings, with greater or lesser cohesiveness, reinforcing the imagined community, or they may be isolated and separate.

The existence of regional mass media also creates and sustains a sense of social space and frames issues in a regional perspective. German media are highly regionalized. The press is dispersed, with no dominant national daily or publishing centre, while radio and television are decentralized and regulated by the Länder. Spanish media are also rather dispersed, with most people reading a regional or local paper. Thus historic nationalities maintain a large output of daily papers and even the national quality *El País* produces separate editions for Catalonia and, since 1997, the Basque Country. Alongside the national radio and television networks are stations sponsored by the autonomous communities, focusing on regional events and providing coverage in both Castilian and the local languages. Belgian media are completely divided on linguistic/regional lines, presenting issues from different perspectives and ensuring that most issues are pressed into the Flemish/Walloon frame of reference (Kerremans, 1997).

In France and Italy television channels, both public and private, are national, with a minimum of regional input. Print media are less centralized, especially in France, but do not often correspond to regions. France's largest provincial paper, *Ouest France*, has common outer pages, with the inside produced in dozens of different versions for very local markets. In the United Kingdom, matters are more varied. England is dominated by London-based media (although there are some regional papers) while Scotland has its own quality and popular papers, although these tend to be regionalized within Scotland. Television has been an important factor in developing regionalism, especially since the advent of commercial television which, on its inception in the 1950s, was allocated to regional companies. The BBC (British Broadcasting Corporation) has 'national regions' in Scotland, Wales and Northern Ireland, with a focus on local political issues and events, and some regional input in England.

Technological change and deregulation have undermined national systems of broadcasting and introduced the global television product, but at the same time they have lowered the threshold for local and regional media. This has led to an increase in local and regional output and a regional perspective on public issues, but once again the effect is very varied, depending on the political content and meaning of regions and regionalism.

THE POLITICS OF REGIONALISM

Regionalism, as a political movement and set of demands, has taken a great many forms and at one time or another been linked to just about every other ideology, from the extreme right to the extreme left, via liberalism, social democracy and christian democracy. To simplify, we might identify six types, whose characteristics can be mixed and matched in individual cases.

First, there is a conservative regionalism, anchored in the idea of affective community, resisting modernization, especially where this takes the form of the uniformizing and secular state. In the nineteenth century, regionalism, especially in France, was often regarded as reactionary and opposed to progress (Mény, 1982) and many French intellectuals still regard the word as politically incorrect, charged with anti-republican connotations (Balme, 1996). The early demands of the Basque movement were for a return to the *fueros*, based on traditional authority and compact (De La Granja, 1995), and this foral principle has proved something of an obstacle in relationships between Basque nationalists and the left. In several countries, regionalism has been an element of christian democratic thought, a way of reconciling tradition with modernity, as well as operationalizing the principle of subsidiarity. Luigi Sturzo's *Partito Popolare* in the years before the advent of Fascism emphasized regionalism as part of its appeal to tradition and stability. It is not, however, one of the base principles of christian democracy (Durand, 1995) and has often been subordinated to the tactical needs of political parties, as in Italy after 1948, or even in the age of Sturzo after the First World War, or exploited for clientelistic ends (Barbera, 1985). Generally, traditionalist and conservative regionalism has been in retreat, as regionalism has increasingly been associated with modernization and change.

One such form of modernization is a 'bourgeois regionalism' (Harvie, 1994) in industrialized and economically advanced regions. In these cases, a dynamic bourgeoisie seeks to free itself from the shackles of an archaic state, or strives to create more modern administrative and political structures to favour industrial development. A historic example would be the Catalan movement in its 'regionalist' phase in the late nineteenth century, when it sought to modernize Spain by 'catalanizing' it (Oltra et al., 1981; Vicens, 1986). A contemporary example might be found in German Länder like Baden-Württemberg, Flanders or even contemporary Catalonia, with their links to the 'Four Motors of Europe', a consortium of regions, each of which is the most technologically advanced in its respective state. This process is more generally found among those regions identified as the centres of the new regional trading order. In the contemporary cases, the lead is often taken not by private industrialists but by the modernizing regional technocracy, often tied to the public sector management and to the planning profession both in government and in universities.

On the left, there is a progressive regionalism. Even in the nineteenth century, there were regionalist movements which stressed the themes of progress, democracy, reform of the state and equality, for example the ephemeral *Félibrige Rouge* in France (Touraine et al., 1981), the progressive movements in Scotland (Keating and Bleiman, 1979) and Wales (Morgan, 1980) or the *Meridionalismo* of Dorso and Salvemini (Galasso, 1978). From the 1960s, there was a new regionalism linked to the libertarian new left, to ecological movements and to popular struggles against plant closures (Keating, 1988, 1992a). This regionalism borrowed from earlier Gramscian ideas and contemporary national liberation movements in the third world, stressing uneven development and internal colonialism (Lafont, 1967). It remained rather weak, however, because of the heterogeneity of its constituent elements and the difficulties of building an alternative paradigm of economic development.

Social democratic movements also contained within them a historic regionalist stream, though this was for many years subordinated to the needs of Jacobin state-building and centralized economic and social management. From the 1960s, this stream slowly expanded but the conversion of the social democratic parties to regionalism had to await the foundering of the old social democratic model of centralized state management under the impact of globalization. Another important factor was experience in opposition, when social democratic parties focused on their territorial power bases and on exploiting the new possibilities that local and regional government provided. This produced important shifts of thinking, in the French Socialist Party, the German Social Democratic Party and the British Labour Party, to which one could add the Italian Communist Party and its successor the *Partito Democratico della Sinistra* (PDS), though enthusiasm for regionalism is stronger in opposition and tends to wane as parties see the prospect of a return to power at the centre.

A right-wing populist regionalism is directed against the centralized state, sometimes against fiscal transfers to poorer regions, and often against immigrants, whether these are from other parts of the state or abroad. In Italy, the first serious territorial opposition arose not in the deprived Mezzogiorno, but in the late 1980s in the North. The *Lega Lombarda*, which later expanded into the Northern League *(Lega Nord)* originated in a combination of social and territorial protest (Biorcio, 1991), based in the lower middle classes and small business people. Although it initially insisted that it did not want to cut off transfers to the south, merely to limit them and ensure that they are well spent (Savelli, 1992), there is no doubt that the League draws on anti-southern sentiment, hence its abysmal performance when it presented candidates in the Mezzogiorno. Its proposals for federalizing Italy drew on antecedents going back to the last century and made some impact in public debate, but federalism was never really consistent with its aim to carve out a distinct macroeconomic space for the north. From the late 1990s, the Lega moved towards separatism and, while some have dismissed the antics of its leader, Umberto Bossi as little more than theatrics, it has begun to establish a solid basis of support for its imagined nation of Padania. It now links this closely into Europe, proposing that Padania join the

European core, including the single currency, leaving the south to fend for itself with its own money (Gruppo Lega Nord, 1996). The social base of the *Lega* remains in the small business sector and small towns of northern Italy, but in the 1990s it has acquired a significant working class following (Biorcio, 1997). After flirting with the *Lega* as a means of attacking the corrupt parties of the old system, big business turned against it (*La Repubblica*, 20 March, 1992). The *Lega* initially espoused an anti-immigrant rhetoric and, while this was toned down in the early 1990s as the party sought to make inroads into the political centre and establish itself as a contender in national politics, it was resumed in the late 1990s, directed at non-European immigrants (*extracomunitari*) and Albanian refugees. Right-wing populism is also found in the Flemish *Vlaams Blok* ,. which combines Flemish separatism with a virulent anti-immigrant line. Some of the French regionalist movements have also ended up on the populist extreme right (Keating, 1985,1988).

Finally, there are 'nationalist' movements in some of the historic territories of Europe. The division between nationalism and regionalism here is by no means clear, and is becoming less so as the state reconfigures (Keating, 1996a). The most important separatist movements — if one excludes the Northern Irish case since it is irredentist rather than separatist — are the peaceful and constitutional Scottish National Party and the Basque *Herri Batasuna*, linked to the violent ETA movement. The Catalan *Esquerra Republicana de Catalunya* (ERC) is also committed to independence, but gains only around 8–10 per cent of the vote. Catalonia's main party, *Convergència i Unió* (CiU), like most of the Belgian movements, favours a new distribution of power within the state and in Europe rather than the establishment of its own state in the classic sense. Such a reformulated nationalism both harks back to the pre-state era in Europe, when Catalonia and the provinces (albeit not the present regions) of what is now Belgium enjoyed wide autonomy under imperial regimes, and forward to the new Europe, which is seen as providing similar opportunities. This ambivalence about independence is also shared by the Italian *Lega Nord*, but in that case it is reflected in wild gyrations in policy rather than a long-term strategy of advance.

It is from the dialectic of these different regionalisms with the state and now the international order that the dynamics of political regionalism are made. Each movement contains a mixture of distinct elements. Each state provides a distinct opportunity structure and set of incentives and constraints, as does the European Union. Regionalism is not necessarily autonomist. There are integrative regionalisms, seeking the full integration of their territories into the nation and the destruction of obstacles to their participation in national public life. There are autonomist regionalisms seeking a space for independent action; and there are disintegrative regionalisms, seeking greater autonomy or even separation. Poor regions have often preferred centralization, especially when this is accompanied by good lines of access to the central state. For example, the Spanish regions of Andalucia and Extremadura, enjoying privileged links with the Socialist government in Madrid in the 1990s, were very cautious about further decentralization, especially in fiscal matters. Italy's Mezzogiorno has notably failed to generate autonomist movements, in large part because of dependence on the centre.

When rich regions dominate a central state they too are liable to be centralist, as in France and the United Kingdom. By contrast wealthy regions which are not politically dominant are likely to be decentralist, as in Lombardy or Catalonia, though even Catalonia has always sought to balance autonomy with access to the centre, most recently in the pact between its governing party CiU and the minority socialist government in Madrid between 1993 and 1995, followed by the pact with the incoming conservative government in 1996.

There is no consistent relationship between the placement of regionalisms on the left–right scale and the degree of integration or disintegration they seek. Generally speaking, regionalism has since the 1960s moved to the left, though there are exceptions such as the christian democracy of the Catalan CiU or the right-wing populism of the *Lega Nord*. This is to be explained partly by the changing relationships between class and territory. Capital, after becoming national in the nineteenth century, has become increasingly international or at least European, and favourable to free trade. Big business leaders overwhelmingly favour less state intervention and welcome the erosion of state power in the face of the market. Where intervention and public action are necessary, they prefer this to be delivered by agencies responsive to business interests rather than politically-controlled bodies in which non-business influence could be a factor. So while not opposing regional policies and mechanisms for promoting growth, they tend to be highly suspicious of regional government, and of regional political movements. Labour, on the other hand, has increasingly territorialized and, faced with capital restructuring, has fallen back on locally-based forms of resistance. This has influenced the parties of the left, which have taken on regional themes and explored ways in which regions could be used to subject capital to greater social control.

There are still two types of regionalism, the conservative and defensive regionalism, rooted in traditional society, insular and resistant to change; and the modern, outward-looking and progressive regionalism, in which tradition is employed as an instrument in modernization. This difference is reflected in popular opinion, in social action and in political movements. Generally, however, regionalism has shifted to the progressive side, seen as a form of democratic maturation (Sharpe, 1993) and an adaptation to the new conditions of modernity (Beaufays, 1985). In this new perspective, functional restructuring and political mobilization coincide in creating a new political space and domain of policy. Yet regions do not exist everywhere and where they do they are the product of political action and region-building.

THE INVENTION OF REGIONS

Regions are not a given fact of life, or a historic relic, but a social construction, constantly being made and remade. Historic elements are often pressed into service, but even their meaning is shaped by contemporary forces. In the context of the present-day restructuring of the state, economy and civil society, the meaning and uses of territory have changed. Even as social and political processes have in some respects deterritorialized, been subsumed in global systems or reduced to the interaction of individuals as consumers, there has been a re-territorialization of politics and the emergence of new political spaces. There are strong reasons why politics tends always to come back to territory: functional, political and normative. The functional reason is that many of the processes of change analysed above, including economic restructuring and cultural revivals, are essentially territorial, even in an age of mass communication and high technology. Government, too, is essentially territorial and even attempts at non-territorial government soon territorialize as they need a framework and boundaries for action. Politically, territory still provides the most effective basis for political mobilization and debate, and the forging of compromises and agreements. It may be, indeed, that the weakening of class and other attachments is enhancing the political significance of territory as an organizing principle in politics and a basis for political identity. Normatively, territory provides a framework for democratic and accountable government and defines the reference group for participation and the exercise of rights in a manner which is inclusive and non-discriminatory.

Yet the constitution of territorial systems varies greatly, depending on the coincidence of the various senses of region, and on political leadership and mobilization, as well as institutional structures. So we get a wide variety of regions and regionalisms. Figure 4.4 indicates some of the differences, taking as indicators just the factors of culture, identity, institutions, distinctive civil society, and a sense of economic regionalism.

Broadly, we can identify three types here. The first are the historic nationalities: Scotland, Wales, Catalonia, Galicia, the Basque Country, Brittany and Corsica, to which we could add the cantons of Switzerland and Flanders, with a strong sense of culture and identity, their own civil institutions and networks, and often a sense of economic regionalism. An extension of this category would include regions with a distinct linguistic or historical identity, but without national pretensions, including Sicily, Sardinia, Val d'Aosta, Trentino-Alto Adige, Friuli-Venezia-Guilia (all in Italy), Navarre, Andalucia and perhaps Aragon and Valencia (in Spain), Languedoc and Alsace (in France), Bavaria and various islands. They vary in their capacity for self-government from the Swiss cantons, with their powerful autonomous institutions, to Brittany, with only a weak regional council, or Scotland and Wales which, up until now, have had only administrative devolution. A second group consists of regions defined primarily by their institutions, which have used these to build around them a political space and an effective system of action. This would include the western German Länder, French regions such as Nord Pas-de-Calais and Rhône-Alpes and the stronger Italian regions such as Emilia-Romagna. A third group consists of administrative regions, which have not succeeded in forging a sense of common identity and which do not correspond to regions in the other senses. This would include the weaker French regions, most of the Italian regions and the weak forms of regional structures found England, Scandinavia and the Netherlands. Finally, there are places where it is difficult to speak of regions at all, including Ireland, Greece and mainland Portugal. This varying map of Europe provides contrasting conditions for the establishment of regions as a system of government.

	Belgium		UK			Spain		France		Germany		Italy	
	Flanders	Wallonia	Scotland	Wales	England	Historic nationalities	Other ACs	Brittany, Corsica	Other regions	Western Länder	Eastern Länder	Special status regions	Other regions
Culture	strong	strong	strong	strong	no	strong	weak/variable	strong	weak	weak/variable	weak	strong	weak/local
Identity	strong	moderate	strong	moderate	weak	strong	weak/variable	fairly strong	weak	weak/variable	weak	strong	weak
Government institutions	strong	moderate	no	no	no	strong	moderate	weak	weak	strong	moderate	moderate	weak
Civil Society	strong	moderate	strong	moderate	no	variable	weak	moderate strong	weak	strong	weak	moderate	weak
Economic regionalism	strong	strong	strong	moderate	weak	variable	weak	strong	weak	strong	strong	moderate	weak

Figure 4.4 Characteristics of regions in Western Europe

5. Regional Government

MODELS OF REGIONAL GOVERNMENT

Regional government in western Europe comes in many varieties. The weakest is functional decentralization, the establishment of ad hoc agencies with specific tasks at a level intermediate between central and local government. This may be a response to functional needs, where a stronger form has been ruled out because existing governments, central or local, fear the establishment of a political rival. Functional forms of regional administration have been used widely in the United Kingdom, where the proliferation of regional agencies by the 1970s led Crowther-Hunt and Peacock (1973) to conclude that a regional level of government was already in existence, though this finding was disputed (Keating, 1979). Regional agencies were also used widely in Italy and France in the 1950s and 1960s, especially for economic development and planning.

Another limited form of regional institutionalization aims to organize the region as a space for social concertation, with a role for the central state, local governments, business, unions, universities and research centres, and other local agents. This model was tried in the United Kingdom from 1965 in the form of the Regional Economic Planning Councils which, except in Scotland and Wales, were abolished in 1979 (Lindley, 1982) and in Ireland between 1969 and 1987 (Laffan, 1996). In Italy and Belgium, the model was superseded by the move to general regional government, but in France the consultative Regional Economic and Social Councils have continued to co-exist with the elected regional governments. A variant of this model provides for regional governments indirectly elected from local municipal bodies, as was the case in France between 1972 and 1986.

Regional administration may also take the form of deconcentrated arms of central government. The most extensive such system is in France, where the regional prefect co-ordinates state services at the regional level, as well as shadowing the work of the regional government through the SGAR (*Secrétariat général pour les affaires régionales*). In the United Kingdom, most central government administration in Scotland, Wales and Northern Ireland is in the hands of the territorial departments, headed by their respective secretaries of state. There is no corresponding arrangement in England, although in the early 1990s Integrated Regional Offices were set up there, in an effort to co-ordinate central government efforts in urban renewal and regional policy (Hogwood, 1995). In Italy and Spain, the state also maintains regional offices but without a general co-ordinating role.

Regional government, however, properly refers to general-purpose, elected political bodies, with their own functions and powers. This represents a decentralization of the state and a transfer of powers to a lower territorial level. The strongest form of such territorial government is federalism, so far found only in Germany, Austria, Switzerland and Belgium. Federalism provides for a constitutional distribution of powers in which each level has its own guaranteed spheres of competence, and neither level is hierarchically superior to the other. It also typically includes a constitutional court to pronounce on conflicts of authority, and for the representation of the federated units in a second chamber of the national legislature. Regional devolution is usually seen as a weaker form, in which the central state transfers some of its powers to lower levels, but retains sovereignty and can, at least in principle, recover the devolved powers. It usually also retains a range of supervisory and over-ride powers to keep regional governments in line. Successive French governments, while presiding over a process of regional devolution, have been at pains to insist that France is still a unitary state and is not heading towards federalization. The distinction has a lot to do with state traditions, notably the contrast between the Germanic state model with its federalist tradition, and the Napoleonic model found in France and Italy, in which decentralization takes the form of devolution within the unitary state (Loughlin and Peters, 1997). The British state, too, has been hostile to the federal principle, with Labour governments in the 1970s and 1990s stressing that devolution to Scotland and Wales would not affect the sovereignty of Parliament and thus the unitary character of the state.

There is certainly a big difference between the regional governments of France and Italy which are the outgrowth of functional decentralization, with an elected element added, and the powerful German Länder. Yet the distinction between federalism and the stronger forms of regionalism is becoming ever more difficult to make. Spain occupies an intermediate position, since it is not formally a federation, but the system of regional government is guaranteed by the constitution and regulated by a constitutional court. Under the Second Republic, the term *Estado Integral* was coined for this form of quasi-federalism, modelled on the German Weimar Republic (Hernández, 1980). Under the 1978 constitution, the term *Estado de las Autonomías* serves the same function, though many observers believe that the system is evolving into a federation (Moreno, 1997). In the 1990s, the debate on regional reform in Italy revolved around the themes of strong regionalism and federalism, to the point that many believed that the distinction had lost its relevance (Mariuca, 1995; Roccella, 1996).

One reason for this convergence is the European tradition of federalism which is not, unlike the United States model of federalism, inspired by a vision of limited government, countervailing powers and a strict delimitation of competences. Rather, it is more organic and integrated, seeing federalism as a principle for sharing power at different levels of society, rather than dividing it. The principle of separation of powers is balanced by that of solidarity and co-operation, reflected in the German constitution where involvement of the Länder in national policy is as important as their autonomous role, and where the territorial distribution of powers is balanced by a commitment to equality of living standards, realized through revenue-sharing and fiscal equalization. The principle of subsidiarity comes into play here, stipulating that tasks should be given to the lowest practicable level in state or civil society, while at the same time recognizing social solidarity and unity.

The distinction between regional devolution and federalism is also called into question by the transformation of the state, the emergence of a European level of government, and the necessary inter-dependence of all the various levels. Europe's destabilizing effects on the territorial distribution of powers are discussed in Chapter 7, as are the efforts by regions and federal units to reclaim lost powers by penetrating both national and European decision-making systems. Inter-dependence is a phenomenon which has affected all federations, but has particular resonance in Europe, where national welfare states require close co-operation among the various levels of government. At the same time, economic restructuring is pitting regions in competition against each other, as discussed in the next chapter, bringing old mechanisms for intergovernmental co-operation and joint policy making under strain. These two conflicting trends are reshaping the meaning of autonomy and policy competence, whether in regionalized or federal states.

Rather than making a sharp distinction between federal and regional models of government, we can see them as a continuum, from the strongest, represented by the German federal system, to the weakest, represented by administrative deconcentration of the central state, or

Federalism		Strong Regionalism	Weak Regionalism		Functional Regionalism	
Germany						
Switzerland	Belgium					
	Austria					
		Spain				
			Italy			
				France	UK	
					Portugal	
						Netherlands
						Sweden
						Finland

Figure 5.1 Models of regional government

purely functional forms of decentralization, as represented in Figure 5.1.

CONSTITUTIONAL STATUS

In the four federal states, the federal principle is guaranteed by the constitution, which also secures the integrity of the individual states. Changing Land boundaries, or merging Länder in Germany is fraught with difficulty, as shown by the failed merger proposal between Berlin and Brandenburg in 1996; the last successful merger was in 1951, when three Länder came together to make Baden-Württemberg (Hoffman and Klatt, 1992). The Spanish and Italian constitutions also entrench the existence of regions but, except in the case of the five special status Italian regions, leave their number and delimitation to special or organic laws and, in the Spanish case, to local initiative. French regions do not feature in the constitution at all and were established by ordinary laws, unlike the communes and departments, whose existence, albeit not their boundaries, are constitutionally entrenched. The weaker forms of region found in other countries are also established under ordinary laws, although the British Labour government has required referendums in Scotland and Wales, as well as for an eventual extension of devolution to England, implying at least an element of local self-determination and entrenchment.

In federal and strong regional systems (Germany, Switzerland, Austria, Belgium, Spain and Italy) regions have legislative powers, as does the proposed Scottish Parliament (but not the Welsh Assembly), but use of legislative powers has in practice been rather limited compared with federations like the United States and Canada. German and Austrian Länder have tended to allow the federal level to take the main responsibility for passing framework laws, while they fill in the details and concentrate on implementation. Italian and Spanish regions have found their legislative freedom limited by the centre's habit of passing rather detailed laws of their own. The Belgian system is rather confused, with no clear hierarchy between federal and regional laws.

Federal and strong regional systems are in principle symmetrical, with general constitutional provisions available to all. In practice, Germany and Austria are largely symmetrical, as is Switzerland, at least in the constitutional status of the cantons, if not their internal operation. Belgium is more complicated, with its two-fold system of devolution, to the three regions of Flanders, Wallonia and Brussels Capital, and to the three language communities, the Flemish, the French and the German. The Flemish region and language community have effectively merged, to produce an integrated territorial government, albeit with some extraterritorial responsibilities for the Flemish population of Brussels. A lack of correspondence between regional and language boundaries has prevented such a merger elsewhere, although the French community has made extensive use of a provision allowing it to delegate the execution of competences to the territorial governments in Wallonia and Brussels (Brassinne, 1994). Regionalized states present more diversity. In Spain, there are differences between the autonomous communities with full powers (Catalonia, the Basque Country, Galicia, Andalucia, Valencia and Canaries) and those with lesser powers. While in principle it is intended that all will accede to the same level of competences, the historic nationalities have always insisted on their *hecho diferencial*, or need for special status. The Basque Country and Navarre have a special fiscal system, the *concierto económico*, a relic of their historic *fueros*, allowing them to collect most taxes locally and pass on a share to Madrid, rather than the other way around. The Canaries also has a special fiscal status, with no value added tax. Another unusual feature of the Basque Country is the application of the federal principle internally, since the three provinces are represented equally in the legislature, despite their huge population differences, and it is the *diputaciones forales*, or provincial assemblies rather than the Basque Parliament which manage the *concierto económico* and taxes. Even France, despite its traditions of republican uniformity, has granted a special statute of autonomy to Corsica. In the United Kingdom, Northern Ireland alone had a devolved legislature between 1922 and 1972, and the Labour Party has been committed since the 1970s to special status for Scotland and, more ambiguously, Wales. Portugal has special status regions in the Azores and Madeira. Denmark accords special status to the Faroe islands and Greenland was permitted, while remaining part of Denmark, to leave the European Community.

A list of regional arrangements for those countries of western Europe with some regional presence, under headings corresponding to the different types is given in Figure 5.2. In some of the smaller countries, such as the Netherlands, Sweden, Finland and Greece, there have been efforts to strengthen the county, provincial or prefecture level, especially in the light of European needs, as a substitute for regional reform but these are not included in the figure as regional entities.

FUNCTIONS

There is a wide variety, not only of regional functions, but of ways in which functions are allocated to regions. Generally speaking, federal constitutions list powers reserved to the centre, with the federated units enjoying the residual competence. The German Basic Law outlines three

Federal States

Germany	16 Länder
Austria	9 Länder
Switzerland	26 cantons (including 6 half cantons)
Belgium	3 regions. 3 language communities

Fully regionalized states

Spain	17 autonomous communities
Italy	20 regions, including 5 special status regions
France	22 regions

Partly regionalized states

Portugal	2 regional governments (Azores and Madeira)
Denmark	2 regional governments (Greenland and Faroes)
United Kingdom	proposed Scottish Parliament, Welsh Assembly

Administrative regionalization

United Kingdom	Scottish, Welsh, Northern Ireland Offices, Integrated Regional Offices, England
France	22 regional prefects

Indirectly-elected regions

Portugal	5 mainland regions

Figure 5.2 Regional government in Western Europe

categories of functions in which the federation is competent: exclusive competences; concurrent competences in which federal laws take precedence; and matters in which the federation can pass framework laws, with the Länder furnishing the details. All other matters fall to the Länder although, in practice, exclusive Land jurisdiction has become limited to education, police, local government organization and a few other matters. Since the federal reform of 1993, Belgian regions and language communities have the residual powers not specifically allocated to the federation, and there is more of an effort than in Germany to separate the two. In the event a complete separation proved impracticable and there are competences reserved for the federal authorities within regional and community matters, an arrangement known as the 'parallel exercise of exclusive competence' (Brassinne, 1994) which has already caused some difficulties. Switzerland and Austria also allocate the residual power to the federated units.

The regionalized states of Spain and Italy have a more complex system for allocating responsibilities. Spain's constitution lists two sets of powers, those to be retained at the centre, and those to be devolved to the regions. Powers not listed in either category may be devolved to autonomous communities proceeding by the fast track immediately, and to other autonomous communities after five years. There is considerable argument over the interpretation of this last category, as the decentralization process continues. The 1948 Italian constitution is more restrictive, laying down a series of regional competences, with the residual power belonging to the state. In 1996, in an effort to reinvigorate the regions as part of the transition to a 'second republic', a new law reversed the principle and gave the regions a general competence outside a list of reserved matters (*Le Regioni*, XXIV.5, 1996). The radical implications of this law were limited, however, by a clause allowing the state back in where matters of national interest or concerning the implementation of European obligations are involved, as well as by the need for decrees to give substance to the new provisions. In any case, the law looked likely to be overtaken by the more radical proposals of the Bicameral Commission, published in 1997, which proposed a federal state (Commissione Parlementare, 1997). French regions have only powers attributed to them by ordinary laws, and are rather circumscribed functionally. The British Labour Government's proposals of 1997 provide for strong devolution in Scotland, whose parliament will have all powers not expressly reserved to the centre, and a much weaker arrangement in Wales, where the assembly will have administrative responsibility in those Welsh Office functions transferred over time by Order in Council. A list of competences in regionalized states is given in Appendix 1. In

France, Italy and Spain, the piecemeal allocation of competences has inhibited regions in developing broad policies addressed to social problems, and has strengthened sectoral linkages with central departments in the various fields, allowing them to intervene in the details of policy.

As a result, some regions, notably in Germany, Austria, Switzerland and, increasingly, Spain, have a broad political role, able to address policy problems and frame solutions in line with local preferences. Belgian regions, although having a broad responsibility for economic matters, planning and physical development, are more restricted, given the presence alongside them of language communities, which are responsible for the 'personalizable' services, including health, education, culture and personal social services. Italian and French regions have been functional rather than general, given their attributed powers and the continued role of the central state. French regions' main responsibilities are in planning, economic development and infrastructure programming, and in professional training. Italian regions also have a planning role, but their main attributed function has been in the health service. Consequently, neither French nor Italian regions have much scope for independent action, but must work closely with national departments within tightly-defined national sectoral programmes.

FINANCE

Regional governments in Europe do not generally have extensive tax-raising powers, but rely heavily on transfers from the centre, or revenue-sharing. States have preferred to assign taxes, keeping control of the base and rates, rather than devolve them to regions and there is rarely provision, as in North America, for regions to decide on which taxes they will levy. There is much wariness about encouraging fiscal competition, and a concern with equalization and solidarity, but changing systems tends to be very slow and difficult, given the inbuilt resistances.

The most complete revenue-sharing arrangement is in Germany, where the main taxes — personal income tax, value-added tax and corporation tax — are determined centrally, subject to the approval of the Bundesrat, representing the Land governments. Revenue is then distributed among the three levels of government according to a three-part formula, with the Land share of income and corporation taxes going back to the regions in which it was raised, and their share of value-added tax distributed according to population. An equalization formula then redistributes funds to poorer Länder. Reunification imposed new strains on this system since, if left unchanged, the western Länder would have lost massively in transfers to the east. The solution, adopted in the framework of the Solidarity Pact, was to increase the federal contribution to equalization sharply, by cutting the federal take of value-added tax from 63 per cent to 56 per cent (Jeffery, 1996d). Länder still have their own taxes, but these raise only small amounts. The German system gives Länder little fiscal autonomy, but they have a large role in approving federal taxes and in negotiating the distribution, all of which must receive the endorsement of the Bundesrat.

Belgium has an extremely complex and evolving system for allocating resources to regions and communities. Regions receive a share of locally-raised income tax, which they can alter within narrow limits, with an equalization mechanism to give poorer regions a larger share. In practice, the Flemish government has a policy of not raising taxes so as to maintain its competitive edge (Hopkins, 1996). They are also assigned a range of 'regional taxes', but without the power to alter the rates — any change in these must be agreed by both levels. Communities also receive a share of the income tax but with no power to alter the rates and no equalization element. They are also assigned the tax on radios and televisions, but their largest source of revenue is a share of value-added tax. A complicated system has been put in place to introduce these provisions over time, and to adjust the shares of the various governments in line with growth of GNP (Brassinne, 1994).

Spanish autonomous communities had only minor taxation powers until the mid-1990s when, under pressure from the Catalan government, Madrid conceded 15 per cent of locally-raised income tax to the regions, with power to raise or lower the rate by up to three per cent. This provision, which is available to regions who choose to use it, was to be raised to 30 per cent under the 1996 pact between the Catalan CiU and the minority government of the *Partido Popular*. Regions also control a range of minor taxes, but have no role in value-added or corporation taxes. State transfers are based on historic service costs, adjusted for economic and population growth and, while there is an equalization scheme, the Inter-territorial Compensation Fund, this is mainly concerned with capital projects. In the Basque Country and Navarre, there is a special provision, the *concierto económico*, whereby the region controls almost all taxes, subject only to European Union regulations, and passes on a contribution to Madrid (Medina, 1991, 1992). This contribution, known as the *cupo*, is negotiated every five years. The Spanish system, both for ordinary regions and for those of the *concierto económico*, has been evolving gradually towards more fiscal autonomy for regional governments, under the pressure notably of the Catalans and some of the wealthier regions.

Italian local and regional governments lost their revenue-raising powers in a reform of 1970 and thereafter were financed directly by the state. Some 85 per cent of the regions' spending was for health, and this was covered by a central grant with rather detailed conditions, most of it being handed on to the local health units. Transfers were determined on the basis of historic spending, with only incremental changes, and the state regularly provided supplementary allocations to cover over-spending, in order to prevent service breakdowns. Under reforms of the early 1990s, regions now get the health service contributions of their own citizens directly, with equalization payments to ensure uniform levels of treatment, but there is still rather detailed control of standards (Buglione et al., 1994; Bosi and Tabellini, 1995). In 1994, regions received about half of their revenue from state transfers, of which about half was for health services (Lucentini, 1996).

French regions have very limited financial powers, consisting of a few assigned taxes. Much of their work, and about two thirds of their spending, is in capital expenditure planning, negotiated with the state in planning contracts. Their main service responsibility is in vocational training, financed by ear-marked central grants.

BUREAUCRACY

An important resource for a regional government is control of the officials charged with helping to frame policy and with carrying it out. German Länder are the most fortunate in this respect, since they administer not only their own policy competences but also most federal legislation. In Switzerland, each level is responsible for administering its own functions, with the cantons accounting for about a third of all public employment (Kriesi, 1995). In Belgium, officials are being transferred to the regions and communities along with competences. At the time of the 1993 reform they still only accounted for two per cent of the civil service (Fitzmaurice, 1996) but by 1995 they were about 40 per cent (De Wachter, 1996).

Spanish regions, too, have built up their own administrative structures to match their devolved functions. A corresponding reduction in central civil servants is made difficult, however, by the fact that not all the autonomous communities have received full powers. Italian regions have few bureaucratic resources, since they have few direct administrative responsibilities; in 1990 they accounted for a mere 2 per cent of public employment (Cassese and Torchia, 1993). In both Italy and Spain, there are proposals to effect a shift of power and shake up the old central bureaucracy by adopting the German system of a single administration under regional control but this has not yet been accepted. French regions have few administrative responsibilities. Until 1982, they were technically not allowed to hire their own staff, although many got around this restriction by setting up presidential cabinets and quasi-public agencies. Since the decentralization reforms of the 1980s, there has been some transfer of personnel, but the state has maintained its own regional structures and there is no question of a single administration under regional control.

POLITICAL CAPACITY

Political capacity refers to the ability of regions to mobilize support for their policy initiatives, and to take decisions on policies and priorities. The ability to mobilize is to a large degree a function of the construction of the region, its sense of identity, and territorial and social coherence. Where a region has a marked linguistic or historic identity, as in the historic nationalities of Spain or Flanders, this is easier, although mobilization can also be organized around economic development themes or modernization. Regions which have no coherence, such as some of the French regions, will find it difficult to mobilize support. Indeed, it has often been suggested that regional boundaries in France were deliberately drawn so as to discourage political mobilization, with historic Brittany divided and cumbersome entities like Languedoc-Rousillon being set up. Even historic regions can be difficult to mobilize, however, where the social structure is fragmented and traditions of collective action are lacking, as in Galicia.

Decision-making capacity has a lot to do with the electoral and party systems. In Germany and Spain, the electoral systems generally produce majority governments or stable coalitions based on programmatic parties. The Belgian political scene is more fragmented, although direct elections to the regions are too recent an experience to generalize. In Italy the former proportional electoral system produced a high degree of fragmentation and militated against clear programmatic choices since party lists were drawn up and coalition strategy decided in Rome. Changes to the system in 1995 were intended to favour strong majorities and stable coalitions, but one effect was simply to make the system so complicated that few electors could understand it. The electoral system for French regions, proportional representation on the basis of the constituent *départements*, both militates against clear majorities and reinforces the tendency for the regions to behave like federations of *départements* rather than purposive entities in their own right.

INTERGOVERNMENTAL RELATIONS

The interdependence of tiers of government and the limitations on the powers of regions mean that relations with other levels of government are crucial. Especially important is the balance between the centre's capacity to control and the regions' ability to exercise influence through the intergovernmental networks.

One type of mechanism is institutional, with a role for subnational governments in national policy-making, through territorially-based second legislative chambers, committees and conferences, and joint policy-making systems. Institutional mechanisms dominate in Germany, characterized by co-operative federalism and an interlocking of levels known as *Politikverflechtung*. The second legislative chamber, the Bundesrat, is a committee of Land governments, voting by majority, with the larger Länder having more votes but not in proportion to their populations. Land governments have delegations in the national capital and are in close contact with federal ministries. There is an elaborate network of sectoral conferences and joint tasks (*Gemeinschaftsaufgabe*) are undertaken through formal co-operation agreements provided for in the constitution. A tradition of consensus, a legalistic culture, and a lack of sharp territorial conflict has made this institutional accommodation possible, although increasing inter-regional competition and the demands of reunification have placed it under some strain.

Belgium's new constitution seeks to reduce the need for institutional linkages by demarcating competences clearly, but it is recognized that many matters of common interest will remain. There is constitutional provision for agreements among governments and for a concertation committee linking the federation with regions and communities. Given the conflict which was at the origin of federalization, it was necessary to stipulate that this committee could act only by consensus, yet the very conflict makes this consensus much more difficult to achieve than in Germany, while the need to agree common positions in Europe further exacerbates the problem (see Chapter 7).

Elsewhere, institutional mechanisms are less important. There are sectoral conferences in Spain, but these are not the main locus of decision-making. Proposals to make the Senate a chamber of territorial representation, as envisaged in the constitution, have never been brought forward and the autonomous communities nominate only a minority of the senators. Italy also has sectoral conferences but these too make little impact. In France, there is no general body for state–regional linkages and the Senate represents only local governments. There is, on the other hand, a great deal of collaboration and joint policy-making. The most formal mechanism for this is the five-yearly planning contracts negotiated with each regional council and forming the framework for both state and regional investment, although since it is the state which transfers the money to the regions it is central priorities that tend to prevail.

A second channel for territorial exchange is bureaucratic. This is especially important in countries with a Napoleonic tradition, with an extensive field bureaucracy of the central state. In France, the regional prefect has the task of keeping an eye on the regional council and reporting irregularities to the appropriate judicial authorities; but at the same time the prefect and the territorial bureaucracy more generally have a role in adapting central regulations to local needs and transmitting local demands to the centre. So a common territorial interest may develop, and a balance of power is worked out which depends on the personalities involved and the weight of the regional politicians. In some cases, the prefect prevails and the regional council is reduced to a secondary role, but in others the regional president emerges as the dominant actor, able to bend national programmes and resources to regional priorities. In Spain and Italy, there is less affinity between state representatives and local political elites. Each Spanish province has a civil governor and there is a delegate of the government in each autonomous community, but in 1996 it was agreed that the civil governors should be replaced by sub-delegates of the latter, with the implication that the autonomous communities would have a role in choosing the delegate. In Italy, there is also a state representative in each region, with the task of liaising with the regional government and ensuring that national priorities are observed. In practice, this control has proved mostly ineffective (Pastori, 1982; Dente, 1985) but nor have the regions themselves been able to forge coherent policies or ensure their adoption by the central administration. In the United Kingdom, the Scottish, Welsh and Northern Ireland Offices serve as a transmission belt for local interests, as well as applying the centre's policies in the periphery.

Partisan links represent a fourth channel of influence. This is particularly important in Spain, where major issues are worked out in party negotiations rather than through the institutions. Under the Socialist government of the 1980s and 1990s, Andalucia, as a bastion of the ruling party, carried weight in Madrid. Under successive minority Socialist and conservative governments from 1993, the mainstream Basque and Catalan nationalist parties, PNV and CiU, bargained for concessions on autonomy as the price for the support of their deputies in the central parliament. Partisan links were also important in Italy before the collapse of the *partitocrazia* in the 1990s but, because the province rather than the region was the main basis for party organization and patronage distribution (Dente, 1985), regional leaders did not carry great weight. On the contrary, they were subject to much dictation from Rome, where the various national party headquarters decided the composition of electoral lists and coalition strategies. Party links are important in Belgium, where the party system is completely regionalized, and national governments represent elaborate coalitions of ideological, linguistic and territorial interests. The interpenetration of the two levels means that national and regional coalitions are worked out together as part of the overall balance. In France, partisan links can be important but, given the weakness and fractiousness of the parties, only as an element in wider networks.

Finally, there are personal links, which are of critical importance in France, where a politician, by accumulating offices at different levels in the system and establishing networks of connections, can accede to the condition of *notoriété*, a combination of personal, partisan and institutional influence (Abélès, 1989). An individual situated at the intersection of diverse networks is able to operate in several systems at the same time and to muster resources from various sources in order to influence policy. Personal influence is also a factor in Germany, where Land leaders are also national politicians, prominent in their parties and with an ability to penetrate the national decision-making system.

Another intergovernmental dimension concerns regions' relations with local governments. In Germany, the Länder have complete control over the system of local government and can alter it at will. In other countries, local governments have their own rights guaranteed in the constitution, and retain direct links with the centre. The strength of local governments has prevented the suppression of the provincial or *département* level in regionalized states. Although arguably it is functionally redundant, politicians at this level have occupied much of the political space once coveted by regionalists. Decentralization reforms in France in the 1980s gave more to the *départements* and cities, whose leaders were well-entrenched in national politics, than to the regions, and proposals for Italy have generally insisted on the need to retain both the provincial and the communal level of government intact. Efforts by the government of Catalonia to abolish its three provinces were rejected by the constitutional court, and the Basque provinces, with their historic rights and fiscal powers, are even more strongly entrenched despite widespread support in the political world for their suppression in favour of a strengthened regional level.

REGIONS AND NETWORKS OF POWER

Regions are now a key level of intervention and action, the nexus of a variety of territorial and sectoral systems of action (Balme, 1996). They represent, not so much a defined series of functions, as the centre of a series of functional interdependencies. This space is unstructured, rather disorganized, and varies from one place to another. Understanding and conceptualizing this field has proved as difficult and contentious as in the analogous case of European integration, since both seem to escape the hierarchical and state-bound categories of political science and public administration.

There has been much talk in recent years of 'networks' as a new mode of policy-making, and of 'governance' as a system of social regulation. Networks are usually seen as a third mode of decision-making and regulation, between the hierarchical control typical of government, and the market relations typical of economic exchange. The term is usually applied to policy sectors, in which actors are in regular exchange and share a body of assumptions and norms. The term 'governance' has been interpreted in a wide variety of ways (Rhodes, 1996) but generally refers to a regime in which power and authority are dispersed and hierarchical regulation is replaced by horizontal negotiation. It also usually includes a blurring of the boundaries between the state on the one hand and the market and civil society on the other. The term has been applied especially in the study of regions, since the fragmented and disorganized nature of regional space makes it difficult to talk of government in the conventional sense. The problem is that this sort of analysis can all too often dissolve into an amorphous pluralism in which the object of inquiry is lost in the complexity and we are left with no appreciative frame or normative criteria to assess it all. Nor is it clear whether governance is a general comment on the state of the world, or an operational concept. Since its defining features are so vague, it is very difficult to use it as a tool of comparative analysis, to measure one system against another, or to say whether it is present or not in any given situation. Perhaps all we can say, rather negatively, is that governance is what exists when government is weak and fragmented. In this sense, some regions have no more than governance, while others have rather 'government' understood as a system of social regulation with an element of authority and the vital factor of political legitimation which, in a democracy, comes from electoral sanction, recognizing that the use of this term does not imply — and never did imply — that government controls all social and economic life or is independent of all external influence.

Another element which eludes pluralist analyses, in which multiple agencies are pursuing their own goals, is the sense of purpose. Regions are not usually a general tier of government, with universal functions of social regulation, but nor are we here dealing with a randomly distributed organizational complex. Regional government has been introduced precisely in order to impose a sense of purpose and a horizontal integration on this untidy mass, but since this is not a sovereign government, let alone the all-powerful state of 'realist' theory, it must work through other institutions and networks. This provides a way of thinking about the power of regions. Political scientists have tended to look at power as a relationship between two individuals such that X has power over Y insofar as X is able to get Y to do something that is more to X's liking and that Y would not otherwise have done (Goodin and Klingemann, 1996). It is thus a relationship among people and a zero-sum game, in that increased power for X means less power for Y. Discussions of power in federal and regional systems have also tended to see it as a zero-sum game, in which a fixed quantity of power is distributed between two levels of government. Another way of thinking about power, however, is not as power *over*, but as power *to*, that is the ability to achieve policy aims. In this formulation, it is possible for two levels to increase their power simultaneously, as they enhance their capacity to address social and economic problems. Alternatively, it is possible to envisage a situation in which neither level has real power to affect social change. Institutional reform can make it possible to extend the public domain and to address economic and social problems otherwise not amenable to resolution. Most analyses of governance and many discussions of government miss out on this dimension, though some observers (for example Le Galès, 1996) use the term governance to imply a purposive coalition of forces engaged in a common project. This approach also implies a refocusing of attention, away from the old concern with autonomy, that is the scope for regional governments to do things on their own, and towards governing capacity, that is the ability to make an impact on social and economic problems, whether through independent action, or by working through intergovernmental or public–private networks.

European regional governments do not, unlike US states and Canadian provinces, have an extensive field of autonomous action in framing and implementing policies. Their role is, rather, concerned with the horizontal integration of decision-making systems and sectoral actors, and the imposition of territorial priorities. This does not, nowadays, involve comprehensive spatial planning or great schemes for the management of social and economic change, but rather the ability to identify priorities and to intervene selectively to mobilize powers and resources. We can appraise the performance of regional government as *government* by examining its capacity to impose a horizontal logic on public policies and integrate sectoral networks in space, always keeping in mind that it does not and never has made claims to monopoly. The first factor influencing this is the coincidence in space of the various systems of action and social regulation and, as we have seen, this varies greatly. Another factor is the strength of institutions, since these do matter even in a world of diffused authority. A measure of autonomy is also required, so that the region is not dominated by the central state, or by the sectoral networks of individual central departments. Yet at the same time the region needs to be connected into other decision-making networks, within the economy, civil society, the state and the European Union. The decision-making structure of the region should be such as to allow priorities to be set politically and carried through, which implies a degree of political stability. Resources need to be available and, more important, disposable, to allow intervention selectively in setting priorities and levering resources from other agencies and governments. Finally, there is an important element of political skill, in operating complex systems and working with other agents.

The interpenetration of regional government and civil society and the need to work with and through other social institutions means that institutional performance depends to a large degree on the constitution of the local society, its values and norms. Implanting institutions where they have no social rooting is unlikely to produce effective policy capacity and mere institutional tinkering is unlikely to change outcomes. Hence the volumes written by jurists about the need to alter the detailed rules of regional government in Italy were largely beside the point, when the problem lay in the mores and corruption of the political class itself, or in the embedded social practices of clientelism. At the other extreme are accounts which attribute a determining role to culture and none whatsoever to institutional design. Putnam (1993) makes a universal claim to the effect that institutional performance is determined by 'civic-ness', a rather ill-defined term which appears to refer to levels of information about politics, participation in voting, lack of clientelist practices, and involvement in associations. This is essentially a cultural explanation resembling Almond and Verba's (1963) notion of the civic culture, which was said to explain variations in democratic performance among countries, or earlier stereotypes of 'primitive societies'. This is a unidirectional mode of explanation, in which long-term cultural traits determine institutional performance, with no scope for a reverse effect of institutions on culture and cultural practices. Nor does it allow any space for political leadership and the building of political communities. The unreliability of this mode of reasoning can be appreciated by looking at Germany, converted in a short period of time from an authoritarian society with no democratic past to a model of democratic stability; at Switzerland, which after the mid-nineteenth century became a byword for stability and democratic consensus (Steinberg, 1996); the Republic of Ireland; or even England, which before the eighteenth century was notoriously liable to revolutions and civil wars. An appreciation of the performance of regional governments must take account of culture, institutions and leadership, seeing these as linked in an essentially political process. Social movements and associations may underpin regional governments, but they are also brought into being by them (Guigni, 1996). Civil society is not entirely independent of the state, supporting it in the way vulgar Marxists saw the capitalist system as supporting the bourgeois state. Rather, civil society and state are mutually dependent, each sustaining the other, an idea closer to the original meaning of the term civil society (Ferguson, 1966) and to European traditions of federalism and subsidiarity. Using this more complex and multi-faceted conception of the power of regional government, we can draw comparisons across and within the states of Europe.

German Länder represent powerful regional governments, with their own resources and bureaucratic capacity. They are not based on strongly felt popular identities, but are linked on the one hand to the local socio-economic world and, on the other, to the intergovernmental system. This is widely seen as an effective way of sharing power and of articulating the territorial principle in an otherwise rather unitary state. Yet the German model is experiencing strains. A high degree of interpenetration and functional interdependency has produced what Scharpf (1988) has called the 'joint decision trap' of multiple veto points and inflexibility. Exposure to global markets and European integration have weakened the national frame and caused a shift from co-operative federalism to a more competitive mode, producing strains in the system of revenue-sharing. With their institutionalized and law-bound mode of operating, Länder may also be less well adapted to the new world of negotiated policy making, and it has proved impossible to change boundaries better to reflect functional realities (Benz, 1992). Finally, reunification has opened up a huge gap in policy capacity between the old Länder of the west, more inclined to competitive federalism, and the new eastern Länder, more dependent on the federal government.

Belgium presents a contrast between Flanders, where a region-building process akin to state-building has been in progress (Van Dam, 1997), and Wallonia, where government is divided between the territorial region and the language community (De Rynck, 1997). Institutional performance is better on the Flemish side, where the territorial principle has allowed more effective policy integration and political mobilization, while on the Walloon side the division between territorial and community decentralization is compounded by the position of Brussels, a francophone city but resented by much of the Walloon elite as the old dominant political and financial capital. The articulation between regional government and civil society has for the same reason been more effective in Flanders, where the associational life is more vigorous. This is not because of any deep-seated cultural feature, but because the Flemish movement from the nineteenth century developed in opposition to the dominant francophone bourgeoisie and included the emerging Flemish elites, while on the francophone side the local elites were the holders of state and economic power. Walloon politics thus took on a stronger class coloration, and was marked by deep social and political divisions. Flemish nationalist efforts to link their present movement back to a glorious mediaeval and early modern past (the Flanders of traders and painters) represents an effort to legitimate their movement in a manner which is common to nation-builders across Europe. The Belgian constitutional reforms have sought to eliminate the joint decision trap inherent in the previous practice of consociationalism by increasing the autonomous scope of regions and communities, while at the same time passing functions upwards to the European Union. Yet the need for joint decision-making and co-operation remains, while the fission of the party system and increasing differentiation of civil society provide few incentives for politicians to engage in the necessary co-operation.

Spanish autonomous communities are also rather heterogeneous. The three historic nationalities stand apart, and even among these there are marked differences. The Generalitat of Catalonia has established itself as a political point of reference for citizens, deriving its legitimacy from the conception of Catalonia as a nation and its links with the distinct civil society. The Basque government has been able to move in the same direction, but less surely because of the persistence of political violence and disputes over the status of the territory and its unity. Many regard the continuing role of the provinces, rooted in the foral tradition, as an anachronism and impediment to the construction of an effective autonomous community. In Galicia, the regional government co-exists with a weak civil society and capacity for collective action. Purposive policy making is frustrated by a pervasive clientelism and an unwillingness on the part of the political elite to change matters. Elsewhere, regional governments are gradually gaining in power and competence. Despite the reluctance of the Madrid ministries, power is shifting slowly and the regions are emerging as an important level of general-purpose government in a federalizing state.

Italian regions have been a disappointment to those who thought that they could serve to transform and democratize the state, as well as overcoming the economic and social gulf between the south and the rest of the country. While Italy has rich local regional traditions, the regional governments do not correspond to any other level of economic and social regulation (Bagnasco and Oberti, 1997) except perhaps in Lombardy (Ritaine, 1996). Nor have the regional governments as institutions been able to fill this gap and impose themselves as centres of new systems of action and policy integration. Putnam (1993) locates the problem in the realm of civic culture, noting large differences in institutional performance between the regions of the south and those of the centre/north. This culture is driven by events in the middle ages, which set the regions on divergent paths from which there is apparently no escape. Most Italian intepretations focus on the failures of the Italian state rather than on the regions themselves. A historical factor of greater immediacy than mediaeval legacies is the conditions of unification in the nineteenth century and the imposition of a specific state model, which served to destroy much of the southern social infrastructure (Sabetti, 1996). Southern elites thereafter sought recourse for their problems in the central state (Davis, 1996) as a safer path than trusting in regional autonomy. Even under the Republic following the Second World War, this recourse to the centre continued as regional political brokers took their problems to Rome, where the main decisions were taken. This was tied into a politics of clientelism and localism oriented to distribution rather than development (Trigilia, 1991) in which the political intermediaries brought back divisible resources, which could be used to buy political support (Bianchi et al., 1995), rather than public goods, which might have favoured development, but from which opponents could not be excluded. This militated against the forging of horizontal links within regions and when regional governments were established they were from the outset subordinated to the *partitocrazia*, ensuring that they would effectively be links in this chain of dependency rather than independent forms of authority. The structure of public administration worked in the same way, with central ministries exercising detailed sectoral control over policies rather than allowing regions to integrate across sectors (Merloni, 1985). A reliance on policies of 'extraordinary intervention' in the Mezzogiorno kept it reliant on the central machine and allowed local political brokers further opportunities to distribute resources selectively. Only in the 1990s were these structures broken, with the dismantling of the system of extraordinary intervention, and the abolition by referendum of central ministries whose powers paralleled those of the regional councils.

In recent years, there is evidence of considerable change. The collapse of the *partitocrazia* has undermined the client networks, although clientelism is unlikely to disappear overnight as a social practice. European integration and the opening of the market have eroded the old structure of territorial management and imposed a new fiscal discipline on the country. There is for the first time a strong regionalist movement from the bottom-up, especially in the north, where it takes the form of the *Lega Nord* and in the centre, where the post-communist *Partito Democratico della Sinistra* (PDS) has taken up the theme of regionalism (Agnew, 1996). There are signs in the south of increasing associationalism (Trigilia, 1996), showing that its lack is not an inherent feature of the society, but a product of specific conditions. As powers have been transferred to the regions along with fiscal responsibilities, there is some evidence of more active policy making and experimentation especially in health, building on the limited advances made in the past (Pastori, 1982). Regions have received new powers and status by the law of 1996 and, above all, they are seen as a key element in the foundation of a new Italian republic in the proposals of the Bicameral Commission of 1997 on constitutional reform. This proposed that Italy be reconstituted as a federal republic, with the state's powers defined and other matters falling to the regions. Regions would have individual statutes with constitutional status, they would enjoy fiscal autonomy and would control their own administration (Commissione Parlamentare, 1997). Regions thus remain a dynamic element in Italian politics and, whatever their past failings, they are likely to be more important in the future.

French regional experience reveals another paradox. While regions have become more important as a level of intervention and integration of public policies, regional governments themselves have benefited little. Rather, the deconcentrated administration of the state, focused on the regional prefect and the SGAR (*Secrétariat général pour les affaires régionales*) has gained in powers (Loughlin and Mazey, 1994; Jouve, 1997). Much regional policy making is highly technical and dealt with by the 'technostructure' (Balme, 1996) itself located within the national administration. As in Italy, sectoral control by ministries is strong, so that French regionalism retains its original functional, rather than a general political character. Even the regions' planning role is dominated by planning contracts with the state (Balme and Bonnet, 1994) and national agencies such as the SNCF (railways) which, to concentrate on the spectacular and prestigious TGV high-speed network, has passed responsibility for financing local and regional services onto the regions.

Regions have gradually raised their political profile, with surveys showing a steady increase in the proportion of people who are well-informed about their activities, from 33 per cent in 1986 to 48 per cent in 1994. By 1994, indeed, some 55 per cent responded that in the future the life of people in the regions will depend more on decisions taken at the regional level than on those taken for France as a whole (OIP, 1994). There are signs of the emergence of a new regional political class prepared to take the region more seriously (Dupoirier, 1994), although to some extent this may reflect the new laws on the accumulation of mandates and the need for senior notables to give up an office; it is usually the regional mandate which they sacrifice (Jouve, 1997). A 1991 survey showed that only 57 per cent of regional councillors actually preferred this to other local mandates, although this had increased from 32 per cent in 1986 (*Le Figaro*, 11 March, 1992) probably because of the law on accumulation of mandates had eliminated the less enthusiastic.

Nor have regions occupied the space created by the decentralization laws of the 1980s. Their role in economic development has been overtaken by *départements* and cities (Keating, 1991b; Le Galès, 1994), which were the main beneficiaries of the reforms. France's centralized state and policy-making system has been put in serious question by globalization and European integration but this has caused something of a defensive reaction on the part of the state elites, who have in some respects sought to recuperate lost powers. The technical bureaucracy and central ministries as well as the general prestige of the state are all a great deal stronger than in Italy and Spain, presenting formidable obstacles to state-transforming decentralization.

Yet within France there is considerable variety, depending on local circumstances, and the strategies of local political leaders (Balme, 1997; Balme et al., 1994). The decentralization laws did enhance the power of politicians and provide opportunities for more horizontal control (Faure, 1994) and in some places it was regional leaders who took advantage of this. They engaged in strategic intervention and concentrated resources, instead of spreading money around evenly. They used their powers and resources to lever those of other agencies, rather than the reverse; and they used their political skills and weight to impose their priorities on regional prefects and technical services. This depends on personality, on the linkages among political elites and institutions characteristic of the French system, and on the ability of regional leaders to mobilize a political majority and a shared regional vision. It also depends on the state response. In some regions, prefects have been accommodating, respecting the prerogatives of regional presidents, while in others they have rigidly imposed central direction. Nord Pas-de-Calais was long considered a strong region, with a rather homogeneous economic and social structure and a dominant Socialist Party committed to region-building. In the 1990s, Rhône-Alpes, with its image of dynamism and growth, is probably the leader, although Aquitaine has also maintained a high profile. Elsewhere, regions are no more than federations of *départements*, or relays for the policies of the central state.

A regional level of government is emerging in many parts of Europe, but its powers and status vary and are largely dependent on the individual state regime. In the past, the key question to ask about territorial government was to do with their degree of autonomy, that is the ability to do things without interference from higher levels. In an interdependent world, autonomy in this sense is less important. More important is policy capacity, that is the ability to act on public issues to change outcomes. Policy capacity depends on the regional government's powers and resources and its ability to link sectoral networks in space. It also depends on its ability to frame a development project and carry it through, and on its links to the external world, the subjects of the next two chapters.

6. The Political Economy of Regionalism

ECONOMIC RESTRUCTURING

One of the driving forces behind the new regionalism is provided by economic restructuring and rapid changes in modes of production. This may seem paradoxical at first sight, since many of these changes are breaking the old link between territory and production as capitalism reconstitutes itself on a global scale. Large-scale manufacturing, exploiting static economies of scale in big, integrated plants, has given way to more differentiated types of production tailored to specific markets. Production has reduced its dependency on proximity to natural resources or waterways, while reduced transportation and communication costs have permitted a geographical dispersion of production, even in the manufacture of components for a single item like an automobile. Multinational corporations operate global investment strategies, reallocating resources across regional and state boundaries, and supplying technology and skilled management where needed. Much has been written about the transition from 'Fordism', characterized by large-scale production of standardized units for national markets, to 'post-Fordism', marked by flexible production, specialization, small work units. Unfortunately, like their predecessors in classical management, Marxism and market liberalism, writers in the post-Fordist school have too often tended to over-generalize their insights, and to extrapolate from modes of material production to the organization of society as a whole. Globalization is another overstretched term, used to capture the rise of multinational corporations, the increase in trade, capital mobility and cultural homogenization. Both ideas draw attention to important changes in production and its attendant social consequences, but neither is an adequate description of current reality. Mass production still characterizes large parts of the world economy, and globalization means something very different in a state like Luxembourg, where foreign trade is equivalent to over 160 per cent of Gross Domestic Product, from the United States, where it is more like 20 per cent.

It remains true that the geography of economic production has been transformed in important ways, but these are highly specific and vary from one sector and one territory to another. Their social effects are mediated by political and cultural elements, and these in turn shape the productive process. Some territorially-based factors of production are becoming less important, enhancing the freedom of firms to choose locations, but many of the new critical factors are themselves territorial, hence the paradox that, at a time of globalization, we can speak of the resurgence of regional economies (Storper, 1995; Scott and Storper, 1992). Some of these factors represent inputs into the production process, such as the presence of complementary industries or component manufacturers, which are more important in the age of just-in-time production techniques, or the availability of a skilled and flexible labour force. Technology, while in principle infinitely mobile, does appear to develop in clusters and the interface between research and application often depends on personal contact and interaction. A good quality natural and built environment is increasingly recognized as an important factor in investment decisions. These factors can be evaluated, quantified and built into investment decisions or public policy. More elusive is the effect of the local *milieu* or social context which appears to add something more, allowing some localities and regions to innovate and remain competitive through successive changes in the productive system (Maillat, 1991). These local effects have been described as 'untraded interdependencies' (Courchene, 1995; Storper, 1995; Morgan, 1995; Scott, 1996), and include labour markets, public institutions, rules of action, understandings and values.

These are critical elements in the production of 'public goods', that is items which are available free to anyone, so that no individual has an incentive to provide them. From the perspective of the individual firm, they constitute 'external economies' of location, reducing transaction costs without charge to the firm. Specific features of the capitalist system of production and exchange may exacerbate the tendency to under-provide public goods. In so far as firms are motivated by short-term profit maximization, they have an incentive to free-ride on public goods and to run-down the stock of social capital, for example by using educated workers while failing to invest in the production of the next generation. Firms which spend money on training, by contrast, risk losing the skilled workers to their rivals. The same might be true of the creation of a good environment or the provision of infrastructure and since these are localized public goods they point to the need for a localized system of public action. Small firms may not have the resources to undertake research and development, and those which do risk having their work appropriated or copied by rivals, patents and copyrights notwithstanding. Transaction costs in providing collective benefits may also be very high for small firms (Johansson, 1991). More generally, innovation is now recognized as a social process, requiring dense interaction and contacts, rapid exchange of ideas and information and feedback mechanisms, producing 'systems of innovation' rather than individual inventors.

Another failing in market capitalism is its dependence on simultaneous and reciprocal exchange as the basis for joint action, when in practice there is a need for non-reciprocal exchange such that we will do things not to our immediate advantage, in the longer-term social good. This affects the financial and banking circuits, so that there is little incentive to lend for long-term projects or for those whose viability is dependent on others making complementary investments in the same location, a problem exacerbated when the lending institutions have no base in, or commitment to, the region. In such a system, everyone could be better off in the long run through co-operation but, once again, we have no incentive to co-operate in the short term. On the contrary, the ethic of individual self-interest gives us a motive to free-ride, and the ethic of competition provides a bias against co-operation. The secret is to provide mechanisms encouraging co-operation in the production of public goods and sustaining social norms, while at the same time retaining the productive advantages of the competitive market. This takes us beyond neo-classical economics, into the field of economic sociology (Thomas, 1972; Swedberg, 1993) with its concern about the social construction of the market and the way in which social trust is fostered (Sabel, 1993; Fukayama, 1995).

The existence of traded and untraded interdependencies within regions suggests a regional logic of production, and has led to a revalorization of the idea of 'industrial districts' first identified by Marshall in nineteenth-century Britain. Here networks or clusters of firms in similar or complementary sectors engage in complex patterns of competition and co-operation, exploiting external economies of scale to remain competitive in the global market, and constantly innovating and improving production methods. Many observers have used this framework to analyse the success of the industrial districts of central Italy, known as the 'Third Italy' to contrast with the north, dominated by large firms and fordist production, and the south, characterized by underdevelopment. In the Third Italy, networks of specialized and flexible small firms and trade associations exploit traditions of craft work and civic values rooted in localities (Garofoli, 1991), harnessing new technology to design skills, so as to compete in world markets. Similar phenomena have been observed in southern Germany, in parts of Scandinavia and elsewhere. The Third Italy literature has come under some criticism (Amin and Thrift, 1994; Ritaine, 1989) for its naïve view of the phenomenon and its social basis. Critics point to low wages and the degree of familial exploitation (Hadjimichaelis and Papamicos, 1991), or note that the model only works in selected sectors and small localities. Few of the more idealistic accounts of industrial districts have withstood critical scrutiny and, since so many of the accounts rely on case studies, it is difficult to sort out what are the essential characteristics. Indeed, it seems that different combinations are important in different places (Storper, 1995), leaving one in doubt whether there is a model at all.

There is also much argument over the origins of industrial districts and the forces which sustain them. Some argue on rational actor grounds that it makes sense for people to co-operate to produce public goods since it is in their own long-term interest. This ignores the collective action problem we have identified earlier, that it makes more sense for an individual to free ride. Others (notably Putnam, 1993) insist on path-dependency, that the fate of a region is determined by patterns of behaviour rooted in past events; a form of reductionism in which history is seen not as something which is happening all the time but as an event located somewhere in the inscrutable past. Others again focus on the role of institutions and the behaviour of individuals and firms in response to the signals and incentives provided by institutions. It is difficult therefore to postulate a single regional logic of production or a model of the performing region. Research shows that differing modes of production can coexist within a single sector with equal efficiency (Storper, 1995). There is no one best practice, and the type of production is influenced by the local social, political and historical context. This does not make spatial analysis redundant but, on the contrary, makes it all the more important to be able to analyse the 'social construction of the market' in specific places while retaining a comparative framework.

The constitution of regions as production systems is also affected by the changing external context. With the concentration of capital in multinationals, the free movement of capital and investment flows and the increased choice of location for investors, competition to attract investment becomes more intense. In a neo-classical world, this would lead to an optimal allocation of resources, as each region exploited its comparative advantage, specializing in those activities in which it was best. It is not necessary, under comparative advantage, for a region to be more productive than other regions in its own sector, merely that it be more productive in this sector than in other sectors, thus making the maximum contribution it can to global output. If, however, we think of a region as a productive system, marked by untraded interdependencies and in competition with other regions, then this focus on *comparative* advantage gives way to the idea of *competitive* advantage, based on absolute advantages (Storper, 1995) of one region over another. Regions are pitted in competition for niches in world markets, for investment and for technological advantage. This has produced what we might call a neo-mercantilism, a return to the belief that one region's gain is another's loss and that regions are in a war of all against all, a sharp contrast to the Ricardian view of comparative advantage in which everyone gains from the division of labour. This has profound implications for policy, as well as for politics, as competition over distributive issues within regions is replaced by competition between regions.

REGIONAL DEVELOPMENT POLICIES. THE NEW PARADIGM

At the same time, there has been a change of thinking about regional development policy. The old paradigm, which guided policy between the 1950s and the 1980s, was based on the state and its command of macro-economic policy and an array of interventionist instruments. Diversionary policies steered large firms away from booming areas into development regions, with the help of grants, tax incentives and development restrictions. The main motor of development was large-scale manufacturing industry, which was intended to generate multiplier effects in the regions and, through the establishment of 'growth poles', to foster complementary development. There was a heavy reliance on infrastructure development, including roads, ports, airports, telecommunications, advance factories and industrial estates. Critics of this approach complained that these policies were ineffective, or merely produced dependent forms of development rather than self-sustaining growth, development alien to the needs and cultural traditions of many regions, based on the assumption that the mass production model of industrialization was the future for everyone. Some critics said that mega-projects were a way for the public purse to finance the restructuring needs of private corporations needing to relocate to coastal sites or to escape high labour costs (Tarrow, 1978; Dunford, 1988). This mode of development encountered increasing difficulties following the oil crises of the 1970s and in the 1980s regional policy expenditures generally declined, a trend reinforced in the 1990s (Bachtler, 1993; Yuill et al., 1993). Diversionary policy is seen as increasingly ineffective in a globalizing economy where firms can locate abroad if they do not have their choice of location at home, and too expensive in a time of fiscal strain.

New thinking about the nature of regional development also encouraged a move to more refined and detailed types of intervention. Automatic grants have generally given way to selective assistance, targeted especially at small firms. There is an emphasis on encouraging endogenous growth rather than mobile investment, on research and development, and on innovation and entrepreneurship (Bachtler, 1993). Services are emphasized as much as manufacturing and there is much encouragement of networks among producers, and of public–private partnerships to mobilize local energies and resources. Labour market policy and training are given prominence. Attraction of inward investment is still emphasized, but even here the stress has moved from grants and subsidies to promoting the competitive advantages of the region as a location to do business (Trigilia, 1996). These types of supply-side policies do not need to be managed centrally and, indeed, require a high degree of local knowledge and connections and a capacity for horizontal integration (Cappellin, 1995a, b; Begg et al., 1995). So policy has been decentralized to regional and local institutions, themselves increasingly in competition with each other.

In the 1980s, this produced a great deal of competition to subsidize industry in various ways, through grants, tax abatements, provision of premises at less than market value and discriminatory local purchasing. Unlike North American jurisdictions, most European states have, at least in theory, controls on this type of competitive subsidization, and the European Commission has also become active in the field under its competition policy, but many regions have sought to push these restrictions to the limit. In recent years, they have tended to become more prudent. French regions which under the decentralization laws had power to aid firms in difficulty and to give tax breaks and subsidies, soon realized that this subjected them to all manner of threats and pressures, and have become very reticent in the matter, limiting themselves to their role in distributing national aid programmes. Spanish regions have been cautious in subsidizing private firms, although there have been complaints from other autonomous communities that the Basque Country and Navarre have used their special fiscal regime to give advantages to incoming investors. German Länder are the main exception to this rule, continuing to grant substantial advantages to investors, even at the cost of conflicts with the European Commission. Generally, policy has moved towards developing the conditions for innovation and growth, focused on key sectors and clusters and the encouragement of institutional co-operation and networking (Bachtler, 1997). Research parks and technology transfer institutions and public–private partnerships are typical instruments in this approach. There has also been a revival of interest in strategic planning (Wannop, 1995) and the role of the region as a key element in economic networks.

Policy has also been influenced by political and ideological trends, notably the declining faith in the state as an instrument of economic and social regulation, and the advance of market-based thinking. A scepticism about large-scale social engineering and a move to the 'small is beautiful' philosophy and locally-tailored solutions have provided some common ground for both right and left. Globalization and free trade are widely accepted and the need to manage the insertion of regions into European and world markets has generally replaced demands for protectionism and defence at all costs of existing productive structures, yet important political differences do remain. Many on the left, while accepting the advantages of local initiative and diversity, still argue for a strong state to allocate resources, regulate spatial competition, and protect weak regions. The left also favours a more interventionist role by the public sector, whether locally or nationally-based, and a stronger social content to development strategies. They also differ on the social content of development strategies, with the right privileging growth of output, and the left emphasizing employment, distribution and the need to maintain social spending. Others emphasize environmental considerations and sustainable development, or the needs of minority cultures or social integration. So there is no one model of economic development, or even one measure of what constitutes development. It is tempting, particularly for politicians, to portray economic development as a non-zero-sum game in which the increment of growth will provide resources for all manner of social needs, so that the objectives can be reconciled in the long run. Apart from the old observation that in the long run we are all dead, this runs into the problem that some growth-maximizing strategies, insofar as they involve demanning, labour market deregulation, reduction of social overheads or cultural assimilation, are in direct conflict with other objectives of regionalist forces. The implications of this are examined later.

THE CONSTRUCTION OF A DEVELOPMENT MODEL

Some accounts of the emergence of regions as systems of development emphasize the demands of the external context. Ohmae (1995) presents a picture of a globally competitive world in which regional nodes will emerge as the economic powerhouses of a neo-liberal trading order, with government and politics as we know it left on the sidelines. This is a form of structural contingency theory, in which form is determined by externally-defined function, a mode of explanation widely criticized in the social sciences (Crozier and Friedberg, 1977) since it ignores the capacity of actors within to change the system. Other accounts privilege internal factors or, as in the case of Putnam (1993) give absolute priority to historically-determined characteristics of regions. This form of path-dependency equally ignores the importance of contemporary politics and the scope for regional actors to manage their relationship with the global economy. A realistic account must avoid the dangers of teleology, path dependency and structural contingency, and focus instead on the nature of internal and external factors, together with their relative weight.

So, while it is true that regions are subject increasingly to the competitive imperative, and that this conditions the strategies open to them, this is not a binding force but a constraint. Regions vary in their dependence on the external market and in their competitive assets, so that those in a strong market position may have more scope for decision making than those that need to attract external capital at all costs. The latter may feel obliged to cut social overheads, to compete on the basis of cheap labour, to reduce environmental standards or generally to prostrate themselves before multinational capital, while the former can be more selective about what sorts of development to accept. Equally important is the political interpretation of the competitive imperative. Politicians have an interest in portraying the region as pitted in deadly competition against its rivals, since this allows them to postulate a common territorial interest, of which they are the guardians. At a time of weakening partisan and class attachments, this provides a basis for political support-building on an extremely wide base. Business interests, similarly, have an interest in the idea of a unitary territorial interest, identifying their interests with those of the region's citizens, closing off political debate, and justifying pro-business policies in taxation, regulation and social intervention. Competitiveness, however, can be interpreted in a variety of ways, and any given development strategy is likely to produce winners and losers within the region. So all the talk of inter-regional competition must be seen as containing an element of objective reality, and an element of social and political invention; the difficulty lies in distinguishing the two.

DEVELOPMENT COALITIONS

Regions are complex constructions which may be considered systems of action and, in some circumstances, as actors themselves in wider arenas. In general, they are not hierarchical structures of government, with line bureaucracies, but rather complexes of actors and 'networks' in which regional governments may have a larger or smaller role. To capture the idea of the region as a system of action, we need a concept broader than that of government, but less vague and pluralistic and more policy-focused than 'governance'. One such concept is the 'development coalition' (Keating, 1991a, 1993, 1997), an idea adapted from the literature on American urban politics, where the conflict between externally-imposed competition and internal political forces has long been a central preoccupation (Kantor, 1995; Stone, 1989; Stone and Sanders, 1987). A development coalition is a cross-class, placed-based alliance of social and political actors dedicated to economic growth in a specific location, its composition varying from one place to another. Development policy will result from a combination of external market influences with local resources and opportunities, mediated by the composition of the coalition, the institutional structure of the region, and cultural factors. An important role may also be played by political choice and leadership. Specifically, we can analyse development coalitions under the headings of territory, institutions, leadership, social composition, culture and external linkages.

TERRITORY

Economic restructuring is one of the main elements in shaping territorial systems of action, but a development coalition does not necessarily correspond to an economically-defined region. We have already noted that functionally-defined regions can differ according to which function is being considered and, even within the realm of economic development, there are those who stress the importance of metropolitan regions and those who prefer more extensive units. Sometimes, there is a competition between development coalitions formed at two levels, as in the rivalry between the city of Barcelona and the Generalitat of Catalonia (Morata, 1996, 1997) or in French regions between local and regional leaders

(Marchand, 1995). A cultural and historic region may also provide the basis for a development coalition, especially where it coincides with an economic region as it does in Catalonia and Flanders and, to some degree, in Scotland. Even where it does not, the new regionalism can serve to redefine identity and politically integrate a region, as may be happening in Wales, where the old Wales, divided into three cultural sub-regions — Anglicized Wales; English-speaking Welsh Wales; and Welsh-speaking Wales — (Balsom and Jones, 1984) is giving way to a new Welsh identity as a European region (Jones, 1997; Snicker 1997). In other cases, mobilization around economic development may be inhibited by a lack of correspondence between the economic and cultural definition of the region, as in Occitania or, to some extent, Brittany. Elsewhere, there is no definable territorial basis for a development project. Even in cases where there is a regional logic of development, the region may be poorly institutionalized, and so fail to provide the common ground for mobilization and exchange, as critics of the Italian regionalization process have noted (Trigilia, 1991).

INSTITUTIONS

Institutions are of critical importance in the new models of regional development. They can, if organized correctly, provide public goods, foster social communication, and provide signals and incentives for cooperative behaviour. Otherwise, they can prove dysfunctional. They also serve to mould the development project by their organizational form and composition. A characteristic form of institution is the specialized regional development agency, operating at arm's length from government and in co-operation with private actors. Such agencies are often preferred because they can concentrate specialized skills and are free of the requirements for uniform procedure and equity to which state bureaucracies must adhere and can thus be more innovative and entrepreneurial. They may also more easily gain the trust and co-operation of private sector partners, with whom they share language and operating assumptions. They are insulated from local political pressure, allowing them to take a longer-term and more strategic view of development and avoid *saupoudrage* — the scattering of credits with something for everyone but not enough anywhere to make a real impact — and clientelism. Italy's regional development agencies in the 1950s, before they fell into the hands of the party patronage machine, would provide an example, as would the activities of the French DATAR. Agencies have also been used to by-pass local political elites considered too conservative or tied to traditional social power centres, as in Scotland in the 1960s, where the Highlands and Islands Development Board was set up by the Labour government to by-pass the landlord class which still controlled the local government system and exercised strong social influence. Agencies are often key actors in less-developed areas, which do not have their own self-sustaining economic networks and indigenous institutions (Bennett and Krebs, 1994). Yet by their very insulation from local pressures, special-purpose agencies can narrow the development agenda, and neglect the social dimension, especially when their make-up provides a large role for private business interests. In other cases, they have been dominated by a technocratic elite concerned with the promotion of a particular model of development irrespective of local conditions and demands; this was a frequent complaint against the policies of the DATAR and other central agencies in France in the 1960s and 1970s.

Where elected regional governments play a role in development policy, the agenda is likely to be wider, since they are accessible to a broader array of social interests. With their constitutional status, democratic legitimacy, and resources, they might be more independent of local producer interests. Policy may be more politicized, and distributional, environmental and other considerations may be brought to challenge development priorities. Yet even here, there is a tendency for economic development to be handled by a rather small core of people within the executive, treated as a specialized function and insulated from legislative input and debate (Kohler-Koch, 1996). Their greater degree of independence from producer interests will tend to make them more directive and less inclined to bargain or negotiate over policy, while their democratic status together with institutional rivalry makes them less inclined to bring in local governments and community interests. This does appear to have happened in some German Länder (Stürm, 1997) and in Flanders (S. De Rynck, 1997; F. De Rynck, 1994). The range of functions of regional governments and their integrative capacity is also important. In France, the regions have relatively few competences and resources and have to rely on their capacity for horizontal co-ordination and selective intervention, yet this capacity is often undermined by the national planning system which makes funding dependent on planning contracts, which require the regions to subsidize national priorities such as universities or railways. Italian regional governments have been in a similarly weak position, and have had to follow national sectoral priorities. Consequently, their role as relays in the allocation of patronage benefits to groups and individuals has prevailed over the needs of spatial planning and priority-setting.

There are specific functional needs which may be filled by regional institutions, where national administration or the private sector does not do so. One of these is in finance, where the tendency to financial centralization and globalization has removed from many regions the capacity to make capital available. German Länder are particularly active here, with their publicly-owned regional banks to which some, like Baden-Württemberg, have added corporations to supply equity participation and loan guarantees (Deeg, 1996). In Scotland, a territorial lobby fought hard in the 1980s to keep control of the Royal Bank in Scottish hands and there have been proposals in Spanish regions for regional banks to tap local savings and pensions. Research is another function which may be institutionalized at regional level, perhaps the best-known example being the Steinbeis Foundation of Baden-Württemberg, supported by the Land government but operating independently to supply and diffuse technology and innovation.

Performing regions are also the nexus of dense networks of associations and groups, providing public goods and information channels and working through co-operation rather than hierarchical command (Cappellin, 1995b). The degree of 'institutional thickness' has been identified as a key factor in development (Amin and Thrift, 1994), as has the extent of associational life (Putnam, 1993). Among the important groups are civic associations, chambers of commerce, co-operatives, business promotion groups and even social bodies which can facilitate communication and foster shared norms. Yet, *pace* Putnam, not all associations are necessarily functional; the Mafia are obviously not, and it is difficult to see how the Orange Order or the Ku Klux Klan might contribute to modernization and growth. Associations may represent rent-seeking by groups within the local society, or efforts to defend locally-entrenched sectors against modernization and change. There is a dynamic to institutionalized exchange which may create incentives to further co-operation by providing regular rewards, but this needs to be fostered by policy and leadership. These associational qualities are variable across time and space. Many observers have attributed the development lag of southern Italy to the lack of associational life and rooted this in turn in immutable historical factors (Putnam, 1993), but recent Italian interpretations have focused on more immediate political reasons, and pointed to an increase in the more positive forms of associationalism in the Mezzogiorno in the 1990s (Trigilia, 1996), especially following the collapse of the old party system, which had served to stifle it by channelling all social demands into the channels of partisan patronage. A 'learning region' (Morgan, 1995) is one in which associations and institutions are used to diffuse innovation and provide incentives to co-operate, rather than encouraging defensive behaviour and the protection at all costs of acquired positions.

LEADERSHIP

Political leadership plays an important role in giving shape to a development coalition, in promoting co-operation and communication and in mobilizing resources at different levels of government and across public and private sectors. Adopting a pro-development role has attractions for regional political leaders, giving them an image of dynamism and modernity and allowing them to pitch their appeals to the regional electorate as a whole, without being confined to class or sectoral interests. Lothar Späth, former minister-president of Baden-Württemberg, made a great deal of political capital out of the image of modernity and high technology. Charles Millon, president of Rhône-Alpes, is another leader known for making development and modernization his trade mark, tying it into a sense of regional identity — the last point in his 1990 electoral programme was to 'reinforce regional identity to give it an image of which Rhone-Alpans can be proud' (Bréchon and Denni, 1992). Yet leadership varies and there is not always an incentive to engage in pro-growth policies, where modernization risks undercutting the support base of the existing political class. States have often used regional reform precisely as a way of eliminating or by-passing conservative local and regional elites, replacing them with dynamic elements known to the French as *forces vives*. In recent years, the European Commission has pursued a similar strategy through its regional development partnerships (Hooghe and Keating, 1994).

It is common to contrast dynamic, pro-development leadership with clientelistic political styles. In a clientelistic system, it is argued, leaders have no incentive to pursue policies of modernization or self-sustaining growth, since this would undermine their own role in attracting and distributing resources from central government and free their clients from dependence. Rather, the incentive for the patron is to attract as much money from the centre as possible and distribute it through party or personal networks, satisfying immediate personal needs while maintaining dependency. Divisible goods, which can be distributed to large numbers of individuals, are preferred to indivisible public goods with diffuse benefits (Bianchi et al., 1995). This has been correctly blamed for much of the failure of development in southern Italy, but some recent interpretations have qualified this picture, pointing out that patron–client systems are in fact a powerful mechanism for achieving horizontal integration within regions and mobilization of resources in governance systems characterized by dispersed authority. The patron, or boss, is thus in a powerful position to head up an effective development coalition, if given the right incentives. Piattoni (1997) finds these incentives in the pattern of competition faced by the patron, arguing that, where patrons face challengers, they may have an incentive to deliver economic growth rather than mere distributive policies. The case is supported by a comparison of the Italian regions of Abruzzo and Molise in the 1980s. In Molise, a traditional patronage system stifled development, while in Abruzzo a dynamic Christian Democrat boss achieved growth and development. A very similar argument is made about Abruzzo by Mutti (1996), and experience of machine politics in American cities — such as Pittsburgh's Renaissance (Weber, 1988) — has confirmed that clientelism may in some circumstances be a means of harnessing diverse interests to a development coalition. In France, too, well-entrenched notables have been able to use their connections to lever resources for development, in contrast to the old distributive game.

Leadership can also come from the private sector. In the 1950s, the CELIB played a key role in mobilizing social forces in Brittany, drawing on the energies of a new generation in industry, commerce, agriculture and the professions. Its example inspired others elsewhere in France and more widely in Europe. The Scottish Council (Development and Industry) was formed in the 1930s by industrialists concerned about the depression and continued to play a key role in economic planning and policy innovation in the 1960s and 1970s. Some business-led groups focus on specific sectors or small business. Elsewhere, business leadership is in the hands of chambers of commerce which, with their general membership, are unwilling to take risks or back projects which would favour some of their members against others. In yet other cases, local business leaders are anti-development, fearing competition and pressure on labour markets, or the entry of multinationals into protected local markets.

SOCIAL COMPOSITION

An important variable in the make-up of regional development coalitions is the representation of the interests of capital and labour. Generally speaking, globalization and the opening of European markets have shifted influence away from labour, which is rather immobile, towards capital, which is increasingly mobile. Since much development policy involves trying to capture capital and anchor it to the region, there is a tendency for policy to tilt to the interests of business, with labour being required to make concessions. In an era in which neo-liberal and market ideas have such high prestige, political leaders need to legitimize themselves by adopting a business-friendly attitude, at least at the level of public discourse, which in turn restructures the arena in a way favourable to capital rather than labour. In the context of inter-regional competition, business is also able to make universal claims to embody the general regional interest in growth, while labour is left making particularist claims to a share of the social product.

Yet these elements, too, are affected by the specific character of particular territories. Some regions, including much of western Germany, have retained their indigenous bourgeoisies, who have a continuing social investment in the place and a lesser inclination to move than firms controlled externally. In the United Kingdom, as we have seen, the entrepreneurial classes of the old industrial regions largely sold out in the course of the twentieth century, their place being taken by conglomerates based in London or overseas. Reindustrialization since the mid-1980s has been undertaken largely by foreign capital. In France, there was a similar drift of industrial control to Paris, echoing the centralization of the state and the financial system. In southern Italy, the absence of an indigenous industrial bourgeoisie has been noted since the nineteenth century, with the lead in the attempts at industrialization since the Second World War being taken by the state. Spanish industrialization started at the periphery, in Catalonia and the Basque Country, under the direction of indigenous elites, but both were torn in their loyalties. Basque financial and, to a lesser extent, industrial capital integrated into the Spanish ruling elite and ended up in the Franco coalition, leaving a section of the bourgeoisie and the small business community to identify with the Basque interest. The Catalan bourgeoisie was at the forefront of the 'regionalist' movement at the turn of the century, but looked to the Spanish state for tariff protection and for repressive measures against their own unruly proletariat. Sections of this bourgeoisie also sided with Franco in the Civil War and afterwards, leaving the small business class to support the conservative nationalist movement. Since the 1970s both Catalonia and the Basque Country have been affected by industrial restructuring, with the decline in old, heavy industry and an increased reliance on outside capital, but with Catalonia showing a dynamism lacking in the Basque case. In both cases, the small business sector generates support for the moderate local nationalist parties.

The existence of a local entrepreneurial class is partly a legacy of history, partly the result of good economic fortune, but there is also a place for politics. In Quebec after the Quiet Revolution, a regional bourgeoisie was fostered by the provincial government as part of a strategy of modernization and taking control out of the hands of the anglophone business class (Latouche, 1991) though, as their firms grow and internationalize, questions have been posed as to whether they will remain québécois. These efforts have been noted by the Catalan governing coalition, *Convergència i Unió* and Flemish politicians, who have made some effort to replicate the strategy. Even the British Conservative government of the 1980s and 1990s made some efforts to rebuild a native business class in Scotland to counteract the political hegemony of the left and the statist orientation of policy since the Second World War.

Business leaders tend to be rhetorically wedded to free market ideology and neo-liberal policies and, these days, to favour free trade. They appreciate the existence of a regional logic of production and the need for spatially-oriented policies but are very suspicious of regional government, especially where this is likely to be controlled by the left (Lange, 1997). So they will support development agencies or partnership schemes as long as these are insulated from political influence and give business a direct role. In 1997, for example, the British Chambers of Commerce called for devolution of regeneration powers to the English regions but insisted that the main 'democratic' body in the regions should be regional chambers comprising appointed representatives drawn mainly from business, strongly rejecting the idea of elected councils (*The Guardian*, 3 September 1997). Small and medium-sized businesses, being less mobile and more committed to place as well as more dependent on the production of local public goods, tend to be more favourably inclined to regionalism and even to its political goals than do large firms. Labour has a similarly ambivalent attitude. As it has become increasingly territorialized and involved in struggles of territorial defence, it has become more interested in local and regional action and opportunities to enhance its influence at the regional level, but at the same time trade union leaders are conscious that open markets and inter-regional competition tend to weaken the power of organized labour. They also tend to insist on maintaining national systems of labour market regulation and social welfare provision.

The need for co-operation in regional development has produced many examples of tripartite collaboration among governments, business and unions. In the Social Democratic stronghold of North Rhine-Westphalia, unions are part of the development coalition and in Baden-Württemberg the arrival of a grand coalition government and the recession of the 1990s led to efforts at concerted action with business and unions, including discussions on labour market flexibility (Deeg, 1996). The 1990s also saw a new spirit of co-operation in Catalonia where in 1993 the employers' organization, *Foment del Treball* and the two main trade unions signed an agreement on a New Industrial Model, pledging co-operation in modernization (Foment del Treball, 1993). Britain's late Conservative government sought to exclude trade unions from the regional development effort, including the Urban Development Corporations and Training and Enterprise Councils, but in Scotland and Wales the strength of the labour movement and the accommodating style forced on the their Secretaries of State by their role in territorial management prevented the complete exclusion of the unions. So the Scottish Economic Council, on which the unions sit, survived the abolition of its regional counterparts in England and in the 1990s the Scottish branch of the Confederation of British Industry got together with the Scottish Trades Union Congress to discuss industrial strategy. In France and Italy, the political divisions of trade unions and the weakness of their regional organization has prevented them from being actors in regional development coalitions. It would be an exaggeration, even in those regions where trade unions are present, to speak of 'regional corporatism' since the conditions for this are not present (Streek and Schmitter, 1991; Anderson, 1992). Neither side of industry has invested heavily enough in the region to permit it to speak authoritatively for its interests, and generally speaking there are not powerful regional governments to act as interlocutors. Instead, we find weaker and varying patterns of social concertation, which help to shape but do not determine policy and outcomes.

CULTURE

The new development paradigm emphasizes the needs of collective action, the production of public goods, and the social norms and customs which encourage these but there are huge difficulties in defining these or describing the conditions for their reproduction. Observers have written of the need for diffuse trust, and of 'social capital' as a feature of territorial societies, but the concepts are elusive, hanging somewhere between the institutional and the cultural. Fukayama (1995) for example, uses trust in a very expansive way, seeing it as the key even to large business corporations, whereas the new regionalist writers tend to use it to refer to a capacity for collective action in the absence of large, rich and powerful institutions like states and corporations. Social capital is equally difficult to pin down. Putnam (1993, p.167) who relies heavily on the idea, defines it in a circular manner, writing that 'social capital here refers to features of social organization, such as trust, norms and networks, that can improve the efficiency of society by facilitating coordinated actions' and then telling us that 'Spontaneous co-operation is facilitated by social capital.' Since it is clear that not all types of trust, norms and networks are functional for growth (organized crime, for instance, is not), we need to know which ones are, and how they are formed and reproduced. Much of the problem stems from a reluctance in the social sciences to invoke cultural explanations. For economists, they violate the individualist, rational actor assumptions that underpin the discipline, while for political scientists and some sociologists they evoke images of stereotyping or even racism. It is true that, where culture has been invoked, it has too often been as a form of determinism, or as an immutable trait of a society. Properly used, however, it can help us understand different sets of norms and patterns action, and can even be incorporated into policy design.

The term culture has a multiplicity of meanings. Narrowly understood, it refers to the arts and entertainment, whether upscale or popular. More generally, it can be understood as the perceptual frames, values and norms used in social life; as the way a society looks at itself and as a filter for what it sees. The two are connected, in that arts and entertainment provide symbols of identity and representations of social norms as well as providing a more or less distorting mirror to society. Culture is also rooted in language, which may provide a social boundary for the reference group, sustain a common discourse and provide the means for the dissemination of common values and norms. Regional cultures come in many forms, and their relationship with development is extremely varied. There are conservative cultures, in which leaders stress the need to preserve the existing social model against the threat of modernization and change. Quebec before the Quiet Revolution, or the regionalist movements of much of nineteenth-century Europe can be seen in this light. Another dominant cultural norm might be provided by escapism, in which symbolic representations of society are divorced from reality and denuded of political significance. One thinks of Scotland in the late nineteenth century and much of the twentieth, dominated by the images of 'tartanry' and the 'kailyard', a literary school in which Lowland Scotland was presented as a small town arcadia, ignoring the realities of industrialism, class conflict and urban stress. It is these representations of culture which led developmentalists for many years to conclude that modernization was incompatible with the preservation of traditional norms and cultural practices. Yet there is a third way of thinking about culture, as a set of images of society which allow a critical debate on social choices and the future, sustaining norms of reciprocity and co-operation which do not serve as obstacles to change. It is this conception of culture which is critical to the new models of regional development and which ensures that not every region adopts the same model (Lindner, 1994).

More specifically, there are three contradictions which a culture needs to bridge in order to satisfy the requirements of the new order: the individual vs. the collective; the outward vs. the inward-looking; and the future vs. the past orientation. Although the new thinking emphasizes the need for social co-operation and collective action, not all collective action is conducive to development. In a market economy, there needs to be a large space for individual competition, and norms of collectivism forged in a era of class struggle may not provide the basis for social co-operation in the modern era, as witnessed by the difficulties of adaptation of old heavy industrial areas formerly dominated by large firms and unionized workforces. Coal miners or steel workers, with their own traditions of class solidarity, are not going to convert themselves overnight into small business people engaged in networks of reciprocity. In other places, the problem is excessive individualism, as in the 'amoral familism' widely identified in peasant societies in southern Europe. The balance between individualism and collectivism, and its institutional expression, are thus critical. A similar dilemma exists between outward and inward-looking aspects of regional culture. A culture that is too closely focused on itself and its maintenance will not provide the basis for innovation and competition in global markets, but a region which is completely cosmopolitanized will lose the source of its collective identity and capacity for common action. Friedmann (1991) talks of 'rooted cosmopolitanism' as a way of bridging the gap, permitting regions to insert themselves in the global trading order without losing their own identities.

The dilemma between past and future images captures the very essence of the problem of modernity (Touraine, 1992a). A society rooted in the past cannot adapt to the present and future, but a society oriented purely to the future has no collective memory or value structure, hence no principles for collective action. A dynamic culture is therefore built out of historic materials, but is open to the future and adaptable. This is not the mere product of chance, or of factors rooted in history, but is the stuff of politics and social action in the present.

There are several candidates for the principle of collective action in the face of global markets. Social class is one, and ethnicity is another. While ethnicity is often seen as an important element in collective action, particularly in immigrant or diaspora communities, it is not, apart from any ethical objections, likely to be effective in meeting the needs of the new development paradigm. The new models of development are essentially territorial, and ethnic groups rarely correspond to territorial units. Ethnicity is a principle of exclusion which might favour some types of co-operation but only by discouraging others. It encourages inward-looking forms of identity and so may discourage social learning and innovation. A form of civic identity and shared culture, open to incomers and able to learn and adapt, is likely to render better performance as well as a more diverse and pluralistic political and social order (Keating, 1996). This is an instance of the 'strength of weak ties' (Granovetter,

1973), facilitating social communication and co-operation rather than constructing barriers.

Culture for this purpose should not be seen in an essentialist or reductionist manner, as something which is inherent to a society or which condemns it to a 'path dependency', but as something which is continually being created and recreated. Nor is the relationship between particular cultural traits and economic and social performance a constant; traits which may be a handicap in one context or historical era may be an advantage in another. Religion provides one example. Religious traditions have bequeathed to modern secularized societies patterns of collective action, corporatist accommodation and social solidarity which have been revalorized as mechanisms for dealing with the issues of contemporary development. Capitalism has been associated since Max Weber with the Protestant ethic of self-help and election, but many of the new performing regions are Catholic in tradition, and perhaps draw on this legacy in fostering social co-operation — one thinks of Quebec, Flanders, Brittany, southern Germany, northern Italy or, more recently, Ireland. Berthet and Palard (1997) have traced the impact of Catholicism and Church leadership on economic development in the Vendée, showing how the very characteristics of this region, notorious as the seat of counter-revolution, could be used to sustain collective action and a specific model of industrialization and modernization. Catalonia's traditions of pactism and accommodation, which are married to a rather individualistic style of social relations compared with other Spanish regions, have similarly been revalorized to project Catalonia as a performing region in the new Europe. Cultural traits can also be converted from handicaps to assets in some cases through the construction of new institutions, providing the appropriate incentives (Mutti, 1996).

Language may have a special role to play here, in facilitating social communication among the group and fostering solidarity. So minority languages, previously considered 'backward' or a handicap to modernization, are now often seen as a resource and an asset (Price et al., 1997). They can, as with other aspects of culture, work both ways. They can close off society, restrict communication and stifle innovation but, if linked to command of global languages and an ability to operate in wider spheres, can underpin the rooted cosmopolitanism of successful regions.

Cultural traits and practices do not survive simply of and by themselves. They are constantly being reinvented, reinterpreted and reinforced, often by leaders eager to establish an image of modernity and change (Bassand, 1991). In many regions of Europe we find the same narrative, of the region having its own special character, a sense of identity, and a capacity for social communication and co-operation which puts it apart. As Sabel

(1993) notes, this very telling of the tale is part of the process of cultural reproduction as people reinvent their own history to shape the future. Nor do patterns of social co-operation necessarily take centuries to be formed and stabilize. On the contrary, stability can come very suddenly after a history of conflict as in the cases of Switzerland (Steinberg, 1996), Germany or Spain, as the very history of instability impresses itself upon actors; subsequently, a further process of historical revision will often present the stability itself as the defining feature of the history. Historical features can also be selected to legitimize a contemporary programme. So Catalonia's heritage as a mediaeval trading nation is pressed into service in the cause of building the modern nation in the European market. In the UK, the 'heritage industry' has been used to tame the old working class culture values in a romanticized vision of the past, or to destroy them entirely in the name of the 'enterprise culture' (Morton and Robins, 1995). Travellers arriving in the old coalfield region of County Durham are now told that they are entering the 'land of the prince bishops'; so a medieaval theme is resurrected in order to efface the memory and reality of two centuries of heavy industry. These complex uses of history are lost in the crude 'path dependency' interpretations of territorial politics.

EXTERNAL LINKAGES

Finally, a development coalition is shaped by the linkages of the region to the outside world and by who controls those links. Regions in a favourable market position will have a wider range of options than those constrained to attract capital by any means available. Relationships to higher levels of government and international regimes are an important element, with varied and complex patterns in different places. Competitive regionalism has tended to destabilize older systems of intergovernmental accommodation and, in particular, to challenge mechanisms of fiscal equalization and resource allocation as regions seek to keep resources which they have won in the development battle. In Germany, the old co-operative federalism has come under strain, as Länder seek their own places in European and global markets (Deeg, 1996; Stürm, 1997) and the system of resource equalization is brought into question (Jeffery, 1997). France's integrated system of territorial politics in which local and regional power brokers play for influence within the state, is similarly challenged by the competitive imperative, which is pushing them towards more autonomous strategies. Spanish autonomous communities are divided between the stronger ones, who want to retain their fiscal surpluses and the poorer ones, who prefer to keep a centralized allocation of resources. In Belgium, the government of Flanders has been pursuing a more independent role, seeing the Belgian state as a drag on its competitive advantages. These factors produce a sharp differentiation among regions, as does their differing ability to operate in the European and international arena, discussed in the next chapter. There is also, however, an internal effect in that competitive regionalism advantages those actors within the region who are best able to master the external linkages. This includes large business, which is more internationalized than small businesses or trade unions. It includes sections of the political elite, who use their international links to enhance their own standing and favour their preferred development strategy. Socially, it includes the multilingual and cosmopolitan elements of the regional society, able to operate in both worlds.

DEVELOPMENT STRATEGIES

From the confluence of the external position of a region and its internal political and social make-up emerges a particular development strategy or policy bias. This is determined neither by the competitive imperative, nor by historical path-dependency, but by the interaction of elements within geographical spaces, and the actions of political and economic agents. Certainly, there are common elements in the new politics of development, such as the competitive ethos, the use of market language to legitimate policy, the minor role for organized labour, and a consequent tendency to social inequality, but there is also variety. The political element stems from the types of regionalist politics identified earlier (Chapter 4), which shape the interpretation and impact of external forces. To illustrate this, we will take four ideal-types of development strategy, not based on any exclusive taxonomy, but derived from an analysis of tendencies and trends. In practice, any given strategy will involve a mixture of elements, and any given region is likely to be found in more than one category, as the discussion will show.

The first strategy is that of 'bourgeois regionalism', a term coined by Harvie (1994) but used in a slightly different way here. This is a development project found in economically strong regions and focused on a local business elite in co-operation with regional governments and agencies. Emphasis is placed on economic competitiveness, productivity, technology and value added, rather than employment, policy is legitimated by reference to market values, and a common regional interest is invoked to overcome class oppositions. Development issues are filtered out of day-to-day politics and taken into special agencies or public–private partnerships, where they will be insulated from social pressures. This is a high-cost growth model, with substantial public spending on infrastructure and other developmental items such as training and education, research and technology transfer to enable the region to compete in ever more advanced sectors. Social policy is entrusted to government departments or municipal governments, who have the prime responsibility for social solidarity and integration; otherwise the social benefits of growth and its distribution are left to 'trickle-down', though where more socially-minded christian democrats are in power this might be given more emphasis. Environmental regulation is likely to be fairly strict, to maintain the advantages to modern industry, and there will be efforts to extend this elsewhere in Europe to prevent other regions gaining a cost advantage. The region seeks to detach itself from other weaker regions in the same state, seeing them as a drag on its growth, pushing for more autonomy and less fiscal equalization. There is an active external policy, but it is functionally specific, with regional leaders seeking resources in the outside world for development, and alliances with like-minded regions in other states. There are strong echoes of this style in the more dynamic and active western German Länder and in Flanders. Italy's *Lega Nord* shares many of the same ideas and assumptions, particularly on the need to detach itself from the south and attack what it sees as a parasitical state, but adds an edge of populism not always found in the other cases. There is an element of bourgeois regionalism in the strategy of the Catalan CiU governing party, but this is only one part of a larger and more encompassing nation-building strategy. The bourgeois model is based on a virtuous circle, in which regions invest heavily, but are able to trade up to higher productive sectors and modes, so recuperating their investments. Like the European social market model, with which is it associated, this strategy is coming under increasing pressure, from the spread of neo-liberal ideology and the difficulty of continually raising productivity to compensate for the high production costs.

A second strategy is the 'sweatshop economy', a low-cost route to competitiveness emphasizing low wages and taxes and a lack of labour market and environmental regulation. The region is a policy-taker, accepting its role in the global division of labour rather than trying to fashion it. There are few institutions for regional planning and those that do exist exclude the interests of labour. Excess labour is absorbed by out-migration or the creation of low-paid service employment. Public policy initiatives and public expenditure are minimized in order to limit production costs. This strategy, associated notably with some of the southern states of the USA, was visible in some parts of southern Europe in the 1990s and was a central element in the British Conservative government's strategy for reindustrialization of the old industrial areas in the late 1980s and 1990s — the term 'sweatshop economy' was used by Conservative former Prime Minister Edward Heath in February 1997 to characterize the policies of his successors in the European market. Such a strategy can yield short-term gains in inward investment and employment, but risks constantly being undercut as other regions in the world enter the competition. Its long-term viability is also in question since it draws on accumulated social investment (in infrastructure, education and public services) without reinvesting for the future. It risks descending into a vicious circle, in which lower labour quality, technology and infrastructure forces the region to enter lower-level production modes, while the dead-weight of social problems continues to act as a drag on production.

The third model is the social democratic project, another high-cost model of competition in which, while policy is still driven by competitive development, social considerations play a larger role. It is found in regions with social democratic political domination, and organized labour and social movements play a larger part in policy, with tripartite collaboration among government, business and unions to secure the conditions for growth. Like the bourgeois model, this depends on a virtuous circle in which social investment pays for high social costs, and the burden of social stress is limited. There is high public investment in development, but priority is given to those elements which simultaneously enhance social equality or access to employment, notably education and training. Employment generation is a prime objective of policy, and is targeted to specific groups who suffer the highest levels of unemployment. Distributional issues generally are regarded as first-order politics, not something to be addressed after growth has been secured. For principled reasons and because social democratic regions tend to be older industrial areas and regions of decline, there is strong support for continued fiscal equalization and inter-regional solidarity. There is not a strong emphasis on external policy or linkages with other regions, but there is support for the creation of a European social space and other measures to regulate inter-regional competition. North Rhine-Westphalia is one example of a Social Democratic region, and others are found in the Scandinavian countries, especially restructuring regions in Sweden. This model too has encountered serious problems in the European market, because of the cost pressures generated by competition and the difficulty in maintaining high social spending in regions with a declining resource base; for this reason this model is still heavily dependent on the presence of an accommodating central state.

Finally, there is the nation-building project, found in regions with aspirations to national autonomy or even independence, such as Catalonia, the Basque Country, Flanders, or Scotland. Here development is regarded both as valuable in itself and a necessary component in building the nation as a system of action and actor in the new Europe. Since nation-building is necessarily rather socially inclusive, this project must seek a broad base of support and cover a wide range of policy areas, though it may well have a 'bourgeois' or christian democratic bias (as in Flanders or Catalonia) or a social democratic bias (as in the emerging coalition in Scotland). Matters of culture and language play a central role and are invoked as the basis for a common regional interest and to rationalize collective action. Policy is legitimated by reference to the national project and territorial solidarity is invoked to overcome class conflict. External policy is emphasized and goes beyond functional co-operation with like-minded regional governments, to include cultural issues and the projection of the region as a national entity.

These strategies are both the product of the constitution of the region as a system of action, and a force helping to sustain and define the region. Successful projects help to institutionalize the region, build confidence and enhance territorial autonomy. Such autonomy must now be defined not merely in relation to the state but also in the new European order.

7. Regions in an Integrated Europe

REGIONALISM AND EUROPE

Globalization and European integration are altering the architecture of the western European state, providing a new context for territorial politics and regional restructuring. Regions are longer confined within their national borders but have become an element in European and international politics. This erosion of the boundary between domestic and international politics was prefigured by earlier functionalist and neo-functionalist scholars of European integration, who argued that functional logic, or the interdependencies among policy spheres, would transcend state-centred politics in the new Europe. Although few people now espouse the strictly functionalist explanation of European integration, rather similar arguments have recently been made in the context of regionalism, with Ohmae (1995) claiming that the functional imperatives of economic restructuring at the global level are breaking down nation-states in favour of trading 'regional states'. A considerable body of work on the Europe of the Regions looks at the combined effects of regional assertion and European integration. Some wishfully see the nation-state as caught in a vice between Europe and the regions, and doomed to disappear — these include both functional determinists who point out that the state is losing its functional rationale, and a variety of utopian thinkers, communitarians and postmodernists, who regard the state as an artificial and oppressive machine and dream of a Europe of peoples (Kearney, 1997). Others present a more complex picture, writing of 'multilevel governance' (Sharpf, 1994; Marks, 1992, 1993) or third level politics (Bullman, 1994), in which different levels of government compete or coexist (Petschen, 1993; Jones and Keating, 1995; Keating and Hooghe, 1996; Engel, 1993, 1994).

161

European integration has important economic and political impacts on the regions, which must be considered separately; the combination of these effects produces a dynamic of its own. The effects of European integration on spatial economic disparities are subject to some controversy. Classical economic theory would suggest that the removal of barriers to trade, capital flows and labour mobility would lead to an equalization of production levels and living standards. Capital would move to depressed areas to take advantage of surplus labour and lower costs, and labour would migrate to growing areas in search of employment and higher wages. Regions hit by foreign competition would move into new sectors of production, according to the principles of comparative advantage, leading to overall increases in output. In practice, matters are more complicated and adjustment less smooth, so that many scholars have argued that integration can increase disparities (Amin and Tomany, 1995a, b). Economies of scale may produce higher returns to capital in booming areas; while outmigration may leave behind the unskilled and the old in the declining regions (Nevin, 1990). Resources freed from the decline of uncompetitive sectors are not necessarily redeployed into new fields. There are practical and cultural obstacles to the free movement of labour around Europe, even compared with the United States, let alone the perfect market model. So there is now a broad, if not universal, consensus that market integration in itself is likely to exacerbate territorial disparities (Molle et al., 1980; Keeble et al., 1988; Camagni, 1992; Steinle, 1992; Begg and Mayes, 1993; Commission of the European Communities, 1991; André et al., 1991; Dunford, 1994), increasing the peripheralization of marginal regions, and producing a new territorial hierarchy. At one time, this was seen as a new centre-periphery cleavage on the continental level, with development concentrated in the 'golden triangle'; other metaphors have included the 'blue banana'. It is clear now that matters are more complex and that winners and losers are scattered across the EU, with pockets of poor performance even within growing regions.

In federal states, including the USA, such disparities are mitigated by the large automatic transfers through federal spending programmes. Poor regions pay less in national taxation and get more back in social spending. In the EU, there is no such automatic compensation mechanism (Mackay, 1993) since total EU spending amounts to well under two per cent of the Union's GDP. Regions cannot use currency devaluation to restore lost competitiveness nor, under the Exchange Rate Mechanism, can states. Considerations of national competitiveness together with EU rules prevent states from intervening to correct disparities through diversionary policies, such as incentives and location controls. EU competition policy may further disadvantage marginal regions, through preventing cross-subsidization of communications services and opening public procurement (Fullarton and Gillespie, 1988). Other EU policies, including agriculture and research spending, also disproportionately benefit the more developed regions (Strijker and de Veer, 1988; Cheshire et al., 1991; Grote, 1992), the notable exception to this being the Structural Funds.

European integration has posed a series of political and constitutional challenges to regions. Competences transferred to the EU include matters in which regions have a direct interest or for which regional governments are constitutionally responsible. Since it is states that are represented in the Council of Ministers and that have the responsibility to implement EU law, national governments have been able to use Europe to re-enter policy domains which they had surrendered to regions. For many years, governments defended their monopoly in European matters with the doctrine that Europe was foreign policy and thus within their exclusive purview, a view which has become untenable as the scope of European regulation has expanded and ramified. Regions have also found themselves obliged to implement European regulations within their sphere of competence, while many other European policies impinge on them indirectly.

There have been two types of reaction on the part of regional interests. A rejectionist regionalism opposes European integration fearing a further loss of democratic control, more remote government and the triumph of market principles. This reaction was common in many regions in the 1970s when, generally speaking, the more remote regions were the most opposed to the European project, and it is still the predominant reaction in Scandinavia. Since the mid-1980s, however, this opposition has tended to transform itself into positive engagement, as regional interests have sought to use the mechanisms of the EU to their benefit, mobilizing political and economic resources, if necessary against the state itself. Europe is widely seen in the regions as a source of material support for economic development, through the structural funds and other initiatives, but there is also a political dimension, as Europe is used as a framework for the international projection of the region, and even as a source of support for minority cultures and languages threatened within large states (Cardus, 1991; de Witte, 1992).

This political dynamic is strongest in those regions with autonomist or minority nationalist aspirations. Some minority nationalist movements note that European integration has reduced the cost of national independence, and propose simply to join the list of member states; this is the case of the Scottish National Party and some Basque nationalists. Others want to replace the existing Union with a federation of regions and small nations, abolishing the existing states; this is the policy of the Welsh nationalist party *Plaid Cymru* and of many Basque nationalists. Europe has even been proposed as a solution to the question of problem regions by taking them out of the state altogether (Drèze, 1993). Others again are more pragmatic, seeing in Europe an arena in which their nationalist aspirations can be expressed and legitimated, while seeking to exert influence at whatever points are available; this is the case of the Catalan governing party, *Convergència i Unió* (CiU), which has been very active promoting the Europe of the Regions concept, and of the governing coalition in Flanders, which has taken the lead in pressing the Europe of the Cultures idea, in which those regions with their own languages and culture will have a special place.

German Länder have also actively pursued the Europe of the Regions idea, not in order to project themselves as stateless nations, but in order to protect institutional rights and competences which are threatened by Europeanization. They took the lead in pressing for changes in the treaties to recognize a regional presence and organized a series of conference on Europe of the Regions in the early 1990s. Since the mid-1990s, however, they have concentrated more on strengthening their position within the German system of co-operative federalism, and using this as a basis for influencing European policies (Jeffery, 1996a).

European integration and regionalism are both forces undermining the nation-state; yet they also represent attempts to create new political arenas at the supranational and subnational level to try and recapture control of at least some of these processes of economic and social change. The shape of these arenas will condition the type of politics that is possible within them, hence a series of conflicts over the shape of the new Europe: the social versus the market vision; the unitary versus the federalist vision; and the Europe of the states versus the Europe of the regions or of the cultures. Regional interests have sought channels of influence into Europe, while the European Union has itself sought to use regions in pursuit of its own policy objectives. The result has been a new dynamic interplay of interests, this time at three levels, among the regions, the EU and the member states. This has spawned a considerable literature examining the ways in which regions can influence policy in the EU (Keating and Jones, 1985; Morata, 1987; Bullman and Eisel, 1993; Petschen, 1993; Bullman, 1994; Jones and Keating, 1995; De Castro, 1994), as well as the use made of regions by the EU itself.

FORMULATING AN INTEREST

Regions, as emphasized above, are political arenas, containing a plurality of interests, but in the international and European arenas they must constitute themselves as actors, formulating a 'regional interest'. In some cases, such as the western German Länder, strong regional governments are able to formulate a regional interest, given legitimacy by democratic election. In others, such as the French regions, regional governments are institutionally weak and rivalled by powerful political figures rooted in the cities and departments as well as a territorial bureaucracy of the central state (Némery, 1993). In some states, of which the only large one is the UK, there are no regional governments at all. Some regions have a capacity to mobilize territorial lobbies encompassing both governmental and private actors. Despite the lack hitherto of elected institutions, Scotland has shown a consistent ability to mobilize a territorial lobby encompassing business, trade unions, municipal governments, religious and other social leaders, and the deconcentrated arms of the central bureaucracy itself (Midwinter et al., 1991). In the Spanish historic nationalities of Catalonia, the Basque Country and Galicia, regional governments are able to draw upon a sense of historic identity to legitimize a regional interest, though with varied results. In some French regions, powerful notables are able to mobilize a lobby around themselves, despite the fragmentation of the system of political representation, with its three levels of sub-national government. In other cases, such as the regions of England, there are neither regional governments nor the capacity to organize lobbies within the civil society. Italian regional governments have been institutionally weak, dominated by the national political parties and poorly linked to the civil society and this has undermined their ability to formulate a regional interest. Belgian regions have had powerful executives accountable to directly elected assemblies, very much like the German Länder. The picture is complicated by the existence of two types of autonomous units: three regions responsible for a wide range of economic matters; and three language communities dealing with cultural matters.

There are some interests common to regions within the EU. These include institutional matters, the design of partnerships in policy implementation and the general principle of subsidiarity and its interpretation. There are also common interests in inter-regional co-operation and cross-border initiatives. Yet regions are also in competition with each other, to attract public funding and private investment, and to shape EU policies to suit their particular interests. So there is a constant tension between promotion of regionalism in general, and the pursuit of regions' individual interests. There is a multiplicity of channels for the pursuit of these collective and individual interests, of varying efficacy depending on the interest to be pursued and the political context. There is not, and cannot be, a single mode of representation of 'regional' interests in the EU.

CHANNELS OF ACCESS

For all the talk of a Europe of the Regions, the most important channel of influence is via national governments. Generally, the better regional interests are integrated into the national policy making system, the better they will be looked after in Brussels. This has posed a particular challenge for the three federal states in the Union, Germany, Belgium and Austria. Germany's problems go back to the early years of the European Community when demands for Land participation in Community affairs led to the appointment of the *Länderbeobachter*, or observer in the German delegation to the Council of Ministers. This arrangement became increasingly unsatisfactory as the pace of European integration speeded up in the 1980s, and the Länder demanded a more formal and powerful role as the price for the ratification in the Bundesrat of the Single European Act and then the Maastricht Treaty. Gradually, participation in EU matters has been brought within the framework and conventions of co-operative federalism which govern domestic intergovernmental arrangements, focused on joint committees and the Bundesrat. Belgian federalization occurred after the establishment of the EU and was altogether more conflictual, as the regions and linguistic communities pressed their particularist interests and sought to expand their scope. So while German Länder have generally worked collectively, Belgian regions usually proceed individually. The Walloon Region and the French Community each appointed an observer to the EU, while Flanders did not.

These consultative mechanisms proved less effective as the Community extended its scope and Belgian and German regions began to demand an input into Treaty revisions. At the initiative of Bavaria, 36 regional presidents, from German and Austrian Länder, Belgian regions, Italian special status regions, and Spanish historic nationalities, met in 1989 in Munich to formulate an input into the Intergovernmental Conference which produced the Treaty of European Union, or Maastricht Treaty (Madariaga, 1995). As a condition of the ratification of the Treaty, the Länder obtained a provision that the Bundesrat would have to approve all further transfers of sovereignty, even those which do not impinge on Länder competences. In Belgium, similar changes were introduced by constitutional amendment in 1993 and 1994, but there general treaty changes need the approval not only of the Senate, which is the federal chamber but, where regional competences are involved, of each regional and community assembly separately.

Another important concession in the Maastricht Treaty was article 146, which allows a state to be represented by a minister of a sub-national government in the Council of Ministers, a clause designed for the federal states of Germany, Belgium and later Austria. It does not, it must be emphasized, allow regions to represent themselves at the Council of Ministers. At the insistence of the French, it was stipulated unambiguously that a regional minister appearing there represents the state and there needs to be a prior agreement among the regions and the state as to what their interest is. In the German case, the Bundesrat is given rights of participation for measures which would require its participation in the domestic sphere. Relevant matters are placed into three categories: exclusive federal competence; mainly Länder competence; and exclusive Länder competence. In the first category, the Bundesrat must be consulted; in the second its position is considered definitive; and in the third a Land representative must represent Germany in the Council of Ministers (Ress, 1994; Morawitz and Kaiser, 1994). In this case, agreement is negotiated among the Länder through a European Ministers' Conference (Jeffery, 1996a) and then adopted in the Bundesrat, if necessary by majority vote, and one of their number is entrusted with representing the common position. The Belgian regions, communities and federal government have laid down detailed arrangements on federal–subnational representation and decision-making in Council of Ministers machinery. Each level represents the Belgian position and casts the vote in matters exclusively under its own jurisdiction, while both levels are involved in matters of joint competence, with one taking the lead, depending on the predominance of interest. The negotiating position is worked out in a coordinating committee in which each government has an effective right of veto. If no agreement is reached, Belgium is obliged to abstain in the Council of Ministers. This gives a much stronger role to individual regions and communities than in the German case. On the other hand, the need to operate within European institutions founded on states and their inability to divide the Belgian vote in the Council, have forced the federal government, regions and communities to work together (Kerremans and Beyers, 1996) and few deadlocks have occurred in practice. Were they to do so, they could pose a threat to the EU as a whole since a Belgian abstention might prevent the Council of Ministers finding enough votes to meet the qualified majority requirement. Austria also has provisions for Land participation in European policy-making though, in line with the more centralized Austrian model of federalism, the national government plays a clear leading role (Morass, 1996). As in Belgium and Germany, participation in the European arena has reinforced the need to forge a national consensus, while guaranteeing the regions a stronger position.

In the regionalized states of Spain and Italy there were until 1996 no general mechanisms to involve regions in the determination of national policy on European matters (Morata, 1995; Desideri, 1995). As a result of the key position of the Catalan and Basque nationalists after the 1996 elections, in which they held the balance of power in the national parliament, new arrangements were negotiated. These provide for a sectoral conference with the autonomous communities to define Spanish positions in the Council of Ministers, as well as representation in working parties. There is a delegate from the autonomous communities in the Spanish Permanent Representation. This did not go as far as demanded by some regionalist forces, notably the Basque nationalists, but represented a major concession from the past position of the Spanish government. The Basque government has pressed for the use of the Maastricht provision for representation but it is generally agreed that this would require a constitutional revision. Few people in Spain wish to reopen the constitutional dossier, least of all the Catalan nationalists, who have not pressed this one. In Italy, the Standing Committee on relations between the state and the regions is empowered to discuss EU matters, but it does so only intermittently and with little result (Desideri and Santantonio, 1996). Further progress will depend on reforms to the Italian state.

Another mechanism for influence via national government is the UK system of administrative devolution. The territorial offices of central government in Scotland, Wales and Northern Ireland, serve the dual role of administering those territories on behalf of the central state, and of lobbying for them within central government. This principle extends to European affairs, where the territorial offices have a role in determining the British position in the Council of Ministers and may be included in the delegation. The weakness of the system is that the offices are not representative of their respective territories, so only lobby within the limits of UK government policy. Nor are they powerful actors within Whitehall or Brussels, so that there is always a danger of the territorial interest being traded off against other objectives which the UK government is pursuing. The Labour Government's devolution proposals provide for participation by the Scottish executive in the UK delegation to the Council, posing a potential political conflict; Wales will continue to be represented in European matters by the Welsh Office. This system does not provide a platform for regions as a whole and the regions of England, lacking even the administrative decentralization of the minority nations, are marginalized from European policy making.

France provides another model of influence via the national state, through its integrated bureaucracy which links local and national policy making, and the cumulation of mandates, by which politicians may simultaneously hold national and local office. To some degree, this unitary system with territorial influence has been extended to the EU (Balme, 1995). A powerful politician like Valéry Giscard d'Estaing, former president of the republic, member of the European Parliament and president of the regional council of Auvergne, was able to pull strings at various levels at the same time. This system is highly uneven in its incidence. While the presence of local politicians in the national parliament provides a powerful institutional defence for the system of local government in France, there is no powerful lobby for the defence of these institutional interests in Europe.

Individual regional interests may also be projected through national governments by partisan links. This is particularly important in southern Europe. Finding itself in a minority following the 1993 general elections, the Spanish socialist central government negotiated a pact with the Catalan CiU, providing access to national policy making and thence to Europe. Other regions, including those controlled by the socialists, were very resentful, especially when the pact was renewed with the succeeding conservative government in 1996, with special attention to Europe. In Belgium, regional interests have access to the federal government through party networks; here the central state has in effect been captured by regionally-based interests

Recent years have seen a spectacular growth in direct links with the EU. These take a variety of forms. Regional and local governments make frequent visits to Brussels, to lobby Commission officials. They engage the services of consultants to help them make a case and find their way through the bureaucracy. Many have opened permanent offices in Brussels and in the ten years to 1996, the number of these grew from just two to 115 (*Europa Magazine*, 1.1996). Some represent individual regions, some represent consortia of regions and some represent municipal governments. Two represent transnational alliances, albeit of non-contiguous regions, Centre-Atlantique, which represents the French regions of Centre and Poitou-Charentes and the Spanish region of Castile and Leon; and the Anglo-French Essex-Picardie. All the west German Länder set up offices between 1985 and 1988, with the eastern Länder following soon after reunification (Jeffery, 1996b). French regions are represented in a variety of ways, on their own, in joint offices, or in some cases by the *département*. In Italy, constitutional provisions prevented the establishment of regional offices before 1996, when the law was changed. Spanish autonomous communities got around a similar prohibition by setting up formally private offices, with public support. The earliest of these, the *Patronat Català Pro-Europa*, was founded in advance of Spanish accession. In 1995, the Constitutional Court ruled that regions could be represented officially in Brussels, an opportunity which was immediately taken up by the Basque government. Some British local governments have set up offices in Brussels but the UK government ruled that the offices for Scotland, Wales and Northern Ireland should be no more than platforms for regional interests, and not have any more political role. The establishment of elected Scottish and Welsh governments will undoubtedly change this, and there is provision in the devolution proposals for Scottish and Welsh offices in Brussels.

These offices are sometimes represented as lobbyists, or forms of direct representation in EU decision-making. Yet the Commission is tied by regulations in deciding on matters like the allocation of structural funds, while political decision-making is in the hands of the Council of Ministers, representing national governments. The offices and the lobbying really serve two more subtle roles. In the first place, they provide information to regions on upcoming initiatives, allowing them to lobby their national governments; and they provide information and regional viewpoints to Commission officials, who are otherwise dependent on national governments for information. They work best when their efforts are most closely tied into those of their national governments and, after some initial suspicion and rivalry, this type of co-operation has generally prevailed. In the second place, they serve a symbolic role in projecting regions and regional politicians in the European arena and presenting them as participants in the policy process. This allows regional politicians to take credit for EU initiatives, particularly funding, that would have come in any case simply by the working of the relevant regulations. The open bureaucracy of the Commission encourages lobbying and visits, while the opacity of the decision-making process and the obscurity of the funding regulations allows a whole variety of actors to take credit for the outcomes.

Regional lobbies are rarely powerful in Brussels on their own. Where they can work with a national government, they can achieve more. They may also be effective when linked with powerful sectoral interests, for example a major corporation based in the region, or a sector with links into the Commission directorates. The best examples of this are in Germany, where sectoral interests are often linked into the system of territorial government in the Länder (Benz, 1997).

Several organizations lobby for regions as a whole at European level. The International Union of Local Authorities and the Council of Communes and Regions of Europe are both wider in scope than the Community and have been closely associated with the Council of Europe which they persuaded to establish a Permanent Conference of Local and Regional Authorities in 1957. In 1986, they opened a joint office to deal with the EC. In 1985, the Council (later Assembly) of European Regions was launched, with 107 members including eleven Swiss cantons. It has pressed for involvement of regions in European decision making, for the principle of subsidiarity, and for institutional changes. Other regional organizations seeking to influence policy making in Brussels are the Conference of Peripheral Maritime Regions; the Association of European Frontier Regions; Regions of Industrial Technology; three Alpine groups and a number of transnational frontier organizations.

The establishment of formal rights of consultation with the Community owed a great deal to the pressure of the European Parliament which, in the course of the reforms of the Community regional fund, stressed the need for greater involvement of regions themselves. In 1988, the Commission established a Consultative Council of Regional and Local Authorities with consultative rights over the formulation and implementation of regional policies as well as the regional implications of other Community policies. Its 42 members were appointed by the Commission on the joint nomination of the Assembly of European Regions, the International Union of Local Authorities and the Council of Communes and Regions of Europe. The Maastricht treaty replaced this with a stronger Committee of the Regions (CoR) with formal rights of consultation on proposals but no formal initiative or veto powers. It consists of 222 members, all of them elected regional or local politicians, and has the same status and powers as the Economic and Social Committee, with which it is organizationally linked. More ardent regionalists had hoped for a regionally-based second chamber of the European Parliament. CoR must be consulted by the Commission on matters falling within its competence, and it can also take up issues on its own initiative. There are five plenary sessions each year in Brussels, and working parties, from which resolutions are generated and passed to the Commission. During its first two years, it adopted 65 main Opinions, about half at its own initiative. These covered both institutional matters, calling for more regional and local involvement in EU institutions and policies, and substantive matters, including regional policy, the environment, training, transportation, culture, information technology, agriculture and rural areas.

While CoR claims to have influenced a number of EU initiatives, several factors weaken its role. Its membership is decided by national governments, and some of these have exercised a strong control, for example in France and the UK, while others, including Belgium, Germany and Spain, have left the matter to regions themselves. The committee includes not just regions but municipal representatives, with different institutional interests (Loughlin, 1996). From the outset, it was rather politicized, not so much on a right–left basis as on a north–south one; at its first meeting a deal was done between the conservative president of Languedoc-Roussillon, Jacques Blanc, and the socialist mayor of Barcelona, Pasqual Maragall, to take the positions of president and first vice-president, rotating half way through the four-year term. There was also a split between the strong regions of Germany, Belgium and, to some extent, Spain, and the weaker ones. The former initially nominated high-ranking politicians, including four German minister-presidents and half the Flemish cabinet, together with Catalonia's Jordi Pujol and Galicia's Manuel Fraga, thinking that substitutes would be allowed for ordinary business (Christiansen, 1996). They resented having to rub shoulders with mere municipal worthies, especially when the majority voted not to allow substitutes. The marginalization of northern European representatives, especially the German Länder, is likely to reduce its influence and to lead those regions that are linked institutionally to their own national states, to use those channels rather than working across national boundaries. Finally, the Committee has the task of representing regions as whole, when regions are increasingly in competition. This may tend to limit it to institutional matters where a common interest can be discerned, though even here the regional–municipal division may cause problems.

THE COMMISSION AND THE REGIONS

Traffic between regional interests and the EU is not all one way. The Commission has itself played an important role in mobilizing regional interests, establishing new networks and creating a dialogue among regions, states and itself. The main stimulus for this has been the EU's regional policy, now subsumed under the structural funds, which by 1993 accounted for a third of the EU budget, less than agricultural spending but far more than any other item. The development of regional and structural policy is the product of two converging logics (Hooghe and Keating, 1994). On the one hand is a policy logic, whose guardian is the Commission. On the other hand is a political and distributive logic, located in the Council of Ministers and intergovernmental negotiations.

The policy logic for an EU regional policy is similar to that for national regional policies of the 1960s and 1970s. It is a mechanism for rectifying the territorial disparities produced by market integration and for achieving allocative efficiency. It is a social compensation for losers in the process of economic restructuring; and it is a device to legitimize the European project in regions where support might otherwise be lacking. The political logic is the need to redistribute resources among member states. Initially, this meant compensating Britain for its disproportionately large net contribution to the Community budget in the 1970s. Later, the policy was extended to compensate the southern European countries for the effects of the single market programme. These different logics produced conflicts between the Commission and member states from the inauguration of the European Regional Development Fund (ERDF) in 1975 (Mawson et al., 1985). In order to gain the consent of member states, the ERDF was divided into fixed national quotas. All regions that were eligible under national regional policies were eligible for ERDF funding. Funds were administered by national governments, who almost invariably refused to treat them as additional to national spending but rather as a reimbursement to themselves for their own regional policy spending. Consequently, the policy was a fiction, a way of dressing up an inter-state transfer mechanism as a European policy.

Over the years, the Commission has sought to increase its own influence over the framing and implementation of the policy, to convert it to a genuine instrument of regional policy, and to ensure the spending is additional to national spending programmes. From the late 1980s, it also sought to co-opt regional interests as partners in designing and implementing programmes. This has produced a three-level contest for control of the policy instrument, among the Commission, member states and regions themselves. In 1988, there was a major reform, again guided by both political and policy logics. The political logic was provided by the need to compensate the countries of southern Europe and Ireland for the adoption of the single market measures in the period to 1993. The policy logic was the Commission's desire to convert the ERDF and other structural funds into a genuine policy. The funds were doubled and the three main ones, the ERDF, the European Social Fund (ESF) and the Guidance Section of the European Agricultural Guidance and Guarantee Fund (EAGGF) brought together (Armstrong, 1995) under the heading of Structural Funds. Five objectives were laid down, three of which are regional in nature. For the first time, the Commission was to draw up its own map of eligible areas, using Community-wide criteria. Funds were to be disbursed only to projects within approved Community Support

Frameworks (CSFs), apart from nine per cent, which was reserved for Community Initiatives sponsored by the Commission. CSFs were to be negotiated between the Commission and member states, with the involvement of regions themselves. Within these, programmes of action were to be framed and administered by partnerships involving Commission representatives, national governments, and representatives from the regions. Additionality was laid down as a general principle, so that spending would have to be over and above national spending. The whole policy was to be guided by the notion of subsidiarity, with the greatest possible involvement of regional and local interests and the social partners in the world of business, labour and voluntary groups. The regulations prescribed an integrated approach to regional development and, since this links spatial policy to technology, environmental policy, education, public procurement and competition policy, it should serve to bring regions into contact with a range of EU policies and directorates. The Commission, in line with contemporary thinking on development policy, also sought to move from infrastructure to human capital, productive investment and indigenous development and this too implies a more active and participative role for regional actors of various sorts.

This potentially provided for greatly enhanced regional involvement in policy making and for stronger direct links between the Commission and regional interests. To some extent, this has happened (Hooghe, 1996). States without regional structures, such as Greece, Ireland and even Sweden have been obliged to create them, or at least some substitute for them, in order to be eligible for funds. Regional and local interests have used the funds to provide a focal point and motif for political mobilization. In some English regions, there have been moves to constitute lobbies in the absence of regional governments, to face the European challenge (Burch and Holliday, 1993). A belief that there is largesse to be had in Brussels explains some of the lobbying and offices in the EU capital. Regional actors have been brought into contact with Commission officials and its thinking on development policy has been diffused through the mechanism of partnership.

Yet the effect of this should not be over-stated. There is no new territorial hierarchy emerging, in which regions are independent actors. For one thing, the Commission itself does not have a consistent definition of what is a region. Its NUTS table (Nomenclature of Territorial Units for Statistics) consists of three levels, each of which is a mere aggregation of national administrative units. Nor does it limit itself to regional authorities, however defined. Some of its initiatives involve municipal governments while others are aimed at the private sector or local action groups within civil society, often at the subregional level (Smith, 1995,

1997). The Commission's objective, following its policy logic, is to get programmes going, to spend the funds in the most effective way possible, and to involve whatever partners are appropriate for the task at hand.

National governments have also found their way back into the act. While the Commission has succeeded in concentrating funds on the neediest regions, there is still a need to make sure that everyone gets something in order to keep national governments on side. Even the new Scandinavian members, although net contributors to the EU budget, had to get a piece of the structural policy, so a new objective 6 was introduced, aimed at areas of sparse population. While there are officially no national quotas, there is an understanding that Britain, for example, will get a large share of the funds for industrial areas, while France will do well in the rural category. The map of eligible areas is in practice negotiated between states and the Commission, a practice which was formalized in 1993. Pressure is exerted by member states to include areas that fall outside the eligibility criteria. Community Support Frameworks (CSFs) are nationally based and negotiated bilaterally with the Commission. In the 1993 changes, it was made possible for states to submit a single document including their overall development plan and the individual applications for assistance, rather than having to have the former approved first. Partnership in the CSFs is decided by member states and this too was formalized in 1993, though the Commission has sought to make this as inclusive as possible.

The result is that the increased regional activity stimulated by the structural funds has followed distinctly national lines. Where national government has taken a permissive stance or been unable to control regional activity, regions have become important actors. In other cases, strong states have largely retained their monopoly on links to the Commission and control of regional policy implementation. At one extreme are the Belgian regions, which deal directly with the Commission on the designation of eligible areas, the allocation of the funds, negotiation of the contracts and implementation. They are not, however, involved in negotiations on changes in the fund regulations, such as those brought about in 1993. The German Länder are also deeply involved, through the mechanisms of co-operative federalism. Individual Länder participate in the design and implementation of CSFs, through the Joint Tasks Framework (*Gemeinschaftsaufgabe*) (Anderson, 1996). At the other extreme are Greece, Ireland and Portugal, which lack a regional tier of government. At the urging of the Commission, there have been some administrative changes, with some involvement of local actors, but there has not been a notable shift of power from central government (Laffan, 1996; Iokamidis, 1996; Holmes and Reese, 1995; Featherstone and

Yannopoulos, 1995). In France and the UK, there has, paradoxically, been some increased centralization since the 1988 reforms, as the structural funds have become financially significant and politically more salient (Balme, 1995; Keating and Jones, 1995; Balme and Jouve, 1996).

The nine per cent of the structural funds budget available for Commission initiatives could potentially be an important instrument to establish links between the Commission and regions. Local, regional or group interests can lobby the Commission to launch an initiative aimed at them, independently of their national governments. For example, the *Rechar* initiative originated in the collaboration between Bruce Millan, Commissioner for Regional Policy, and a coalition of British local governments from coal-mining areas (McAleavey, 1993).

Another mechanism for the organization of subnational interests is networking. *Recite* (Regions and Cities of Europe), launched in 1991, funds 37 networks covering a range of subjects, and with a variety of partners. *Roc Nord* is a network, through which the Danes share their expertise in economic and environmental planning with Crete. *Quartiers en crise* promotes exchanges among 25 cities on problems of social exclusion. In *Dionysos*, ten French, Italian, Spanish and Portuguese wine-growing regions are pooling their resources and organizing the transfer of technology to the least developed regions. The INTERREG programme promotes cross-border co-operation. In addition to this special network programme, networks have emerged in the cohesion policy instrument. This goes from extensive and relatively general networks, like that for the Objective 2 regions, to more specific ones as the one around the *Rechar* initiative. They leave Europe densely organized — with most local and nearly all regional authorities involved in several networks simultaneously. This organizational activity does not, however, cluster around clearly identifiable regional authorities. On the whole, the contacts, the partnership arrangements, and the Commission's sectoral and spatial initiatives have succeeded in mobilizing local and regional interests. Yet, it has been difficult for regional authorities to get a comprehensive overview of cohesion policy. Subnational interests have been drawn into the European arena in diverse ways, and degree and form of participation have tended to follow distinctly national patterns. Their influence similarly is still largely determined by their linkages into national government. Direct contact with the Commission is a supplement, not a substitute for this.

Europe has provided a powerful theme for the redefinition of regions as actors and interests, yet their influence remains limited and they have yet to define a clear role. Much hope has been invested in the concept of subsidiarity, adopted by the EU in the Maastricht Treaty to mark the limits of European intervention. The concept is highly charged politically and subject to a variety of interpretations. Initially, it represented a principle for regulating the scope of authority in a unitary society. Later it was used by the Catholic Church as a means to resist the encroachment of the secular state. It has been widely applied to describe a specifically European model of federalism which rests, not on the limitation of government or the division of powers as in American federalism, but rather on the sharing of powers in a co-operative framework, bounded by an overall principle of solidarity. It is in this sense that the principle has been invoked in the debates on European integration, but differences of interpretation remain. Some governments sought to interpret the principle as indicating a watertight delimitation of functions. Britain, notably, interpreted the principle as a limitation on the prerogatives of the EU, and a defence of those of the member states, an interpretation vigorously disputed by the German Länder as well as by home rulers in Scotland and Wales.

In the preparation for the 1996–7 Intergovernmental Conference, the Committee of the Regions sought a tighter definition of regional rights, with a stronger role for the Committee of the Regions, and a right of access to the Court of Justice. They also wanted the principle of subsidiarity to be justiciable. This was part of a strategy, pressed by the German Länder since the late 1980s, of establishing the regions as a 'third level' of the European polity (Jeffery, 1996a) with extensive recognition and independent rights of participation. The demands received little support in the Commission and none from member governments and little was achieved. Regional strategies and regional influence thus continue to be shaped by national political arenas. Europe does alter the balance within these arenas, by intruding into regional competences, and, by way of reaction, forcing regions to re-establish their role and defend their competences. It does not, however, break the national mould, or allow regions to short-circuit state channels by constituting themselves as actors directly within the EU policy making structure. In the wider European space, however, regions are seeking to escape the national framework and penetrate national boundaries, notably by inter-regional networking and cross-border co-operation.

INTER-REGIONAL CO-OPERATION

The gradual building of a European economic and political space has led regions to seek to re-evaluate their position and to seek out new alliances and partnerships. By combining their efforts, they hope to increase their influence with EU institutions and to promote their common interests both in institutional reform and in substantive European policies. Regions also seek to learn from each other and to exploit complementary assets and skills in pursuing their own development projects. This is part of an emerging phenomenon of para-diplomacy, in which regions are challenging the monopoly of the state in transnational relations (Hocking, 1997). It is not to be confused with traditional diplomacy, which covers the whole range of state interests and seeks to present a united front to the world. Paradiplomacy is functionally specific, usually limited to matters of common economic or cultural interest, although in the case of minority nations it does extend to the promotion of the territory as something more than a mere region and serves to legitimize nationalist aspirations. This is notably the case in Catalonia, the Basque Country and in Flanders, which has moved from a dialogue with other regions to seeking states as partners (S. De Rynck and Maes, 1995). These challenges are not welcomed by states, which have sought to restrict the international activities of regions through constitutional, legal and political means. France, Spain and Italy have been particularly reticent in establishing a legal framework for the transnational activities of regions, although gradually these restrictions have been relaxed. Conflict is especially likely over matters pertaining to state sovereignty or national identity, ideas which are interpreted very strictly in France, where the constitutional court even ruled that French deputies in the European Parliament could not have territorial constituencies, because this would imply a divided representation of France abroad. Federal states are more accommodating, especially Belgium, where the 1993 constitution gives the regions and communities full responsibility in external matters within their spheres of competence.

There are two levels of co-operation: multi-purpose associations of regions; and more focused alliances of specific regions. There are three principal multi-purpose associations. The Council of Local Authorities and Regions of Europe is a European-wide body bringing together subnational governments on matters of common interest. The Congress of Local and Regional Authorities of Europe comes under the aegis of the Council of Europe and its 286 members come from all its 40 member states. Founded in 1994 to replace an earlier body confined to western Europe, it is divided into two chambers, one for regions and the other for local governments. Its main task is the promotion of local democracy and it has adopted charters and conventions on local self-government; transfrontier co-operation; participation of foreigners in local public life; regional and minority languages; urban issues; young people; and mountain areas. It is particularly active in the countries of central and eastern Europe. The Assembly of European Regions was founded in 1985 and, while it does cover the whole of Europe, its main focus has been on the institutions of the European Union. It played an important role in formulating a regional input to the negotiations leading to the Maastricht Treaty, with its provisions for greater regional participation and it prepared a further list of demands for the 1996 Intergovernmental Conference, including a stronger subsidiarity clause, a right of recourse for regions to the Court of Justice, and a firmer legal basis for inter-regional co-operation. Its responsibility in institutional development has been taken over to some degree by the Committee of the Regions, but it still plays a role in these matters, as well as in lobbying on policy issues. Like CoR, however, it is weakened by its heterogeneous membership and particularly by the division between the strong regions, which have succeeded in inserting themselves into the decision-making process through national constitutional amendment (in Germany, Austria and Belgium) and the weak regions, which have more interest in European-wide fora for regional interest articulation. Universal associations also come up against the old problem of just what constitutes a region and what the political implications of this are. Regions like those in France, which are essentially economic planning units, come up against German Länder, which are units of general government. Both contrast with regions which have a cultural specificity or national pretensions, such as Scotland, Flanders or Catalonia. These efforts have, nonetheless, raised the profile of regions, provided an interlocutor for the Commission, and established the legitimacy of regional intervention directly into the European political space, without the necessity to work through national governments.

A more focused effort is provided by groups of regions with a narrower geographical or sectoral focus, able to emphasize common interests and define policy proposals. These started to appear in the 1970s, as the completion of the common market forced policy makers to look at the issue of economic restructuring in a European context. The first was the Association of European Frontier Regions, founded in 1971 (Balme, 1996). In 1973 the Conference of Peripheral Maritime Regions was set upon the initiative of the Breton group, CELIB. This was followed by the association of traditional industrial regions RETI (*Régions de tradition industrielle*) — later 'tradition' was replaced by 'technology' to give a more dynamic image while retaining the same initials. Another association brings together capital-regions of Europe. The Foundation Europe of the Cultures, founded in 1992, is an initiative of the Flemish government, interested in promoting an alternative to the Europe-of-the-Regions scenario which, it felt, paid insufficient attention to regions with their own culture or language and reduced them to the level of mere administrative regions. These groups have served to exchange experiences and formulate demands, and have given birth to more specific initiatives among their members, focused on sectoral issues.

The more limited inter-regional initiatives are of two types, those which focus on general sectoral interests, and cross-border initiatives. Both were given a huge impulse by the Single Market Programme of the 1980s and have continued to expand in number and scope in the 1990s. A number of initiatives came out of the Conference of Peripheral Maritime Regions, notably the Atlantic Arc, focused on the threats and opportunities faced by regions from the shift of gravity towards central Europe (Balme et al., 1996). The most celebrated initiative is the Four Motors of Europe, founded as an alliance of high technology regions by Baden-Württemberg, Lombardy, Rhône-Alpes and Catalonia, to exploit the advantages of the single market. This is an ambitious scheme, to promote the interests of dynamic regions, which feel themselves neglected by the Commission's emphasis on declining areas (Kukawka, 1996; Morata, 1996). The aim is to establish trans-European networks for research, innovation and production, applying in the single market the lessons learned from territorially-bound industrial districts. Accordingly, much emphasis is placed on education, technology and the transfer of knowledge. In this way, regions can gain from external knowledge, pool experiences and provide a mutual stimulus to innovation, all critical factors in the new regional development paradigm. They can also combine to lobby European institutions and simultaneously pressure their own national governments. These initiatives have received a very high political profile and, to judge from their own publicity, have made a huge impact on policy and development in Europe. Outside observers are generally more reserved (Borrás, 1993), noting that much of the activity is symbolic and emphasizing the obstacles to co-operation inherent in different legal, administrative and political structures and systems of innovation.

Cross-border initiatives are by far the most common type of inter-regional co-operation. There appears to be a strong functional logic for this, especially where economic or cultural regions are bisected by national boundaries, some of them of quite recent origin. While the first projects, such as those of the upper Rhine and the Saarland–Lorraine–Luxembourg, date to the 1970s, initiatives have proliferated since the start of the Single Market Programme and the 'borderless Europe'. A strong boost was given by the Commission when, as part of the Single Market initiative, it established the INTERREG scheme as a Programme of Community Initiative, giving it a high degree of control. 'Euroregions' have been established across the French–Belgian–British frontier and the Spanish–French frontier, and working groups have proliferated across the Alpine boundaries. Since the end of the Cold War and expansion of the EU, similar initiatives have been taken in Sweden, Finland and the Baltic states. By the late 1990s, indeed, there was not a border in western Europe that was not covered by some sort of transfrontier programme. Typically, cross-border initiatives have a functional basis, focused on common problems and opportunities, notably in economic development, promotion, infrastructure, environment and sometimes culture, but they also have a strong political component, founded on the desire of regional politicians to project themselves on a wider stage, or to escape the restrictions of national politics. Their success or failure depends on the appropriateness of the functional linkages established, as well as on the political dynamics, including the attitude of national and local governments.

The functional logic of cross-border co-operation rests on the existence of complementary assets within each region, precise projects to realise them, and the availability of resources to carry these out. These conditions are not always present. Regions with completely different economic structures have little to co-operate about, and regions with identical structures do not need to co-operate. Co-operation requires a degree of complementarity and an observable opportunity to exploit these. It also requires that the regions in question have the requisite powers and resources. Given the variations in the structure, competences and financial powers of regions in various countries, co-operation can be a real practical problem.

Co-operation is most likely in areas such as infrastructure and environmental policy, where it can produce positive-sum outcomes. It is also important for small and medium-sized businesses (Eisel et al., 1996), where the logic of industrial districts can be extended transnationally; large firms have their own connections, are linked more directly into global networks, and do not depend on the external economies of scale provided by proximity. Yet in matters of economic development, neighbouring regions tend to be competitors, making co-operation very difficult. Sectoral interests on either side of the border will resist rationalization if this is a threat to them, and it is to the interests of their own constituents rather than those of the cross-border region as a whole that politicians must attend. A typical example would be the existence of two airports, one on either side of the border and neither large enough to serve the needs of an expanding economy. Yet rationalizing in one large airport would mean local politicians in the losing area giving up a local asset and employer and, whatever the compensating gains, this is difficult to sell. To overcome this problem, an external incentive is needed and it is here that EU funding, however small in scale, is important.

Success is also critically dependent on individual political entrepreneurs. Frequently, a cross-border initiative will be attributed to the actions of a prominent politician, or a link between two individuals, and its success will depend on their continued interest. Regional politicians, for their part, have used these initiatives to project a European image and build political capital. National governments, on the other hand, have tended to be very reticent and, especially in centralized states like France and Italy, have sought to limit independent initiatives and channel them through the capital. So cross-border initiatives between northern France and Belgian regions have required an immensely complicated set of committees on the French side, in order to bring in regional and local governments, the regional prefect, national ministries and even the French Foreign Ministry, such is the sensitivity of dealing with foreign governments. On the Belgian side, given the extensive powers of regions and communities in foreign affairs within their sphere of competence, matters are much more simple.

Despite the apparent functional logic of restructuring, then, it is not easy to mount public policies across national borders. Frequently, joint programmes amount to little more than parallel efforts, separately mounted, or the relabelling of existing activities. Only in specific projects, such as a river crossing or an environmental clean-up, is genuinely joint action commonly found. On the other hand, cross-border working does serve to alter the context of politics and redistribute political assets within national systems. State governments may seek to defend the border by controlling joint initiatives, insisting on their presence at meetings, and even routing all financial programmes back through the centre, but they cannot control informal contacts and exchanges. Telephone communication, travel and attendance at conferences and meetings is creating a new class of European-minded officials, operating at the interface of the state and Europe, whose ideas are permeating into policy. They may even be able to set up their own circuits of information, as for example in the case of France, where regional officials, unable to get the necessary information for the gatekeepers in Paris, sometimes get it from the Belgian contacts across the border. This is a subtle process. European borders are not disappearing under the impact of functional restructuring, and will not do so as long as national political and legal systems exist, but they are increasingly penetrated and national governments are losing their monopoly of control over them.

There is no automatic spillover from functional integration across the border into political and social integration. Rather, political considerations are prior and linkages are dominated by public officials. In a case like the border between the Irish Republic and Northern Ireland, functionally-based common interests are not able to overcome entrenched political divisions or even attenuate them (Tannam, 1995). Where there is a strong political commitment to Europe, on the other hand, this provides an incentive for transfrontier initiatives and a context and support system for them. Nor is there much evidence of spillover in the other direction, from political linkages into civil society and the actions of firms, except in a few very active cases, such as the partnership between Hessen and Emilia Romagna (Eisel et al., 1996). Large firms already operate in the global economy and have little interest in small-scale cross-border initiatives, while small firms lack the resources and contacts. Only where they are involved in specific projects with a tangible reward are they likely to participate actively in inter-regional initiatives. Inter-regional co-operation is a learning process and rapid results should not be expected.

European integration and regionalism have much in common. Both are impelled by a combination of economic/functional forces and political motivations, which combine to produce further dynamics. Like regions, Europe represents an unstructured political space, sectorally divided. There are numerous pressure points for exerting influence but not all are equally effective. Regional governments and other interests have been in a learning process, trying a variety of strategies to see what works best. So far there is no one formula for success and regions are aiming at a moving target, since Europe itself has been evolving so rapidly and continues to do so. Once again, it would be a mistake to pitch regions against the state in a necessarily antagonistic relationship, or assume that, if either Europe or the regions are gaining power, the states must be losing it. Rather, we are seeing an interpenetration of territorial policy spaces, as Europe is increasingly regionalized, regions are europeanized, and the state is both regionalized and europeanized.

8. Conclusion

DO REGIONS MATTER?

The easiest conclusions to write are those with the most sensationalist message. It would be immensely gratifying to write that the European state system was being overturned by the rise of regions. Slightly less gratifying but equally easy would be to fall back on the certainties of 'realist' theory and affirm that the nation state was, and ever shall be, the sole basis for authority and public policy in Europe. What emerges from this overview is more subtle and elusive. States have never, except in the minds of Jacobin enthusiasts and realist dogmatists, been the sole basis of political authority and action. Territorial politics has always been present and has never fitted easily into the procrustean bed of the nation state. In the present era, states continue to maintain a formidable arsenal of powers and resources, yet there are changes taking place, regions are emerging and politics is being reshaped. The emergence of regions has been traced, looking at two forces, the functional logic of economic change and public policy, and the political dynamics within the regions themselves. History shapes these trends, but does not determine them, as historical materials can be used, reinterpreted and even invented. These have produced varied outcomes in different places. Here we have a serious problem in the study of comparative territorial politics. Since the focus of the enquiry is on combinations of effects in different places, everywhere is unique and systematic comparison is impossible. That is why in this book I have examined general trends and then illustrated them by reference to specific examples, avoiding the temptation to make sweeping generalizations about the new territorial politics.

I think that I have shown that regions do matter, that territorial politics is restructuring, but that the nation state is here to stay for the time being. The old systems of territorial accommodation based on the nation-state have been eroded by social and economic change, more dramatically in

184

some states than in others, and new systems are slowly emerging. The new territorial politics is focused less on territorial management and national integration, and more on territorial competition, within national arenas but also within Europe and the wider market. This process is less sensational when examined in the light of European historical experience, in which the meaning of territory has continually been redefined and states have taken successive forms. While it is too early to talk of a new Hanseatic Europe or a return to the mediaeval order, history does teach us that state forms are contingent and temporary.

Regions matter because they have become a key level in functional transformation, notably as a nexus of interdependencies. The transformation of the state has affected not only the relationship between government and civil society, but also the territorial expression of this. Hierarchical systems of territorial government, with a rigid demarcation of competences, characteristic of eras of limited government and stability, have long since given way to complex systems of interdependence and intergovernmental policy making as new problems arise which do not correspond to the functional divisions of government. Dente (1997) characterizes this as a transition from an era in which both the problem and the solution are known, to one in which the problem is known but the solution is to be found. In the 1990s, we have experienced a further transition, to an era in which neither the nature of problems nor solutions are fully known, and in this context there is a premium on experimentation and even organizational redundancy (Dente, 1997). Regions and federal units, competing not only with each other for economic resources in the market, but also with other levels of government in the provision of solutions to policy problems, are one reflection of this.

Regions matter politically, as they constitute a meeting place and an arena for negotiation of functional and territorial systems of action, in economics, society and politics. They provide, in many instances, a basis for identity, especially where they possess their own language, culture or strong historical traditions. Regions may provide a framework for political mobilization, and they are emerging as a system of government. Finally, they are in many cases constituting themselves as actors in state and European arenas, where a development coalition has been able to formulate a regional interest and its own project. These meanings of regionalism are diverse and do not always coincide. Where they do, we have strong regionalism; elsewhere the territorial principle is reflected at other levels or not articulated at all. Regionalism is not, for this reason, to be dismissed, any more than cities or nation states should be dismissed as mere reifications of complex phenomena. Thinking about the future must be more speculative.

THE FUTURE

The future of the regions, like their past, will depend on developments in the state system, in Europe and in the regions themselves. The new context has changed the political economy of regionalism in important ways. Dependency on the state has given way to more complex patterns of dependency on the state, the global market and the European Union. Of these, dependency on the state remains primary as fiscal transfers within states dwarf those at the European level and are likely to continue to do so (Davezies, 1997). State monetary and fiscal policies are still the main public policy influence on well-being. Yet all this could change should Europe move to economic and monetary union, with a single currency and, effectively, a single monetary and fiscal policy regime. In that case, some regions, especially strong regions in weak states, might consider the state shell redundant and seek independence of some sort within the EU. The scenario is the subject of much debate in Belgium and has been evoked in Spain, while the Scottish National Party already favours independence in Europe. This will not happen purely because of economic change. It is unlikely, for instance, that any German Länder or French regions will seek national independence. The preconditions are the existence of a territorial fault line within the state, an organized nationalist movement, and a rather weak state without the capacity effectively to resist or to present an attractive pole of identity.

Economic and monetary union would also deprive states of some of their remaining instruments for managing their spatial economies and coping with asymmetric shocks. Given the economic disparities within the single currency area — much larger than those within any member state — this would encourage demands for more active regional policy at the EU level, paralleling the demand for more attention to unemployment and social issues. At the same time, the stronger and more dynamic regions, faced with the disciplines of competition within the monetary union, would seek to limit their liabilities towards their own poor compatriots and seek to escape to some degree from the national frame. This scenario has been rehearsed in Flanders as well as in Northern Italy.

Another possibility is economic and monetary union only for a core of central countries (Pintarits, 1995; Keating and Pintarits, 1997) with some countries (the United Kingdom, Denmark, Sweden) opting out for political reasons and others (like Italy, Spain and Portugal) failing to qualify. This could extend to a Europe of concentric circles, with the outer circles, including the countries of central and eastern Europe, ever less tightly integrated. In this case the boundary between those inside the single currency area and those outside it could be a source of tension, with strong regions in the 'outs' (such as northern Italy) and those with national aspirations (like Scotland, Catalonia and the Basque Country) seeking membership of the core, thus potentially breaking with their host states. Further out, tensions could arise in Poland, between western regions seeking closer links with the EU core, and eastern areas more inclined to protectionism.

An alternative scenario is for the collapse of the single currency plans in the face of popular resistance and mass unemployment. In this case, a renationalization of territorial politics is likely. Active EU regional policy will no longer be needed as a compensation for market integration, and this could be returned to the member states, while regional movements focus their attention on national capitals.

Political developments within the regions themselves are likely to continue to be very diverse. Over recent years, we have seen region- and nation-building projects in various partes of Europe, the former including German Länder, Spanish autonomous communities and some of the French regions, the latter including Scotland, Catalonia, the Basque Country and Flanders. The ultimate goals of many of these projects are often unspecified, apart from the search for ever more autonomy and increased policy capacity. These movements will not go away, but states may find it difficult to accommodate them without building a new model of the state.

THE REGIONAL STATE

The new regionalism, along with developments in Europe and the global economy, is transforming the state as a system of action and mechanism for making and implementing public policy. The constitutional implications of this are less clear. There is a trend to territorial decentralization and regional governments, experienced in France, Spain, Belgium and Germany, and now extending to Italy and the United Kingdom. We might interpret this as the triumph of the federal principle, a European dream going back to the last century or further, with three levels of government: Europe, the state and the region; but the emerging phenomenon is too complex to fit into traditional models of federalism, even in their European form. Regions are not emerging everywhere, so that a European-wide 'third level' is not a possibility; already the juxtaposition of strong regions with mere local governments in the Committee of the Regions is causing problems. Where regions exist, they differ greatly in their nature, from the French functional/planning regions to the general-purpose governments of the German Länder; from administrative creations to historic nations; from the massive North Rhine-Westphalia, to uniprovincial Spanish autonomous communities. Even within states, there is a huge disparity in the size, constitutional status and social reality of regions. So if there is to be a new model of the state, it is likely to be asymmetrical, a national and European mosaic more akin to the pre-modern Europe than the uniform nation state inherited from the nineteenth century. Already there are trends to asymmetry in Spain, the United Kingdom and even France, with its special status for Corsica.

Such a differentiated political order will solve some problems, but raise others. By tailoring institutions more closely both to the emerging functional systems, regions can increase policy performance. By matching them to a sense of popular identity, they can enhance democratic efficacy and overcome the alienation from government which characterizes modern Europe. This, however, requires that the functionally effective units correspond to the sense of popular identity; sometimes they do and sometimes not. Regional devolution and institutions tailored to specific needs can also help recognize the multiple identities of individuals and groups, which are a feature of contemporary reality, and defuse conflicts over nationalism and the control of space, as has happened in Spain and, perhaps less successfully, in Belgium. By strengthening smaller units, it can also bring government closer to the citizen, encourage participation and foster policy innovation and experimentation.

On the other hand, such a variable-geometry state and Europe would increase the complexity of government, making it less comprehensible to the citizen and increasing the power of political brokers, able to operate in and span the diverse systems of action. Only a strengthening of democratic control by territorial governments and assemblies can counteract the tendency for policy to disappear into obscure networks, dominated by functional specialists. This is why the functional criteria for delimiting policy systems should never be determinate; nor should it, as opposed to a sense of political community, determine the territorial boundaries of regions. A variable-geometry Europe would also risk exacerbating inequalities, as rich regions and those which are best equipped politically and institutionally, took most advantage of the situation. In a political free market, with unbridled competition among regions, within a neo-liberal trading order — as envisaged by market regionalists like Ohmae (1995) — the result would be perilous for social solidarity both within and between regions. An asymmetrical political order also raises questions about the equality of citizen rights and liberties, previously secured by the nation state. Only a strengthened European political and social space could provide a forum in which to address these issues and mobilize resources to deal with them. This ties in closely with the continuing argument between exponents of a neo-liberal Europe and those pressing for a more social vision (Hooghe, 1997). So once again the fortunes of the regions and Europe are inextricably linked.

Appendix 1. Allocation of Functions to Regional Governments

Germany

Functions retained by Federation
Exclusive Powers:
foreign affairs and defence;
citizenship in the Federation;
freedom of movement, passport matters, immigration, emigration and
    extradition;
currency, weights and measures, time standards;
unity of customs and trading area, foreign trade and commerce;
federal railways and air transport;
posts and telecommunications;
legal status of Federation employees;
industrial property rights, copyrights and publishing law;
co-operation between the Federation and the Länder on police, protec-
    tion of the constitution and matters which endanger the foreign
    interests of the Federation, and establishment of the Federal Criminal
    Police Office;
statistics for federal purposes.

Concurrent powers
civil law, criminal law, execution of sentences, organization of courts
    and legal professions;
registration of births, deaths and marriages;
law of association and assembly;
residence and settlement of aliens;
weapons and explosives;

protection of German cultural assets against migration abroad;
refugee and expellee matters;
public welfare;
citizenship in the Länder;
war damage and reparations;
benefits to war-disabled and dependents of those killed in war;
war graves of soldiers and victims of war and despotism;
economic matters, including industry, commerce and finance;
nuclear energy;
labour law;
training and research;
expropriation;
public ownership of land, resources and means of production;
prevention of abuse of economic power;
agriculture and forestry;
land and housing;
communicable diseases;
hospitals;
protection of food, drink and tobacco, and of plants and animals;
shipping;
road traffic;
non-federal railways;
waste disposal, air quality and noise abatement.

Belgium

Functions retained by Federation:
economic union;
monetary union;
foreign policy;
national defence;
justice;
national police;
social security;
federal cultural institutions;
federal scientific institutions;
certain matters pertaining to population, the militia, civil protection, control of communes in German-speaking region or with a special language status, employment and work, and the civil service;
pensions;
most public health;
overseas development;
public debt;

fiscal matters, except those of communes and regions;

federal co-ordinating power in various matters such as scientific research.

Spain

Functions transferred to autonomous communities:

organization of own institutions;

local government boundaries and supervision of local government when
provided for by state law;

town and country planning and housing;

public works of interest to autonomous community;

internal railways;

ports for pleasure craft and non-commercial airports;

agriculture, in accordance with overall economic planning;

forestry and mountains;

environmental protection;

hydraulic works and canals of local interest;

inland fisheries and game;

local and regional fairs;

economic development, within overall national policies;

artisanship;

museums, libraries and musical conservatoires;

monuments of regional interest;

culture and regional languages;

tourism within the region;

sport;

social assistance;

health;

protection of community's own buildings in co-ordination with local
police.

Matters reserved for State:

intellectual and industrial property;

customs and external commerce;

monetary system, basic rules on credit, banking and insurance;

weights and measures, time standards;

general economic planning and co-ordination;

state finance and debt;

stimulation and general co-ordination of scientific research;

general regulation of health matters, pharmaceutical standards;

basic rules of social security system, without prejudice to role of autonomous communities in implementation;

basic rules on public administration and civil servants;

sea fisheries, without prejudice to role of autonomous communities in this;

mercantile marine, ports and airports of general interest, air traffic control, meteorological services;

railways and land transport crossing boundaries of autonomous communities;

hydraulic works affecting more than one autonomous community;

basic legislation on environmental protection, without prejudice to right of autonomous communities to impose stricter requirements;

public works of general interest or affecting more than one autonomous community;

basic rules for mining and energy;

arms and explosives;

basic rules on press, radio and television, without prejudice to role of autonomous communities;

defense of Spanish art and cultural works against exportation and exploitation, state museums, libraries and archives;

public security, without prejudice to right of autonomous communities to establish their own police forces where provided for in their statutes of autonomy;

regulation of academic and professional qualifications;

state statistics;

authorization of referendums.

Functions which may be devolved
Matters not reserved to the state may be devolved to autonomous communities proceeding under the fast track, and to other autonomous communities after a period of five years from their establishment.

Italy
The constitution of 1948 provided a list of powers to be devolved to the regions, as follows:

city limits;

urban and rural police;

fairs and markets;

public charities and health and hospital insurance;

vocational training;

local museums and libraries;

town planning;

tourism and hotels;

regional trams and motor services;
roads, acqueducts and public works of regional interest;
lake navigation and ports;
mineral and spa waters;
quarries and peat bogs;
hunting;
lake and river fisheries;
agriculture and forestry;
artisanship;
other matters indicated by constitutional laws.

Law 1124 of 1996 provided that the regions would have all functions and competences relative to looking after the interests and promoting the development of their respective communities and all localizable competences, except for:
foreign affairs and external trade (except for promotion);
defence, armed forces, weapons and explosives;
relations between the state and religious confessions;
civil status and registration of births, deaths and marriages;
electoral consultation and referendums (except regional referendums);
currency, monetary policy and equalization;
customs, protection of national borders, international disease control;
public order and security;
administration of justice;
posts and telecommunications;
production and distribution of energy at national level;
social security;
scientific research;
university education, school regulation, scholastic programmes, general
   organization of scholastic instruction and legal status of teaching
   personnel.
Also excluded are activities already attributed by the state to independent
   agencies; related to the planning, execution and maintenance of
   infrastructures designated by the state as of national interest; of
   national importance related to civil protection, defence, the environment, public health or historic heritage; functions aimed at the
   implementation of obligations derived from the Treaty on European
   Union or international agreements.

France

Competences devolved to regions
regional planning, planning contracts with state;
tourism;
natural environment;
definition of priorities in housing;
aid to enterprises, subject to national limits;
energy conservation and innovation;
regional transport planning;
small airports;
regional railway services;
canals and waterways;
fisheries;
planning and financing buildings of high schools and agricultural and
    fisheries colleges;
implementation, financing and regional planning of vocational training
    programmes;
heritage sites, regional museums and archives.

United Kingom

Proposed functions of Scottish Parliament
Legislative and administrative control of:
Health including the National Health Service in Scotland and public and
    mental health;
Education and training including pre-5, primary, secondary, further and
    higher education; and training policy and programmes;
Local government, social work and housing including local government
    structure and finance; social work; the voluntary sector; housing
    policy; area regeneration; building control; and the statutory planning
    framework;
Economic development and transport including responsibility for the
    economic development of Scotland; financial and other assistance
    and support for Scottish business and industry; promotion of trade
    and exports; inward investment; tourism; functions in relation to the
    energy sector; the administration of the European Structural Funds;
    and a range of road, rail, air, sea transport and inland waterways
    matters;
The law and home affairs including most civil and criminal law and the
    criminal justice and prosecution system including police and prisons;
    fire services; legal aid; parole, the release of life-sentence prisoners
    and alleged miscarriages of justice; certain Crown, church, ceremo-

nial and local government electoral matters; and civil defence and
emergency planning;

The environment including environmental protection policy and matters
relating to air, land and water pollution; the natural and built heritage;
and water supplies, sewerage, flood prevention and coastal protection;

Agriculture, fisheries and forestry including The Scottish Office's
existing responsibilities for promoting agriculture and fisheries
inScotland and those of the Forestry Commission in Scotland;

Sport and the arts including the Scottish Sports Council, the Scottish Arts
Council and the national institutions;

Research and statistics in relation to devolved matters.

Powers that may be transferred to Welsh Assembly
Administrative control in:
economic development;
agriculture, forestry, fisheries and food;
industry and training;
education;
local government;
health and personal social services;
housing;
environment;
planning;
transport and roads;
arts, culture, the Welsh language;
the built heritage;
sport and recreation.

Appendix 2. Regions in 6 Countries

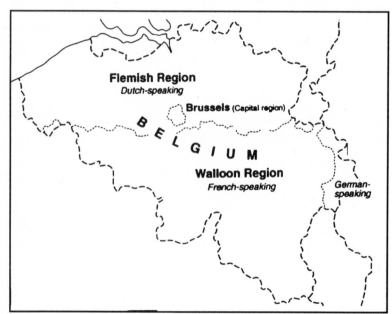

Bibliography

Aarebrot, F. (1982), 'Norway: Centre and Periphery in a Peripheral State', in S. Rokkan and D. Urwin (eds), *The Politics of Territorial Identity. Studies in European Regionalism*, London: Sage.

Abélès, M. (1989), *Tranquille jours en '89*, Paris: Odile Jacob.

Agnew, J. (1987), *Place and Politics. The Geographical Mediation of State and Society*, London: Allen and Unwin.

Agnew, J. (1990), 'From political methodology to geographical social theory? A critical review of electoral geography, 1860–1987', in R.J. Johnston, F.M. Shelley and P.J. Taylor (eds), *Developments in Electoral Geography*, London: Routledge.

Agnew, J. (1994), 'The dramaturgy of horizons: geographical scale in the "Reconstruction of Italy" by the new Italian political parties', *Political Geography*, 16.2, pp.99–121.

Agnew, J. (1996), 'Mapping Politics: how context counts in electoral geography', *Political Geography*, 15.2, pp.129–146.

Agnew, J. (1997a), 'Transnational Liberalism and the New Geopolitics of Power', International Studies Association, Toronto, March 1997.

Agnew, J. (1997b), 'European Landscape and Identity', in B. Graham (ed.), *Modern Europe: Place, Culture and Identity,* London: Edward Arnold.

Agnew, J. and S. Corbridge (1995), *Mastering Space. Hegemony, territory and international political economy,* London: Routledge.

Agranoff, R. (1993), 'Intergovernmental Politics and Policy: Building Federal Arrangements in Spain', *Regional Politics and Policy*, 3.2, pp. 1–28.

Aja, E., J. Tornos, T. Font, J.M. Perulles and E. Albertí (1985), *El sistema jurídico de las comunidades autónomas*, Madrid: Tecnos.

Allardt, E. (1982), 'Reflections on Stein Rokkan's Conceptual Map of Europe', Stein Rokkan Lecture 1, Institute of Comparative Politics, University of Bergen.

Allum, P. (1973), *Politics and Society in Postwar Naples*, Cambridge: Cambridge University Press.

Almond, G. and S. Verba (1963), *The Civic Culture*, Princeton: Princeton University Press.

Amin, A. and N. Thrift (1994), 'Living in the Global', in A. Amin and N. Thrift (eds), *Globalization, Institutions, and Regional Development in Europe,* Oxford: Oxford University Press.

Amin, A. and J. Tomany (1995a), 'The Challenge of Cohesion', in A. Amin and J. Tomany (eds), *Behind the Myth of European Union. Prospects for Cohesion,* London: Routledge.

Amin, A. and J. Tomany, (1995b), 'The Regional Dilemma in a Neo-liberal Europe', *European Urban and Regional Studies*, 2.2, pp.171–88.

Anderson, B. (1983), *Imagined Communities: Reflections on the Origins and Spread of Nationalism*, London: Verso.

Anderson, J. (1992), *The Territorial Imperative. Pluralism, Corporatism and Economic Crisis,* Cambridge: Cambridge University Press.

Anderson, J. (1996), 'Germany and the Structural Funds. Unification Leads to Bifurcation', in L. Hooghe (eds), *Cohesion Policy and European Integration*, Oxford: Clarendon.

Anderson, P. (1994), 'The Invention of the Region, 1945–1990', *EUI Working Paper EUF No. 94/2*, Florence: European University Institute.

André, C., J-F. Drevet and E. Landaburu (1989), 'Regional Consequences of the Internal Market', *Contemporary European Affairs* 1.1–2, pp.205–14.

Armstrong, H. (1995), 'The Role and Evolution of European Community Regional Policy', in B. Jones and M. Keating (eds), *The European Union and the Regions*, Oxford: Clarendon.

Bachtler, J. (1993), 'Regional Policy in the 1990s. The European Perspective', in R.T. Harrison and M. Hart (eds), *Spatial Policy in a Divided Nation*, London: Jessica Kingsley.

Bachtler, J. (1997), 'New Dimensions in Regional Policy in Western Europe', in M. Keating and J. Loughlin (eds), *The Political Economy of Regionalism*, London: Frank Cass.

Badie, B. (1995), *La fin des territoires. Essai sur le désordre international et sur l'utilité sociale du respect,* Paris: Fayard.

Bagnasco, A. and M. Oberti (1997), 'Le trompe-oeil des régions en

Italie', in P. Le Galès and C. Lequesne (eds), *Les paradoxes des régions en Europe*, Paris: La Découverte.

Balme, R. (1995), 'French Regionalization and European Integration: Territorial Adaptation and Change in a Unitary State', in B. Jones and M. Keating (eds), *The European Union and the Regions*, Oxford: Clarendon.

Balme, R. (1996), 'Introduction. Pourquoi le gouvernement change-t-il d'échelle?', in R. Balme (ed.), *Les politiques du néo-régionalisme*, Paris: Economica.

Balme, R. (1997), 'La région française comme espace d'action publique', in P. Le Galès and C. Lequesne (eds), *Les paradoxes des régions en Europe*, Paris: La Découverte.

Balme, R. and L. Bonnet (1994), 'From Regional to Sectoral Policies: The Contractual Relations Between the State and the Regions in France, *Regional Politics and Policy*, 4.3, pp.51–71.

Balme, R., S. Brouard and F. Burbaud (1996), 'La coopération inter-régionale atlantique et la genèse de l'espace européen', in R. Balme (ed.), *Les politiques du néo-régionalisme*, Paris: Economica.

Balme, R. and B. Jouve (1996), 'Building the Regional State: Europe and Territorial Organization in France, in L. Hooghe (ed.), *Cohesion Policy and European Integration*, Oxford: Clarendon.

Balme, R., P. Garraud, V. Hoffman-Martinot and E. Ritaine (1994), *Le territoire pour politiques: variations européennes*, Paris: l'Harmattan.

Balsom, D. and B. Jones (1984), 'The Faces of Wales', in I. McAllister and R. Rose, *The Nationwide Competition for Votes. The 1983 British Election*, London: Frances Pinter.

Barbera, A. (1985), '1970–85; como superare le insufficienze del decentramento', *Democrazia e diritto*, XXV.1, pp.41–49.

Barucci, P. (1974), 'Introduzione', in P. Barucci (ed.), *Il Meridionalismo dopo la ricostruzione, 1948–57*, Milan: Guiffré.

Bassand, M. (1991), 'Introduction' in M. Bassand (ed.), *Identité et développement régional*, Berne: Peter Lang.

Beaufays, J. (1985), *Théorie du régionalisme*, Brussels: S.Story-Scientia.

Begg, I. and D. Mayes (1993) 'Cohesion, Convergence and Economic and Monetary Union in Europe', *Regional Studies*, 27.2, pp.149–65.

Begg, I., M. Lansbury and D.G. Mayes (1995), 'The case for decentralized industrial policy', in P. Cheshire and I. Gordon (eds) *Territorial Competition in an Integrating Europe*, Aldershot: Avebury.

Bennett, R.J. and G. Krebs (1994), 'Local Economic Development Partnerships: An Analysis of Policy Networks in EC–LEDA Local Employment Strategies', *Regional Studies*, 28.2, pp.119–140.

Benz, A. (1992), 'Redrawing the Map? The Question of Territorial

Reform in the Federal Republic', *German Politics*, 1.3, pp.38–57.

Benz, A. (1997), 'Les régions allemandes dans l'Union européenne: de la politique conjointe à la gouvernance polycentrique', in P. Le Galès and C. Lequesne (eds), *Les paradoxes des régions en Europe*, Paris: La Découverte.

Bergman, E., G. Maier and F. Tödtling (1991), 'Introduction', in E. Bergman, G. Maier and F. Tödtling (eds), *Regions Reconsidered. Economic Networks, Innovation and Local Development in Industrialized Countries*, London:Mansell.

Bernardy, A.A. (1930), *Rinascita Regionale*, Rome: Istituto Nazionale Fascista/ Libreria del Littorio.

Berthet, T. and J. Palard (1997), 'Culture politique réfractaire et décollage économique. L'exemple de la Vendée du Nord-Est', *Revue française de science politique*, 47.1, pp.29–48.

Bianchi, G., R.J. Grote and S. Pieracci, (1995), 'Dalla economica alla coesione istituzionale. Sussidiarietà funzionale e reti socio-istituzionali nelle politiche regionali', in G. Gorla and O.V. Colonna (eds), *Regioni e Sviluppo: Modelli, politiche e riforme*, Milan: Franco Angeli.

Biarez, S. (1989), *Le pouvoir local*, Paris: Economica.

Biorcio, R. (1991), 'La Lega come attore politico: dal federalismo al populismo regionalista', in R. Mannheimer (ed.), *La Lega Lombarda*, Milan: Feltrinelli.

Biorcio, R. (1997), *La Padania Promessa*, Milan: Il Saggiatore.

Bogdanor, V. and W. Field (1993), 'Lessons of History: Core and Periphery in British Electoral Behaviour, 1910–1992', *Electoral Studies*, 12.3, pp.203–224.

Bonenfant, T. (1992), 'Bretagne. Des campagnes électorales éclatées', in P. Habert, P. Perrineau and C. Ysmal (eds), *Le vote éclaté. Les élections régionales et cantonales des 22 et 29 mars 1992*, Paris: Presses de la Fondation Nationale des Sciences Politiques.

Bonora, P. (1984), *Regionalità. Il concetto di regione nell'Italia del secondo dopoguerra (1943–1970)*, Milan: Franco Angeli.

Borrás, S. (1993), 'The "Four Motors for Europe" and its Promotion of R&D Linkages. Beyond Geographic Coniguity in Interregional Agreements', *Regional Politics and Policy*, 3.3, pp.163–76.

Bosi, P. and G. Tabellini (1995), 'Il finanziamento di regioni ed enti locali', *Quaderni regionali*, XIV.1, pp.195–236.

Bourjol, M. (1969), *Les institutions régionales de 1789 à nos jours*, Paris: Berger-Levraut.

Brassinne, J. (1994), *La Belgique fédérale*, Brussels: CRISP.

Braudel, F. (1986), *L'identité de la France. Espace et Histoire*, Paris: Arthaud-Flammarion.

Bréchon, P. and B. Denni (1992), 'Rhône-Alpes. La naissance politique d'une région', in P. Habert, P. Perrineau and C. Ysmal (eds), *Le vote éclaté. Les élections régionales et cantonales des 22 et 29 mars 1992*, Paris: Presses de la Fondation Nationale des Sciences Politiques.

Brockliss, L. and D. Eastwood (1997), 'Introduction. A union of multiple identities', in L. Brockliss and D. Eastwood (eds), *A Union of Multiple Identities. The British Isles, c.1750 – c.1850*, Manchester: Manchester University Press.

Brown, A., D. McCrone and L. Paterson (1995), *Politics and Society in Scotland*, London: Macmillan.

Brunstein, W. (1988), *The Social Origins of Political Regionalism*, Berkeley: University of California Press.

Buglione, E. and G. France (1984), 'Skewed Fiscal Federalism in Italy: Implications for Public Expenditure Control', in A. Premchand and J. Burkhead (eds), *Comparative International Budgeting and Finance*, New Brunswick (USA): Transaction Books.

Buglione, E., C. Desideri, A. Ferrara, G. France, G. Meloni, V. Santantonio and V.V. Comandini (1994), 'Per un nuovo regionalismo', *Le Regioni*, XXII.5, pp.1337–87.

Bullman, U. (ed.) (1994), *Die Politik der dritten Ebene. Regionen im Europa der Union,* Baden-Baden: Nomos.

Bullman, U. and D.Eisel (1993) 'Europa der Regionen. Entwicklung und Perspectiven', *Aus Politik und Zeitgeschichte*, 21, pp.3–15.

Burch, M. and I. Holliday (1993), 'Institutional Emergence: The Case of the North West Region of England', *Regional Politics and Policy*, 3.2, pp.29–50.

Caciagli, M. (1977), *Democrazia Cristiana e Potere nel Mezzogiorno. Il sistema democristiano a Catania*, Rimini: Guaraldi.

Camagni, R. (1992) 'Development Scenarios and Policy Guidelines for the Lagging Regions in the 1990s', *Regional Studies* 26.4, pp. 361–74.

Camilleri, J. and J. Falk (1992), *The End of Sovereignty? The Politics of a Shrinking and Fragmenting World*, Aldershot: Edward Elgar.

Cappellin, R. (1995a), 'Una politica regionale nazionale "orientata al mercato" tra i nuovi modelli organizzativi e federalismo', in G. Gorla and O.V. Colonna (eds), *Regioni e Sviluppo: Modelli, politiche e riforme*, Milan: Franco Angeli.

Cappellin, R. (1995b), 'Regional Development, Federalism and Interregional Cooperation', in H. Eskelinen and F. Snickers (eds), *Competitive European Peripheries*, Berlin: Springer.

Cardús, S. (1991), 'Identidad cultural, legitimidad política e interés económico', in *Construir Europa. Catalunya*, Madrid: Encuentro.

Caronna, (1970), *Guido Dorso el il Partito Meridonale Rivoluzionario,* Milan: Cisalpino-Goliardica.

Cassese, S. and L. Torchia (1993), 'The Meso Level in Italy', in L.J. Sharpe (ed.), *The Rise of Meso Government in Europe*, London: Sage.

Chauvel, L. (1995), 'Valeurs régionales et nationales en Europe', *Futuribles*, 200, pp.167-201.

Cheshire, P., R. Camagni, J.-P. Gaudemar and J. Cuadrado Roura (1991), '1957 to 1992: moving toward a Europe of regions and regional policy', in L. Rodwin and H. Sazanami (eds), *Industrial Change and Regional Economic Transformation. The experience of Western 'Europe*, London: Harper Collins.

Christiansen, T. (1996), 'Second Thoughts on Europe's "Third Level": The European Union's Committee of the Regions', *Publius*, 26.1, pp.93–116.

Chubb, J. (1982), *Patronage, Power and Poverty in Southern Italy. A tale of two cities*, Cambridge: Cambridge University Press.

CIRES (1996), Centro de Investigaciones sobre la Realidad Social, surveys *Identificación Supranacional,* Madrid: CIRES.

Ciuffoletti, Z. (1994), *Federalismo e regionalismo. Da Catteneo alla Lega*, Rome: Laterza.

Clark, M. (1996), 'Sardinia: Cheese and Modernization', in C. Levy (ed.), *Italian Regionalism. History, Identity and Politics,* Oxford: Berg.

Clément, R. (1988), 'Les élections municipales. Une démarche unitaire conforme aux intérêts des habitants', *Economie et Politique*,140, pp.46–9.

Collinge, M. (1987), 'Le sentiment d'appartenance: une identité fluctuante', *Cahiers du CACEF*,130, pp.7–23.

Commission des Communautés Européenes (1991) *Les Régions dans les Années 90. Quatrième rapport périodique sur la situation et l'évolution socio-économique des régions de la Communauté*, Luxembourg: Office for Official Publications of the European Community.

Commissione Parlamentare per le Riforme Costituzionali (1997), *Progetto di legge constituzionale*, Rome: Camera dei Deputati, no.3931, Senato della Repubblica, no.2583, 30 June 1997.

Conze, W. (1962), 'The German Empire', in *The New Cambridge Modern History. Vol. XI. Material Progress and World-Wide Problems, 1870–1898*, Cambridge: Cambridge University Press.

Courchene, T. (1995), *Celebrating Flexibility: An Interpretative Essay on the Evolution of Canadian Federalism*, C.D. Howe Institute, Benefactors Lecture, 1994, Montreal.

Crowther-Hunt, Lord and A.T. Peacock (1973), Royal Commission on the Constitution, 1969–1973 (Kilbrandon Commission), *Memorandum of Dissent, volume 11, Cmnd.5460–1*, London: Her Majesty's Stationery Office.

Crozier, M. and E. Friedberg (1977), *L'acteur et le système. Les contraintes de l'action collective,* Paris: Seuil.

Cuadrado Roura, J. (1981), 'La política regional en los planes de desarrollo', in R. Acosta España (ed.), *La España de las Autonomías* Tomo 1, Madrid: Espasa-Calpe.

Daalder, H. (1981), 'Consociationalism, center and periphery in the Netherlands', in P. Torsvik (ed.), *Mobilization, center-periphery structures and nation-building, A volume in commemoration of Stein Rokkan*, Bergen: Universitetsforlag.

Davezies, L. (1997), 'Interregional Transfers from Central Government Budgets in European Countries. A Fragmented Cohesion Process?, Conference on *Territorial Politics in Europe: A Zero-Sum Game?*' Robert Schuman Centre, European University Institute, Florence, April 1997

Davis, J.A. (1996), 'Changing Perspectives on Italy's "Southern Problem"', in C. Levy (ed.), *Italian Regionalism. History, Identity and Politics,* Oxford: Berg.

De Castro Ruano, J.L. (1994), *La emergente participación política de las regiones en el proceso de construcción europea*, Vitoria: Instituto Vasco de Administración Pública.

De La Granja, J.L (1995), *El nacionalismo vasco: un siglo de historia*, Madrid: Tecnos.

De Rynck, F. (1994), 'Belgio. Il case della regione delle Fiandre', in F. Merloni and A. Bours (eds), *Amministrazione e Territorio in Europa. Una ricerca sulla geografia amministrativa in sei paesi*, Bologna: Il Mulino.

De Rynck, S. (1997), 'Culture civique et rendement institutionnel: les régions belges', in P. Le Galès and C. Lequesne (eds), *Les paradoxes des régions en Europe*, Paris: La Découverte.

De Rynck, S. and R. Maes (1995), 'Belgium: Regions, Communities and

Subregional Authorities in the Single European Market', in J.J. Hesse (ed.), *Regions in Europe*, Baden-Baden: NOMOS.

De Smet, R., R. Evalenko and W. Fraeys (1958), *Atlas des élections belges 1919–1954*, Brussels: Institut de Sociologie Solvay.

De Wachter, W. (1996), 'La Belgique d'aujourd'hui comme societé politique', in A. Dieckhoff (ed.), *Belgique. La force de désunion*, Paris: Editions Complexe.

De Winter, L. and P. Frognier (1997), 'L'évolution des identités politiques territoriales en Belgique durant la période 1975–1995', in S. Jaumain (ed.), *La réforme de l'Etat... et après?*, Brussels: Presses de l'Université de Bruxelles.

de Witte, B. (1992), 'Surviving in Babel? Language Rights and European Integration', *Israel Yearbook on Human Rights* 21, pp.103–26.

Dearlove, J. (1979), *The reorganisation of British local government. Old orthodoxies and a new perspective*, Cambridge: Cambridge University Press.

Deeg, R. (1996), 'Economic Globalization and the Shifting Boundaries of German Federalism', *Publius*, 26.1, pp.27–52.

Dente, B. (1985), *Governare la frammentazione,* Bologna: Il Mulino.

Dente, B. (1997), 'Federalismo e politiche pubbliche', in A. Martinelli (ed.), *Terzo rapporto sulle priorità nazionali*, Milan: Fondazione Rosselli and Mondadori.

Desideri, C. (1995), 'Italian Regions in the European Community', in B. Jones and M. Keating (eds), *The European Union and the Regions*, Oxford: Clarendon.

Desideri, C. and V. Santantonio (1996), 'Building a Third Level in Europe: Prospects and Difficulties in Italy', *Regional and Federal Studies*, 6.2, pp.96–116.

Deutsch, K. (1966), *Nationalism and Social Communication. An Inquiry into the Foundations of Nationality,* Cambridge, MA: MIT Press.

Deutsch, K. (1969), *Nationalism and Its Alternatives,* New York: Knopf.

Dicey, A.V. and R.S. Rait (1920), *Thoughts on the Union between England and Scotland*, London: Macmillan.

Dogan, M. (1967), 'Political Cleavage and Social Stratification in France and Italy', in S.M. Lipset and S. Rokkan, *Party Systems and Voter Alignments*, New York: Free Press.

Drevet, J.-F. (1991), *La France et l'Europe des régions*, Paris: Syros.

Drèze, J. (1993), 'Regions of Europe', *Economic Policy*, 17, pp.265–308.

Dunford, M. (1988), *Capital, the State and Regional Development,*

London: Pion.

Dunford, M. (1994), 'Winners and Losers: the new map of economic inequality in the European Union', *European Urban and Regional Studies*, 1.2, pp.95–114.

Dunford, M. and G. Kafkalas (1992), 'The global–local interplay, corporate geographies and spatial development strategies in Europe', in M. Dunford and G. Kafkalas (eds), *Cities and Regions in the New Europe* (London: Belhaven).

Dupoirier, E. (1994), 'The First Regional Political Elites in France (1986–1992): A Profile', *Regional Politics and Policy*, 4.3, pp.25–32.

Dupoirier, E. and B. Roy (1995), 'Le fait régional en 1994', *Annuaire des Collectivités Locales, 1995*, Paris: Librairies Techniques.

Durand, J.-J. (1995), *L'Europe de la Démocratie chrétienne*, Paris: Editions Complexe.

Durkheim, E. (1964), *The Division of Labour in Society*, New York: Free Press.

Eisel, D., U. Bullman, H. Bennewitz, O. Dobrev, A. Grasse and B. Paeschke (1996), 'La deuxième vague de coopération inter-régionale en Allemagne: les partenariats de la Hesse', in R. Balme (ed.), *Les politiques du néo-régionalisme*, Paris: Economica.

Eley, G. (1986), *From Unification to Nazism. Reinterpreting the German Past*, London: Allen and Unwin.

Emerson, R. (1928), *State and Sovereignty in Modern Germany*, New Haven: Yale University Press.

Engel, C. (1993), *Regionen in der EG*, Bonn: Europa Union Verlag.

Engel, C. (1994), 'Regionen im Netzwerk europäischer Politik', in U. Bullman (ed.), *Die Politik der dritten Ebene. Regionen im Europa der Union*, Baden-Baden: Nomos.

Erbe, M. (1994), 'Die historische Dimension Regionaler Identität', in G. Bassong, M. Erbe, P. Frankenberg, C. Grivel and W. Lilli (eds), *Westeuropäische Regionen und Ihre Identität. Beitrage aus interdisziplinärer Sicht*, Mannheim: J&J.

Eurobarometer (1991), *Eurobarometer 36.0*, Luxembourg: Office of Publications of the European Communities.

Eurobarometer (1995), *Eurobarometer 43.1*, Luxembourg: Office of Publications of the European Communities.

Faure, A. (1994), 'Les élus locaux à l'épreuve de la décentralisation', *Revue française de science politique*, 44.3, pp.462–79.

Featherstone, K. and G. Yannopoulos (1995), 'The European Community and Greece: Integration and the Challenge to Centralism', in B. Jones and M. Keating (eds), *The European Union and the Regions*, Oxford: Clarendon.

Ferguson, A. (1966), *An Essay on the History of Civil Society, 1767* (Edinburgh: Edinburgh University Press).

Fieldhouse, E. (1995), 'Thatcherism and the changing geography of political attitudes, 1964–87', *Political Geography*, 14.1, pp.3–30.

Fitzmaurice, J. (1996), *The Politics of Belgium. A Unique Federalism*, London: C. Hurst.

Flogatis, S. (1979), *La notion de décentralisation en France, en Allemagne et en Italie*, Paris: R. Pichon et R. Durand-Auzias.

Flory, T. (1966), *Le mouvement régionaliste français*, Paris: Presses universitaires de France.

Foment del Treball Nacional, Comissió Obrero Nacional de Catalunya, Unió General de Treballadors de Catalunya (1993), *Un Nou Model Industrial. Situació i actuacions a l'àmbit de Catalunya.*

Frankenberg, P. and J. Shuhbauer (1994), 'Raumbezogene Identität in der Geographie', in G. Bossong, M. Erbe, P. Frankenberg, C. Grivel and W. Lilli (eds), *Westeuropäische Regionen und ihre Identität. Beitrage aus interdisziplinärer Sicht*, Mannheim: J&J.

Friedmann, J. (1991), 'The Industrial Transition: A Comprehensive Approach to Regional Development', in A. Bergman, G. Maier and F. Tödtling (eds), *Regions Reconsidered. Economic Networks, Innovation, and Local Development in Industrialized Countries*, London: Mansell.

Fry, M. (1987), *Patronage and Principle. A Political History of Modern Scotland*, Aberdeen: Aberdeen University Press.

Fukayama, F. (1995), *Trust: The Social Virtues and the Creation of Prosperity*, London: Hamish Hamilton.

Fullarton, B. and A. Gillespie, (1988), 'Transport and Telecommunications', in W. Molle and R. Cappelin (eds) *Regional Impact of Community Policies in Europe*, Aldershot: Gower.

Galasso, G. (1978), *Passato e presente del meridionalismo*, Naples: Guida.

Ganci, M. (1978), *La nazione siciliana*, Naples: Storia di Napoli e della Sicilia.

Garaud, P. (1992), 'Le kaléidescope des candidatures et des campagnes', in P. Habert, P. Perrineau and C. Ysmal (eds), *Le vote éclaté. Les élections régionales et cantonales des 22 et 29 mars 1992*, Paris: Presses de la Fondation Nationale des Sciences Politiques.

García Barbancho, A. (1979), *Disparidades Regionales y Ordenación del Territorio*, Barcelona: Ariel.

Garofoli, G. (1991), 'Local Networks, Innovation and Policy in Italian Industrial Districts', in E. Bergman G. Maier and F. Tödtling (eds), *Regions Reconsidered. Economic Networks, Innovation and Local Development in Industrialized Countries*, London: Mansell.

Garside, P. and M. Hebbert (eds) (1989), *British Regionalism 1900– 2000*, London: Mansell.

Gerstlé, J. (1992), 'La région prise entre nation et département', in P. Habert, P. Perrineau and C. Ysmal (eds), *Le vote éclaté. Les élections régionales et cantonales des 22 et 29 mars 1992*, Paris: Presses de la Fondation Nationale des Sciences Politiques.

Giard, J. and J. Scheibling (1981), *L'enjeu régional*, Paris: Messidor/ Editions Sociales.

Goguel, F. (1970), *Géographie des élections françaises sous la troisième et la quatrième république*, Paris: Armand Colin.

Good, M. Hoover (1976), *Regional Reform in Italy: The Politics of Subnational Reorganization*, Providence, Rhode Island: PhD thesis, Brown University.

Goodin, R. and H.-D. Klingemann (1996), 'Political Science: The Discipline', in R. Goodin and H.-D. Klingemann (eds), *A New Handbook of Political Science*, Oxford: Oxford University Press.

Gore, C. (1984), *Regions in question: space, development theory and regional policy*, London: Mansell.

Gottman, J. (ed.) (1980), *Centre and Periphery. Spatial Variations in Politics*, Beverly Hills: Sage.

Gourevitch, P. (1978), 'Reforming the Napoleonic State: The Creation of Regional Governments in France and Italy', in S. Tarrow and P.J. Katzenstein (eds), *Territorial Politics in Industrial Nations*, New York and London: Praeger.

Gramsci, A. (1978a), 'Some aspects of the southern question', in Q. Hoare (ed.), *Antonio Gramsci. Selections from Political Writings (1921–1926)*, London: Lawrence and Wishart.

Gramsci, A. (1978b), 'Operai e contadini', from *L'Ordine Nuovo*, 3 January 1920, reprinted in V. Lo Curto (ed.), *La questione meridionale*, 2nd edition, Florence: G. D'Anna.

Granovetter, M. (1973), 'The Strength of Weak Ties', *American Journal of Sociology*, 78, pp.1360–80.

Grivel, C. (1994), 'Identitatsräume', in G. Bossong, M. Erbe, P. Frankenberg, C. Grivel and W. Lilli (eds), *Westeuropäische Regionen und ihre Identität. Beitrage aus interdisziplinärer Sicht*, Mannheim: J&J.

Grote, J. (1992), 'Diseconomies in Space: Traditional Sectoral Policies of the EC, the European Technology Community and Their Effects of Regional Disparities', *Regional Politics and Policy* 2. 1&2, pp.14–46.

Gruppo Lega Nord per la Padania independente, Senato della Repubblica (1996), *Le ragioni della Padania*, Foligno:author.

Guigni, M.G. (1996), 'Federalismo e movimenti sociali', *Rivista Italiana di Scienza Politica*, XXVI.1, pp.147–70.

Guillorel, H. (1981), 'France: Religion, periphery, state and nation-building', in P. Torsvik (ed.), *Mobilization, center–periphery structures and nation–building, A volume in commemoration of Stein Rokkan*, Bergen: Universitetsforlag.

Guillorel, H. (1991), 'The social bases of regionalism in France: the Breton case', in J. Coakley (ed.), *The Social Origins of Nationalist Movements. The Contemporary West European Experience*, London: Sage.

Habert, P., P. Perrineau and C. Ysmal (eds) (1992), *Le vote éclaté. Les élections régionales et cantonales des 22 et 29 mars 1992*, Paris: Presses de la Fondation Nationale des Sciences Politiques.

Hadjimichaelis, C. and N. Papamicos, (1991), '"Local" Development in Southern Europe: Myths and Realities', in E. Bergman, G. Maier and F. Tödtling (eds), *Regions Reconsidered. Economic Networks, Innovation and Local Development in Industrialized Countries*, London: Mansell.

Hagen, R.M., K. Johannessen, L. Marthinsen, E. Mikkelsen and H. Skram (1991), *Historik Atlas*, volume 15 of R.K. Mykland (ed.), *Norges Historie*, Oslo: J.W.Cappelens.

Haggard, S. and B. Simmons (1987), 'Theories of International Regimes', *International Organization*, 41.3, pp.491–511.

Hansen, T. and T. Bjørkland (1997), 'The Narrow Escape — Norway's No to the European Union', mimeo, University of Oslo.

Harvie, C. (1994), *The Rise of Regional Europe*, London: Routledge.

Harvie, C. (1995), *Scotland and Nationalism. Scottish Society and Politics, 1707–1994*, second edition, London: Routledge.

Hayward, J. (1969), 'From functional regionalism to functional representation in France: The Battle of Brittany', *Political Studies*, XV11.

Heath, A., J. Curtice, R. Jowell, G. Evans, J. Field and S. Witherspoon

(1991), *Understanding Political Change. The British Voter 1964–1987*, Oxford: Pergamon.

Hechter, M. (1975), *Internal Colonialism. The Celtic fringe in British national development, 1536–966*, London: Routledge and Kegan Paul.

Heiber, H. (1993), *The Weimar Republic*, Oxford: Blackwell.

Hernández, A. (1980), *Autonomía e integración en la segunda república*, Madrid: Encuentro.

Hobsbawm, E. and T. Ranger (eds), (1983), *The Invention of Tradition*, Cambridge: Cambridge University Press.

Hocking, B. (1997), 'Regionalism: an International Relations Perspective', in M. Keating and J. Loughlin (eds), *The Political Economy of Regionalism*, London: Frank Cass.

Hoffman, A. and H. Klatt (1992), *Die Bundesrepublik Deutschland. Eine kleine politische Landeskunde*, Munich: Aktuell.

Hogwood, B. (1995), 'Regional Administration in Britain since 1979: Trends and Explanations', *Regional and Federal Studies*, 5.3, pp. 267–91.

Hogwood, B. and M. Keating (eds) (1982), *Regional Government in England*, Oxford: Clarendon.

Holmes, M. and N. Reese (1995), 'Regions within a region: the paradox of the Republic of Ireland', in B. Jones and M. Keating (eds), *The European Union and the Regions*, Oxford: Clarendon.

Hooghe, L. (1991), *A Leap in the Dark: Nationalist Conflict and Federal Reform in Belgium*, Cornell University, Western Societies Program, occasional paper no. 27, Ithaca: Cornell University.

Hooghe, L. (ed.) (1996), *Cohesion Policy and European Integration. Building Multi-Level Governance*, Oxford: Clarendon.

Hooghe, L. (1997), 'The Structural Funds and Competing Models of European Capitalism', Conference on *Territorial Politics in Europe: A Zero-Sum Game?*, Robert Schuman Centre, European University Institute, Florence, April 1997.

Hooghe, L. and M. Keating (1994), 'The Politics of EU Regional Policy', *Journal of European Public Policy*, 1.3: 368–93.

Hopkins, W.J. (1996), *Regional Autonomy in the European Union*, PhD thesis, Faculty of Law, University of Sheffield.

Houthaeve, R. (1996), 'Spatial Planning in Flanders. Looking for Strengths and Weaknesses Through its Regional Approach', in J. Alden and P. Boland (eds), *Regional Development Strategies. A European Perspective*, London: Jessica Langley.

Indovina, F. (1973), 'Le forze sociali e l'uso dell'ente regionale', in E. Rotelli (ed.), *Dal Regionalismo alla Regione*, Bologna: Il Mulino.

Ingrao, P. (1973), 'Regioni per unire', in E. Rotelli (ed.), *Dal Regionalismo alla Regione*, Bologna: Il Mulino.

Institut de Ciènces Politiques i Socials (1995), *Sondeig d'Opinió, 1994*, Barcelona: author.

Iokamidis, P. (1996), 'EU Cohesion Policy in Greece: The Tension Between Bureaucratic Centralism and Regionalism', in L. Hooghe (eds), *Cohesion Policy and European Integration*, Oxford: Clarendon.

Jacquemain, M., R. Doutrelepont and M. Vendekeere (1990), 'Identités sociales et comportement électoral', *Bundel*, XXXII.1, pp.63–79.

Jacquemain, M., R. Doutrelepont and M. Vendekeere (1994), 'L'identité wallonne saisie par l'enquête. Une approche constructiviste de l'identité collective', *Bundel*, XXXVI.3/4, pp.343–60.

Jeffery, C. (1996a), 'Farewell the Third Level? The German Länder and the European Policy Process', *Regional and Federal Studies*, 6.2, pp.56–75.

Jeffery, C. (1996b), 'Regional Information Offices in Brussels and Multi-Level Governance in the EU: A UK–German Comparison', *Regional and Federal Studies*, 6.2, pp.183–203.

Jeffery, C. (1996c), 'Conclusions: Sub-National Authorities and "European Domestic Policy"', *Regional and Federal Studies*, 6.2, pp.204–19.

Jeffery, C. (1996d), 'The Territorial Dimension', in G. Smith, W.E. Paterson and S. Padgett (eds), *Developments in German Politics 2*, London: Macmillan.

Jeffery, C. (1997), 'The Decentralisation Debate in the UK: Role-Modell Deutschland?', *Scottish Affairs*, 19, pp.42–54.

Jiménez Blanco, J., M. Garcia Ferrando, E. Lopez Aranguren and M. Beltrán Villalva (1977), *La conciencia regional en España*, Madrid: Centro de Investigaciones Sociológicas.

Johansson, B. (1991), 'Economic Networks and Self-Organization', in E. Bergman, G. Maier and F. Tödtling (eds), *Regions Reconsidered. Economic Networks, Innovation, and Local Development in Industrialized Countries*, London: Mansell.

Johnston, R.J. (1985), *The Geography of English Politics*, London: Croom Helm.

Johnston, R.J. and C.J. Pattie (1997), 'The Region is not Dead: Long Live the Region — Personal Evaluations and Voting at the 1992 British General Election', *Space and Polity*, 1.1, pp.103–15.

Jones, B. (1997), 'Wales. A Developing Political Economy', in M. Keating and J. Loughlin (eds), *The Political Economy of Regionalism*, London: Frank Cass.

Jones, B. and M. Keating (eds) (1995), *The European Union and the Regions*, Oxford: Clarendon.

Jouve, B. (1997), 'France: From the Regionalized State to the Emergence of Regional Governance?', in M. Keating and J. Loughlin (eds), *The Political Economy of Regionalism*, London: Frank Cass.

Kantor, P. (1995), *The Dependent City Revisited. The Political Economy of Urban Development and Social Policy*, Boulder: Westview.

Kearney, R. (1997), *Postnationalist Ireland. Politics, Culture, Philosophy*, London: Routledge.

Keating, M. (1975a), *The Role of the Scottish MP*, PhD thesis, London: Council for National Academic Awards; and Glasgow: Glasgow College of Technology.

Keating, M. (1975b), 'The Scottish Local Government Bill', *Local Government Studies*, 4.

Keating, M. (1979), 'Is there a regional level of government in England?', *Studies in Public Policy*. no. 49 Glasgow: Centre for the Study of Public Policy, University of Strathclyde.

Keating, M. (1984), 'Labour's Territorial Strategy', in I. McAllister and R. Rose, *The Nationwide Competition for Votes. The 1983 British Election*, London: Frances Pinter.

Keating, M. (1985), 'The Rise and Decline of Micronationalism in Mainland France', *Political Studies*, XXXIII.1, pp.1–18.

Keating, M. (1986), 'Revendication et Lamentation. The Failure of Regional Nationalism in Languedoc', *Journal of Area Studies*, 14.

Keating, M. (1988), *State and Regional Nationalism. Territorial Politics and the European State*, London: Harvester-Wheatsheaf.

Keating, M. (1991a), *Comparative Urban Politics. Power and the City in the United States, Canada, Britain and France*, Aldershot: Edward Elgar.

Keating, M. (1991b), 'Local Economic Development Politics in France', *Journal of Urban Affairs*, 13.4, pp.443–59.

Keating, M. (1992a), 'Do the Workers Really Have No Country? Peripheral Nationalism and Socialism in the United Kingdom, France, Italy and Spain', in J. Coakley (ed.), *The Social Origins of Nationalist Movements*, London: Sage.

Keating, M. (1992b), 'Regional Autonomy in the Changing State Order: A Framework of Analysis', *Regional Politics and Policy*, 2.3, pp.45–

61.

Keating, M. (1993), 'The Politics of Economic Development. Political Change and Local Development Policies in the United States, Britain and France', *Urban Affairs Quarterly*, 28.3, pp.373–96.

Keating, M. (1995a), 'Size, Efficiency and Democracy: Consolidation, Fragmentation and Public Choice', in D. Judge, G. Stoker and H. Wolman (eds), *Theories of Urban Politics*, London: Sage.

Keating, M. (1995b), 'Local Economic Development. Policy or Politics?', in N. Walzer (ed.), *Local Economic Development. Incentives and International Trends*, Boulder: Westview.

Keating, M. (1996), *Nations against the State.The New Politics of Nationalism in Quebec, Catalonia and Scotland*, London: Macmillan.

Keating, M. (1997), 'The Political Economy of Regionalism', in M. Keating and. J. Loughlin (eds), *The Political Economy of Regionalism*, London: Frank Cass.

Keating, M. and D. Bleiman (1979), *Labour and Scottish Nationalism*, London: Macmillan.

Keating, M. and P. Hainsworth (1986), *Decentralisation and Change in Contemporary France*, Aldershot: Gower.

Keating, M. and L. Hooghe (1996), 'By-passing the Nation State? Regions in the EU Policy Process', in J.J. Richardson (ed.), *Policy Making in the European Union*, London: Routledge.

Keating, M. and B. Jones (eds) (1985), *Regions in the European Community*, Oxford: Clarendon.

Keating, M. and B. Jones (1995), 'Nations, Regions and Europe: The UK Experience', in B. Jones and M. Keating (eds), *The European Union and the Regions*, Oxford: Clarendon.

Keating, M. and S. Pintarits (1997), 'Regions and the European Union', *Comparative Social Research*.

Keeble, D., J. Offord and S. Walker (1988), *Peripheral Regions in a Community of Twelve Member States*, Luxembourg: Offices of Publications of the European Community.

Keohane, R. (1989), *International Institutions and State Power*, Boulder: Westview.

Kerremans, B. (1997), 'The Flemish Identity: Nascent or Existent?', *Res Publica*, XXXIX.2, pp.303–14.

Kerremans, B. and J. Beyers (1996), 'The Belgian Sub-National Entities in the European Union: Second or Third Level Players?', *Regional and Federal Studies*, 6.2, pp.41–55.

Kilbrandon (1973), Royal Commission on the Constitution, 1969–1973

(Kilbrandon Commission), *Report, volume 1, Cmnd.5460*, London: Her Majesty's Stationery Office.

King, R.L. (1987), 'Regional government: the Italian experience', *Environment and Planning C: Government and Policy*, 5, pp. 327–46.

Kohler-Koch, B. (1996), 'Regionen als Handlungseinheiten in der europäischen Politik', *Welt Trends*, 11, pp.7–35.

Kriesi, H. (1995), *Le système politique suisse*, Paris: Economica.

Kukawka, P. (1996), 'La Quadrige européen ou l'Europe par les régions', in R. Balme (ed.), *Les politiques du néo-régionalisme*, Paris: Economica.

Laffan, B. (1996), 'Ireland: A Region without Regions — the Odd Man Out?', in L. Hooghe (ed.), *Cohesion Policy and European Integration. Building Multi-Level Governance*, Oxford: Clarendon.

Lafont, R. (1967), *La révolution régionaliste*, Paris: Gallimard.

Lange, N. (1997), *Wirtschaftsinteressen im Spannungsfeld zwischen Regionalismus und europäischer Integration*, unpublished doctoral thesis, University of Mannheim.

Latouche, D. (1991), 'La stratégie québécoise dans le nouvel ordre économique et politique internationale', Commission sur l'avenir politique et constitutionnel du Québec, *Document de travail numéro 4* , Quebec: Commission.

Laurent, A. and C.-M. Wallon-Leducq (1992), 'La double inconstance. Partis, électeurs et double vote', in P. Habert, P. Perrineau and C. Ysmal (eds), *Le vote éclaté. Les élections régionales et cantonales des 22 et 29 mars 1992*, Paris: Presses de la Fondation Nationale des Sciences Politiques.

Le Bras, H. (1995), *Les Trois France*, Paris: Odile Jacob.

Le Galès, P. (1994), 'Regional Economic Policies: An Alternative to French Economic Dirigisme?', *Regional Politics and Policy*, 4.3, pp.72–91.

Le Galès, P. (1996), 'Régulation, gouvernance et territoire', Association française de science politique, Aix en Provence, April 1996.

Le Galès, P. (1997), 'Gouvernement et gouvernance des régions: faiblesses structurelles et nouvelles mobilisations', in P. Le Galès and C. Lequesne (eds), *Les paradoxes des régions en Europe*, Paris: La Découverte.

Lenoir, R. and J. Lesourne (eds), (1992), *Où va l'état?* Paris: Le Monde Editions.

Lepschy, A.L., G. Lepschy and M. Voghera (1996), 'Linguistic Variety in Italy', in C. Levy (ed.), *Italian Regionalism. History, Identity and*

Politics, Oxford: Berg.
Lilli, W. and R. Hartig (1995), 'Le rôle des aspects culturels et interactionnels dans la définition de l'identité régionale', *Sciences de la Societé,* 34, pp.125–35.
Lindley, P. (1982), 'The framework of regional planning, 1964–1980', in B. Hogwood and M. Keating (eds), *Regional Government in England,* Oxford: Clarendon.
Lindner, R. (1994), 'Einleitung', in R. Linder (ed.), *Die Wiederkehr des Regionalen. Uber neue Formen kultureller Identität,* Frankfurt: Campus.
Lipset, S.M. and S. Rokkan (1967), *Party Systems and Voter Alignments,* New York: Free Press.
Lopez-Aranguren, E. (1982), *La conciencia regional en el proceso autonómico español,* Madrid: Centro de Investigaciones Sociológicas.
Loughlin, J. (1994), 'Nation, State and Region in Western Europe', in L. Beckemans (ed.), *Culture: the Building-Stone of Europe 2002,* Brussels: Presses Interuniversitaires.
Loughlin, J. (1996), 'Representing the Regions in Europe: The Committee of the Regions', *Regional and Federal Studies,* 6.2, pp.147–165.
Loughlin, J. and S. Mazey (1994), 'Introduction', *Regional Politics and Policy,* 4.3, pp.1–9.
Loughlin. J. and B.G. Peters (1997), 'State Traditions, Administrative Reform and Regionalization', in M. Keating and J. Loughlin (eds), *The Political Economy of Regionalism,* London; Frank Cass.
Lucentini, E. de Sanctis (1996), 'Entrate Regionali', in *Annuario 1996 delle autonomie locali,* Rome: Edizioni delle autonomie locali.
Lyttleton, A. (1996), 'Shifting Identities: Nation, Region and City', in Levy, C. (ed.), *Italian Regionalism. History, Identity and Politics,* Oxford: Berg.
Mack Smith, D. (1986), *A History of Sicily,* London: Chatto and Windus.
Mackay, R.R. (1993), 'A Europe of the Regions: A Role for Nonmarket Forces?', *Regional Studies,* 27.5, pp. 419–431.
MacLaughlin, J. (1986), 'The political geography of "nation-building" and nationalism in social sciences: structural vs. dialectical accounts', *Political Geography Quarterly,* 5.4, pp.299–329.
Madariaga, J.A. (1995), 'Las regiones en la Unión Europea', *Revista Española de Derecho Constitucional,* 45, pp.85–131.
Maillat, D. (1991), 'The Innovation Process and the Role of the Milieu', in E. Bergman, G. Maier and F. Tödtling (eds), *Regions Reconsidered. Economic Networks, Innovation and Local Development in*

Industrialized Countries, London: Mansell.

Marchand, M.-J. (1995), 'La région et ses partenaires en matière d'intervention économique', *Annuaire des Collectivités Locales, 1995*, Paris: Librairies Techniques.

Mariuca, L. (1995), 'Relazione introduttiva', *Regione e Governo Locale*, XVI.4, pp.425–52.

Marks, G. (1992), 'Structural Policy in the European Community', in A. Sbragia (ed.), *Euro-Politics. Institutions and Policymaking in the 'New" European Community*, Washington: Brookings.

Marks, G. (1993), 'Structural Policy and Multilevel Governance in the European Union', in A. Cafruny and G. Rosenthal (eds), *The State of the European Community. The Maastricht Debates and Beyond*, Boulder: University of Colorado Press.

Marks, G. (1997), 'Territorial Identities in the European Union', mimeo, University of North Carolina at Chapel Hill.

Martel, P. (1994), 'Histoire d'Occitanie/ Histoires d'Occitanistes', in G. Bassong, M. Erbe, P. Frankenberg, C. Grivel and W. Lilli (eds), *Westeuropäische Regionen und Ihre Identität. Beitrage aus interdisziplinärer Sicht*, Mannheim: J&J.

Mawson, J., M.R. Martins and J. Gibney (1985), 'The Development of the European Community Regional Policy', in M. Keating and B. Jones (eds), *Regions in the European Community*, Oxford: Clarendon.

McAleavey, Paul (1993), 'The Politics of European Regional Development Policy: The EC Commission's Rechar Initiative and the Concept of Additionality' *Regional Politics and Policy* , 3.2, pp. 88–107.

McCrone, D. (1992), *Understanding Scotland. The Sociology of a Stateless Nation*, London: Routledge.

McKenzie, E. (1994), *Privatopia. Homeowner Associations and the Rise of Residential Private Government*, New Haven and London: Yale University Press.

Medina Guerrero, M. (1991), *Los regimenes financieros en la constitución de 1978*, Bilbao: Instituto Vasco de Administración Pública.

Medina Guerrero, M. (1992), *La incicendia del sistema de financiación en el ejercicio de las competencias de las comunidades autónomas*, Madrid: Centro de Estudios Constitucionales.

Mény, Y. (1982), 'Introduction' in Y. Mény (ed.), *Dix ans de régionalisation en Europe. Bilan et perspectives,* Paris: Cujas.

Merloni, F. (1985), 'Perché è in crisi il regionalismo', *Democrazia e Diritto*, 1, pp.59–81.

Midwinter, A. M. Keating and J. Mitchell (1991), *Politics and Public Policy in Scotland,* London: Macmillan.

Ministro per gli affari regionali (1982), *Rapporto 1982 sullo stato delle autonomie,* Roma: Istituto Poligrafico e Zecca dello Stato.

Mintzel, A. (1990), 'Political and Socio-economic Developments in the Postwar Era: The Case of Bavaria, 1945–1989', in K. Rohe (ed.), *Elections, Parties and Political Traditions. Social Foundations of German Parties and Party Systems, 1867–1987,* New York: Berg.

Mitchell, J. (1990), *Conservatives and the Union. A Study of Conservative Party Attitudes to Scotland,* Edinburgh: Edinburgh University Press.

Mitchell, J. (1996), *Strategies for Self-government. The Campaigns for a Scottish Parliament,* Edinburgh: Polygon.

Modica, E. (1972), *I Comunisti per le autonomie,* Rome: Edizioni per le autonomie e i poteri locali.

Molle, W., A. van Holst and H. Smit (1980), *Regional Disparity and Economic Development in the European Community,* Farnborough: Saxon House.

Molle, W. and R. Cappellin (eds) (1988), *Regional Impact of Community Policies in Europe,* Aldershot: Gower.

Mommsen, W. (1995), *Imperial Germany, 1867–1918. Politics, Culture and Society in an Authoritarian State,* London: Arnold.

Montero, J.R. and M. Torcal (1990), 'La opinión pública ante el estado de las autonomías: una visión panorámica', *Informe Pi i Sunyer sobre Comunidades Autónomas,* Barcelona: Civitas.

Morass, M. (1996), 'Austria: The Case of a Federal Newcomer in European Union Politics', *Regional and Federal Studies,* 6.2, pp.76–95.

Morata, F. (1987), *Autonomia regional i Integració Europea,* Barcelona: Generalitat de Catalunya.

Morata, F. (1995), 'Spanish Regions in the European Community', in B. Jones and M. Keating (eds), *The European Union and the Regions,* Oxford: Clarendon.

Morata, F. (1996), 'Barcelone et la Catalogne dans l'arène européenne', in R. Balme (ed.), *Les politiques du néo-régionalisme,* Paris: Economica.

Morata, F. (1997), 'The Euro-region and the C6 Network: The New Politics of Sub-national Co-operation in the West Mediterranean Area', in M. Keating and J. Loughlin (eds), *The Political Economy of Regionalism.* London: Frank Cass.

Morawitz, R. and W. Kaiser (1994), *Die Zusammenarbeit von Bund und*

Ländern bei Vorhaben der Europäischen Union, Bonn: Europa Union Verlag.

Moreno, L. (1997), *La federalización de España. Poder político y territorio*, Madrid: Siglo Veintiuno.

Morgan, K.O. (1980), *Rebirth of a Nation. Wales, 1880–1980*, Oxford: Oxford University Press.

Morgan, K. (1992), 'Innovating by networking: new models of corporate and regional development', in M. Dunford and G. Kafkalas (eds), *Cities and Regions in the New Europe* (London: Belhaven).

Morgan, K. (1995), 'The Learning Region. Institutions, Innovation and Regional Renewal', *Papers in Planning Research,* no. 157. Cardiff: Department of City and Regional Planning, University of Wales College of Cardiff.

Morton, D. and K. Robins (1995), *Spaces of Identity. Global media, electronic landscapes and cultural boundaries*, London: Routledge.

Mutti, A. (1996), 'Politiche di sviluppo per le regione meridionali', *Il Mulino*, XLIV.357, pp.83–97.

Némery, J.-C. (1993), 'Les institutions territoriales françaises à l'épreuve de l'Europe', in J.-C. Némery and S. Wachter, *Entre l'Europe et la décentralisation. Les institutions territoriales françaises,* Paris: DATAR/éditions de l'aube.

Nevin, E.T. (1990), 'Regional Policy', in A.M. El-Agraa (ed.) *The Economics of the European Community,* 3rd edn., New York: Philip Allan.

Norton, A. (1994), *International Handbook of Local and Regional Government. A Comparative Analysis of Advanced Democracies*, Aldershot: Edward Elgar.

Ohmae, K. (1995), *The End of the Nation-State: The Rise of Regional Economies*, New York: The Free Press.

OIP (1994), Observatoire Interrégional du Politique, 'Enquête OIP 1994', in *L'Identité des Régions en France et en Europe, Actes de la journée d'étude organisée par l'Observatoire Interrégional du Politique et la Région Midi-Pyrénées*, Toulouse, 26 January, 1996, Toulouse: Privat.

OIP (1995), Observatoire Interrégional du Politique, *L'identité des régions en France et en Europe*, Toulouse: Privat.

OIP (1997), Observatoire Interrégional du Politique, *Enquête OIP 1997. Le fait régional*, Paris: OIP.

Oltra, B., F. Mercadé and F. Hernández (1981), *La ideología nacional catalana*, Barcelona: Anagrama.

Oneto, G. (1997), *L'invenzione della Padania. La rinascita della communità più antica d'Europa,* Ceresola: Foedus.

Osiander, A. (1994), *The States System of Europe, 1640–1990. Peacemaking and the Conditions of International Stability,* Oxford: Clarendon.

Paddison, R. (1983), *The Fragmented State. The Political Geography of Power,* Oxford: Blackwell.

Page, E. (1995), 'Patterns and Diversity in European State Development', in J. Hayward and E. Page (eds), *Governing the New Europe,* Cambridge: Polity.

Parisot, J.-C. (1996), 'La construction des identités régionales: l'exemple de la Picardie', *Annuaire des Collectivités Locales, 1996,* Paris: Librairies Techniques.

Pastori, G. (1980), 'Le regioni senza regionalismo', *Il Mulino,* 268, pp. 204–26.

Pastori, G. (1982), 'Gli studi di diritto amministrativo in materia regionale', *Le Regioni,* X.6.

Paterson, L. (1994), *The Autonomy of Modern Scotland,* Edinburgh: Edinburgh University Press.

Pattie, C. and R. Johnston (1995), '"It's not like that round here": Region, economic evaluations and voting at the 1992 British General Election', *European Journal of Political Research,* 28, pp.1–32.

Pelling, H. (1967), *Social Geography of British Elections, 1885–1910,* London: Macmillan.

Perrineau, P. (1992), 'La demande de renouvellement du système politique', in P. Habert, P. Perrineau and C. Ysmal (eds), *Le vote éclaté. Les élections régionales et cantonales des 22 et 29 mars 1992,* Paris: Presses de la Fondation Nationale des Sciences Politiques.

Petschen, S. (1993), *La Europa de las regiones,* Barcelona: Generalitat de Catalunya.

Piattoni, S. (1997), 'Local Political Classes and Economic Development. The Cases of Abruzzo and Puglia in the 1970s and 1980s', in M. Keating and J. Loughlin (eds), *The Political Economy of Regionalism,* London: Frank Cass.

Pintarits, S. (1995), *Macht, Demokratie und Regionen in Europa, Analysen und Szenarien der Integration und Desintegration,* Marburg: Metropolis.

Piore, M.J. and C.F. Sabel (1984), *The Second Industrial Divide. Possibilities for Prosperity,* New York: Basic Books.

Plan Urbain (1986), Commissariat général du plan, Délégation à l'aménagement du territoire et à l'action régionale (DATAR), *Mutations Economiques et Urbanisation*, Paris: Documentation Française.

Price, A., C. O'Torna and A. Wynne Jones (1997), *The Diversity Dividend. Language, Culture and Economy in an Integrated Europe*, Brussels: European Bureau for Lesser Used Languages.

Putnam, R. (1993), *Making Democracy Work. Civic Traditions in Modern Italy*, Princeton: Princeton University Press.

Putnam, R., R. Leonardi and R. Nanetti (1985), *La pianta e le radici. Il radicamento dell'istituto regionale nel sistema politico italiano*, Bologna: Il Mulino.

Ress, G. (1994), 'The Constitution and the Maastricht Treaty: Between Cooperation and Conflict', *German Politics*, 3.3, pp.47–74.

Rhodes, M. (ed.) (1995), *Regions and the New Europe*, Manchester: Manchester University Press.

Rhodes, R.A.W. (1996), 'The New Governance: Governing without Government', *Political Studies*, 44.4, pp.652–67.

Ritaine, E. (1989), 'La modernité localisée. Leçons italiennes sur le développement régional', *Revue française de science politique*, 39.2, pp.154–77.

Ritaine, E. (1994), 'Territoire et politique en Europe du sud', *Revue française de science politique*, 44.3, pp.75–98.

Ritaine, E. (1997), 'La capacité politique des régions en Europe du Sud', in P. Le Galès and C. Lequesne (eds), *Les paradoxes des régions en Europe*, Paris: La Découverte.

Ritter, G.A. (1980), *Wahlgeschichtliches Arbeitsbuch. Materialen zur Statistik des Kaiserreichs 1871–1918*, Munich: C.H. Beck.

Ritter, G.A. (1990), 'The Social Bases of the German Political Parties, 1867–1920', in K. Rohe (ed.), *Elections, Parties and Political Traditions. Social Foundations of German Parties and Party Systems, 1867–1987*, New York: Berg.

Ritter, G.A. and M. Niehuss (1991), *Wahlen in Deutschland, 1946–1991. Ein Handbuch*, Munich: C.H. Beck.

Roccella, A. (1996), 'La Chiesa ambrosiana di fronte al regionalismo', *Le Regioni*, XXIV.3, pp.575–98.

Rohe, K. (1990a), 'German Elections and Party Systems in Historical and Regional Perspective: An Introduction', in K. Rohe (ed.), *Elections, Parties and Political Traditions. Social Foundations of German Parties and Party Systems, 1867–1987*, New York: Berg.

Rohe, K. (1990b), 'Political Alignments and Realignments in the Ruhr,

1867–1987: Continuity and Change of Political Traditions in an Industrial Region', in K. Rohe (ed.), *Elections, Parties and Political Traditions. Social Foundations of German Parties and Party Systems, 1867–1987*, New York: Berg.

Rohe, K. (1992), *Wahlen und Wählertraditionen in Deutschland*, Frankfurt: Suhrkamp.

Rokkan, S. (1966), 'Electoral Mobilization, Party Competition and National Integration', in J. LaPalombara and M. Weiner (eds), *Political Parties and Political Development*, Princeton: Princeton University Press.

Rokkan, S. (1967), 'Geography, Religion and Social Class. Crosscutting Cleavages in Norwegian Politics', in S.M. Lipset and S. Rokkan (eds), *Party Systems and Voter Alignments*, New York: Free Press.

Rokkan, S. (1980), 'Territories, Centres, and Peripheries: Toward a Geoethnic–Geoeconomic–Geopolitical Model of Differentiation within Western Europe', in J. Gottmann (ed.), *Centre and Periphery. Spatial Variations in Politics,* Beverly Hills: Sage.

Rokkan, S. and D. Urwin (1982), 'Introduction: Centres and Peripheries in Western Europe', in S. Rokkan and D. Urwin (eds), *The Politics of Territorial Identity. Studies in European Regionalism*, London: Sage.

Rokkan, S. and D. Urwin (1983), *Economy, Territory, Identity. Politics of West European Peripheries,* London: Sage.

Rose, R. and D. Urwin (1975), 'Regional Differentiation and Political Unity in Western Nations', *Contemporary Political Sociology Series, 06–007*, London: Sage.

Rotelli, E. (1973), 'Dal regionalismo alla regione', in E. Rotelli (ed.), *Dal regionalismo alla regione*, Bologna: Il Mulino.

Ruffilli, R. (1980), 'La tradizione regionalista: crisi e rinnovamento', in M. Rosa (ed.), *Decentramento dello stato. Il caso italiano*, Rome: Città Nuova.

Sabel, C.F. (1993), 'Studied Trust: Building New Forms of Cooperation in a Volatile Economy', in R. Swedberg (ed.), *Explorations in Economic Geography*, New York: Russel Sage Foundation.

Sabetti, F. (1996), 'Path Dependency and Civic Culture: Some Lessons From Italy About Interpreting Social Experiments', *Politics and Society*, 24.1, pp.19–44.

Salerno, G. (1983), 'Governo, Parlamento, Regioni ed Enti Locali', *Annuario 1983 delle Autonomie Locali*, Rome: Edizioni delle Autonomie.

Salvi, S. (1996), *L'Italia non esiste*, Florence: Camunia.

Savelli, G. (1992), *Che cose vuole la Lega*, Milan: Longanesi.

Scharpf, F. (1988), 'The Joint-Decision Trap: Lessons from German Federalism and European Integration', *Public Administration*, 66, pp.239–78.

Scharpf, F. (1994), 'Community and Autonomy: Multi–level Policy–Making in the European Union', *Journal of European Public Policy*, 1.2, pp.219–42.

Schmidt, V. (1990), *Democratizing France. The Political and Administrative History of Decentralization*, Cambridge: Cambridge University Press.

Schmidtke, O. (1993), 'The Populist Challenge to the Italian Nation-State: The Lega Lombarda/Nord', *Regional Politics and Policy*, 3.3, pp.140–62.

Schmidtke, O. (1995), 'The Lega Nord — A Territorial Movement Beyond Regionalism', in N.A. Sørensen, *European Identities. Cultural Diversity and Integration in Europe since 1700*, Odense: Odense University Press.

Schonhardt-Bailey, C. (1991), 'Lessons in Lobbying for Free Trade in 19th Century Britain: To Concentrate or Not', *American Political Science Review*, 85.1, pp.37–58.

Scott, A.J. (1996), 'Regional Motors of the Global Economy', *Futures*, 28.5, pp. 391–411.

Scott, A.J. and M. Storper (1992), 'Industrialization and Regional Development', in A.J. Scott and M. Storper (eds), *Pathways to Industrialization and Regional Development*, London and New York: Routledge.

Senelle, R. (1990), 'Memo from Belgium', *Views and Surveys*, no.198, Brussels: Ministry of Foreign Affairs.

Sharpe, L.J. (1993), 'The European Meso; an appraisal', in L.J. Sharpe (ed.), *The Rise of Meso Government in Europe*, London: Sage.

Sked, A. (1989), *The Decline and Fall of the Habsburg Empire, 1815–1918*, London: Longman.

Smith, A. (1995), *L'Europe politique au miroir du local. Les fonds structurels et les zones rurales en France, en Espagne et au Royaume-Uni*, Paris: L'Harmattan.

Smith, A. (1997), 'L'échelon infrarégional: lieu privilégié des fonds structurels?', in P. Le Galès and C. Lequesne (eds), *Les paradoxes des régions en Europe*, Paris: La Découverte.

Smith, A.D. (1986), *The Ethnic Origins of Nations*, Oxford: Blackwell.

Snicker, J. (1997), *Cymru am Byth? Mobilising Welsh Identity, 1979–*

c.1994, unpublished D.Phil. thesis, University of Oxford.

Specht, E. (1898), *Die Reichstags-Wahlen von 1867 bis 1897*, Berlin: Carl Henmanns.

Spruyt, H. (1994), *The Sovereign State and Its Competitors*, Princeton: Princeton University Press.

Steinberg, J. (1996), *Why Switzerland?*, 2nd edn, Cambridge: Cambridge University Press.

Steinle, W.J. (1992), 'Regional Competitiveness and the Single European Market', *Regional Studies* 26.4, pp. 307–18.

Stöhr, W. (1990), *Global Challenge and Local Response. Initiatives for local economic regeneration in Europe*, London: Mansell.

Stone, C.N. (1989), *Regime Politics. Governing Atlanta, 1946–1988*, Lawrence: University of Kansas Press.

Stone, C.N and H.T. Sanders (eds) (1987), *The Politics of Urban Development*, Lawrence: University of Kansas Press.

Storper, M. (1995), 'The Resurgence of Regional Economies, Ten Years Later: The Region as a Nexus of Untraded Interdependencies', *European Urban and Regional Studies*, 2.3, pp.191–221.

Strange, S. (1982), 'Cave! hic dragones: A Critique of Regime Analysis, *International Organization*, 36.2, pp.479–96.

Streek, W. and P. Schmitter (1991), 'From National Corporatism to Transnational Pluralism: Organized Interests in the Single European Market', *Politics and Society*, 19.1, pp.133–64.

Strijker, D. and J. de Veer (1988) 'Agriculture', in W. Molle and R. Cappellin (eds) *Regional Impact of Community Policies in Europe,* Aldershot: Avebury.

Stürm, R. (1997), 'Regions in the New Germany', in M. Keating and J. Loughlin (eds), *The Political Economy of Regionalism*, London: Frank Cass.

SVIMEZ (1954), Associazione per lo Sviluppo dell'Industria nel Mezzogiorno, *Statistiche sul Mezzogiorno d'Italia, 1861–1953*, Rome: ZVIMEZ.

Swedberg, R. (1993), 'Introduction', in R. Swedberg (ed.), *Explorations in Economic Geography*, New York: Russel Sage Foundation.

Tannam, E. (1995), 'EU Regional Policy and the Irish/Northern Irish Cross-Border Administrative Relationship', *Regional and Federal Studies,* 5.1, pp. 67–93.

Tarrow, S. (1967), *Peasant Communism in Southern Italy*, New Haven: Yale University Press.

Tarrow, S. (1978), 'Regional Policy, Ideology, and Peripheral Defense:

The Case of Fos-sur-Mer', in S. Tarrow, P.J. Katzenstein and L. Graziano (eds), *Territorial Politics in Industrial Nations*, New York and London: Praeger.

Taylor, A.J.P. (1948), *The Habsburg Monarchy, 1809–1918. A History of the Austrian Empire and Austria-Hungary*, London: Hamish Hamilton.

Tema Nord (1995), *Regional Development in the Nordic Countries — NOGRAN Periodic Report 1994/5*, Copenhagen: Nordic Council of Ministers.

Thiesse, A.-M. (1994), 'Le régionalisme de la Troisième République en France (1871–1940)', in G. Bassong, M. Erbe, P. Frankenberg, C. Grivel and W. Lilli (eds), *Westeuropäische Regionen und Ihre Identität. Beitrage aus interdisziplinärer Sicht*, Mannheim: J&J.

Thomas, M.D. (1972), 'Growth Pole Theory: An Examination of Some of its Basic Concepts', in N.M. Hansen (ed.), *Growth Centers in Regional Economic Development*, New York: Free Press. London: Collier-Macmillan.

Tilly, C. (1990), *Coercion, Capital and European States, AD 990–1990*, Oxford: Blackwell.

Tilly, C. (1994), 'Entanglements of European Cities and States', in C. Tilly and W.P. Blockmans (eds), *Cities and the Rise of States in Europe, AD 1000 to 1800*, Boulder: Westview.

Tilly, C. and W.P. Blockmans (eds) (1994), *Cities and the Rise of States in Europe, AD 1000 to 1800*, Boulder: Westview.

Todd, E. (1990), *L'invention de l'Europe*, Paris: Seuil.

Todd, E. (1991), *The Making of Modern France. Politics, Ideology and Culture*, Oxford: Blackwell.

Touraine, A. (1992a), *Critique de la modernité*, Paris; Fayard.

Touraine, A. (1992b), 'L'état et la question nationale', in R. Lenoir and J. Lesourne (eds), *Où va l'état?*, Paris: Le Monde Editions.

Touraine, A., F. Dubet, Z. Hegedus and M. Wieviorka (1981), *Le pays contre l'état. Luttes occitanes*, Paris: Seuil.

Trigilia, C. (1991), 'The paradox of the region: economic regulation and the representation of interests', *Economy and Society*, 20.3, pp.306–27.

Trigilia, C. (1996), 'Una nuova occasione storica per il Mezzogiorno?', *Le Regioni*, XXIV.1, pp.93–101.

Urwin, D. (1982), 'Germany: From Geographical Expression to Regional Accommodation', in S. Rokkan and D. Urwin (eds), *The Politics of Territorial Identity. Studies in European Regionalism*, London: Sage.

Urwin, D. (1983), 'Harbinger, Fossil or Fleabite? "Regionalism" and the West European Party Mosaic', in H. Daalder and P. Mair (eds), *Western European Party Systems. Continuity and Change*, London: Sage.

Van Dam, D. (1997), 'Les mouvements sociaux d'hier, germes du nationalisme', in S. Jaumain (ed.), *La réforme de l'Etat... et après? L'impact des débats institutionnels en Belgique et au Canada*, Brussels: Editions de l'Université de Bruxelles.

Versmessen, E. (1995), 'In the Kingdom of Paradoxes; the Belgian Regional and National Elections of May 1995', *Regional and Federal Studies*, 5.2, pp.239–46.

Vicens Vives, J. (1986), *Los catalanes en el siglo XIX*, Madrid: Alianza.

Wald, K. (1983), *Crosses on the Ballot. Patterns of British Voter Alignment since 1885*, Princeton: Princeton University Press.

Waller, B. (ed.) (1990), *Themes in Modern European History, 1830–1890*, London: Unwin Hyman.

Wannop, U. (1995), *The Regional Imperative. Regional Planning and Governance in Britain, Europe and the United States*, London: Jessica Kingsley.

Watkins, S. Cott (1991), *From Provinces into Nations. Demographic Integration in Western Europe, 1870–1960*, Princeton: Princeton University Press.

Weber, E. (1977), *Peasants into Frenchmen. The modernization of rural France*, London: Chatto and Windus.

Weber, M.P. (1988), *Don't call me boss. David L. Lawrence. Pittsburgh's Renaissance Mayor*, Pittsburgh: Pittsburgh University Press.

Welhofer, E.S. (1986), 'Class, territory and party: political change in Britain, 1945–1974', *European Journal of Political Research*, 14.

Wilson, C. (1962), 'Economic Conditions', in *The New Cambridge Modern History. Vol. XI. Material Progress and World-Wide Problems, 1870–1898*, Cambridge: Cambridge University Press.

Woods, D. (1995), 'The crisis of Center-Periphery Integration in Italy and the Rise of Regional Populism: The Lombard League in Comparative Perspective', *Comparative Politics*, 27.2: 187–204.

Ysmal, C. (1989), *Les partis politiques sous la Ve République*, Paris: Montchrestien.

Yuill, D., K. Allen, J. Bachtler, K. Clement and F. Wishlade (1993), *European Regional Incentives, 1993–4*, 13th edn, London: Bowker-Saur.

Zaggario, V. (1981), 'La tradizione meridionalista e il dibattito sulle

autonomie nel secondo dopoguerra', in G. Mori (ed.), *Autonomismo meridionale: ideologia, politica e istituzioni,* Bologna: Il Mulino.
Zariski, R. (1972), *Italy. The Politics of Uneven Development,* Hinsdale: Dryden.

Index

A

Abruzzo 149
accumulation of mandates 134
agrarian politics 24
agriculture 163
Åland islands 55
Alava 43
Albigensians 28
Aleanza Nazionale 99
Alsace 110
Alsace-Lorraine 31
Aménagement du territoire 49
anarchism 25, 33, 53
Andalucia 68, 91, 99, 108,
   110, 117
annales school 4, 8
Aquitaine 135
Aragon 19, 91, 95, 110
Arana, Sabino 28
art 84
Assembly of European
   Regions (AER) 171, 179
Association of European Frontier
   Regions 171, 179
Atlantic Arc 180

Ausgleich 29
Austria 10, 17, 41, 113, 167
Austro-Hungarian Empire 17,
   24, 27, 30, 37
autonomous communities
   121, 168
Auvergne 169
Azores 117

B

Baden-Württemberg 40, 99,
   105, 147, 148, 151, 180
Baltic states 181
Barcelona 22, 58, 144
Basic Law 40, 117
Basque Country 19, 24, 28, 29,
   31, 34, 37, 54, 67, 69,
   76, 82, 90, 94, 95, 98,
   99, 102, 103, 110, 117,
   121, 141, 150, 160, 165,
   178, 187
Basque language 26
Basque nationalism 36, 59,
   105, 163
Bavaria 31, 33, 34, 36,

231